WWII MEMORIES OF AN UNDEFEATED FIGHER ACE

*The story of air battles over Europe
and life between the deadly duels.*

# CLAYTON KELLY GROSS

FOREWORD BY GEN. ROBERT LEE SCOTT AUTHOR OF *GOD IS MY CO-PILOT*

PORTLAND • OREGON

*About the cover painting:*

Some years ago, Portland, Oregon, artist Ron Weil painted an impression of my victory over the ME-262 jet and surprised me with it. I was thrilled, but mentioned that his depiction was not quite historically accurate. He came to my home bearing models and we spent time reconstructing the engagement to match my recollection (later confirmed by Kurt Lobgesong, the German pilot).

The painting is currently in the Oregon National Guard Museum.

Copyright © 2006 by Clayton Kelly Gross

Cover painting by Ron Weil
Cover and interior design by Masha Shubin

All rights reserved. No part of this book may be reproduced or transmitted in any form or by any means whatsoever, including photocopying, recording or by any information storage and retrieval system, without written permission from the publisher and/or author. Contact Inkwater Press at 6750 SW Franklin Street, Suite A, Portland, OR 97223-2542.

www.inkwaterpress.com

ISBN 978-1-59299-186-0

Publisher: Inkwater Press

Printed in Canada.

# DEDICATION

This book is dedicated to three beautiful women…

### ELIZABETH THERESA GROSS
Who gave me life and prayed that I would keep it.

### GWENDOLYN AVON GROSS
The beauty I married at flight school graduation and who inspired me to live through the war to continue the marriage. It lasted 53 wonderful years before her death.

### RAMONA HARRIET GROSS
Another beautiful woman I found after losing Gwen. This wonderful lady has kept me young for over eight years of our marriage. Her encouragement and work have helped immeasurably in telling this story.

For your many, many hours at the computer and the dictionary to translate my writing to readable form, I thank you, Love!

# TABLE OF CONTENTS

Dedication ................................................... iii
Prologue ...................................................... ix
Foreword ..................................................... xi
Wisdom ...................................................... xiii
Author's Introduction ............................... xv

CHAPTER 1
The Beginning ............................................. 1

CHAPTER 2
School Days ................................................. 5

CHAPTER 3
The First Draw to the Sky ....................... 13

CHAPTER 4
Air Corps Career ....................................... 19

CHAPTER 5
Where are the Airplanes? ........................ 24

CHAPTER 6
Basic and Advanced Training ................. 31

CHAPTER 7
Two Huge Steps…Graduation and
    Marriage ................................................. 43

CHAPTER 8
A Fighter Pilot! ................................................................. 48

CHAPTER 9
Training to Fight .............................................................. 53

CHAPTER 10
The 354th Fighter Group ................................................. 58

CHAPTER 11
Hayward, California ........................................................ 65

CHAPTER 12
Life and Training in the Great Northwest ..................... 74

CHAPTER 13
Training Missions Till Ready .......................................... 85

CHAPTER 14
On The Way to War ......................................................... 94

CHAPTER 15
This is England! ............................................................. 104

CHAPTER 16
I'm A Public Speaker? ................................................... 115

CHAPTER 17
Combat Readiness/Life ................................................. 120

CHAPTER 18
Gains & Losses for the 354th ........................................ 127

CHAPTER 19
Memorable February Missions… ................................ 131

CHAPTER 20
Missions and Life ........................................................... 142

CHAPTER 21
Emotions ........................................................................ 148

CHAPTER 22
More Action? ................................................................. 154

CHAPTER 23
Picadilly Circus, The Best Show in London ...................... 161

CHAPTER 24
Contemplation ................................................................. 167

CHAPTER 25
Scores in the Air and Then D-Day! ................................. 173

CHAPTER 26
Another Victory – War Is Hell! ....................................... 180

CHAPTER 27
Post D-Day – Orders Home! ............................................ 190

CHAPTER 28
Back to the War ............................................................... 198

CHAPTER 29
Paris! ................................................................................ 207

CHAPTER 30
Parties, Mud and Five Down ........................................... 212

CHAPTER 31
I Get Shot Down .............................................................. 222

CHAPTER 32
Back to Fighting With Big Changes – P-47's .................. 234

CHAPTER 33
Musings at the End of 1944 ............................................. 244

CHAPTER 34
Party Time in France ....................................................... 252

CHAPTER 35
P-51's Cheer the Bitter Winter ........................................ 261

CHAPTER 36
Patton Moving – Germany on the Run! ........................... 270

CHAPTER 37
Last Victory – A Jet! ....................................................... 275

CHAPTER 38
Winding Down and It Ends ................................................. 286
CHAPTER 39
Trip Home After V-E Day 1945 ........................................... 292
Postscript ................................................................................ 300
Epilogue ................................................................................. 302
Glossary ................................................................................. 305
Index ...................................................................................... 307

# PROLOGUE

**"SO IT WAS THAT** the war in the air began. Men rode upon the whirlwind that night; slew and fell like archangels upon the astonished earth. Surely the last fights of mankind were the best. What was the heavy pounding of your Homeric Swordsman, what was the creaking chariots, besides this swift rush, this crash, this giddy triumph, this headlong sweep to death?"

> The above was written by prolific English writer H. G. Wells (and prophet?) in his book, *"THE WORLD SET FREE"* in 1913 and published in 1914 *before* World War I began. Only a decade after the Wright Brothers' 120-foot flight and before others envisioned the use of aircraft against each other, he pretty well described what Rickenbacher et al did in the First World War and what I did in the second War – the subject of this book.

One of America's early and most famous Aces, Robert Lee Scott, Jr. became a friend of the Author.

# FOREWORD

IN 1989 GENERAL BOB Scott traveled from his Arizona residence to Oregon for a week visiting and of golf. I had located a first edition of GOD IS MY CO-PILOT and one day brought it for his autograph. We had been discussing my book efforts during the round. In the book, his autograph contained the following message:

> "Endorsed especially to Clayton Kelly Gross (Ace) and Gwen, with the hope that you write that book. If you do not, remember – you leave a gap in history.
>
> Best wishes,
> Bob Scott"

Fifteen years later, I traveled to Macon, Georgia for the General's 95th birthday – yes, we played a round of golf! I carried the manuscript of this book with me and after reading it, he wrote the following:

"Dear Lord, let me grow up to be a fighter pilot and in time to be an ACE! FIVE DOWN AND GLORY WAS EVER MY DREAM!

So it was with CLAYTON KELLY GROSS and thousands of young men who looked to the sky. Though we grew up far apart from Washington to Georgia, we became good friends, enjoying hundreds of golf games and many evenings of fine dining. Geography means nothing to fighter pilots!

For Clayton Kelly Gross and I both became ACES. The aerial victory that moved him to that lofty plateau of "five kills" nearly killed him. You'll read of that. His final victory was over Kurt Lobgesong in a Luftwaffe ME-262, the world's first operational jet. Later in life, Clayton Kelly Gross went to Germany and found his once enemy and they became friends. Such is a strong characteristic among fighter pilots.

Clayton and I share a strong belief in God – who perhaps put us on this earth to do just what we have done. The tales are good and I believe you will enjoy the memories he shares in his book.

Brig. Gen. Robert L. Scott, Jr."
*God is My Co-Pilot*

# WISDOM

"Only the dead have seen the end of war."
*Plato, Fifth Century BC*

"What then of death? Is not the taps of death but first call to the reveille of eternal life! We live in deeds – not years. There are no practice games in life."
*Gen. George S. Patton, Jr.*

"The essence of war is violence and moderation in war is imbecility."
*Lord McCaulay, 1831*

*General Nathan F. Twining, USAF, reported* " – a top fighter pilot once said that fighter pilots fall into two broad categories…those who go out to kill and those who secretly desperately know they are going to get killed – the hunters and the hunted."

"It's not whether you win or lose…it's whether I win or not!"
*Author Unknown*

16-Victory German Ace, Franz Stigler – Friend and drinking Buddy who got me started on this book.

Painting of Stigler's ME-109

# AUTHOR'S INTRODUCTION

For many years following my World War II service, the thought of recording my experiences did not enter my mind. I did in fact, find efforts by some of my compatriots to be less than thrilling to me. More than once, I stated, when asked, that I would not consider it. It was *not* because I wanted to put it out of mind as some claim. To the contrary, there has hardly been a period of time since the war when I did not think of that most exciting part of my being. Still, it took one of our erstwhile enemies to change my mind.

In 1976, I was selected to chair that reunion edition of the American Fighter Aces in Portland, Oregon. A local aviation 'buff' told me of a German Ace living in Vancouver, Canada, and I contacted and invited him to attend and speak to the American Aces. Franz Stigler was a 16-victory Luftwaffe Ace and the first one of those I had heard admit to flying against us. Those I had met at previous meetings usually followed any discussion of combat with the information that their victories were all "Eastern front" – the Russians. I often wondered where the survivors of the Western front battles had gone. During and after the 1976 meeting, Franz and I became good friends and drinking buddies. After all, we were fighter pilots! As we sat in a bar, any bar, any place, he would tell me of an exciting experience and invariably that would lead to one of my stories. These were *not* the standard, "there I was at 30,000 feet, flat on my back and bleep on the air speed"--- stories. Too many of those were probably what bored me in some pilot-written books. These stories were the more human side of life between "battles to the death" in the skies.

I would laugh at his, tell one of mine, he would laugh and we would order another drink. They were good tales that you would enjoy. I think Franz said it first, laughing at one of my efforts, he said in his heavy German accent, "Ve shood poot dat in a Buch." I agreed and we shook on it. We would write the best book to come out of the war!

I started immediately. That was 20 years ago. I had the advantage of all my records, and places to search for those I did not have. I bought and read every air war book available. As my collection of stories increased, so did calls to my German friend. How are you coming on "the Buch"? He wasn't. He had only memory to search. He had none of the myriad of places to go that I had.

One of his stories would explain that and give you, dear reader, an idea of what started this effort. Franz was a top Luftwaffe pilot as evidenced by the fact that he was flying the ME-262 jet at the end of the war. Only their best were trusted with the Jets. He landed after a final mission and was met by his crew chief who told him, "no more fuel and no more ammunition". "In that case," said Franz. "You don't need pilots."

Now the Russians were closing rapidly from the East and our forces were rapidly coming from the West. No German in his right mind wanted to be captured by the Russians, our friend included. He got a motorcycle and like any dashing and single fighter pilot, put two girls on the back and headed West. He related, "I had not gone ten kilometers when we found American troops who took my motorcycle *and* both girls."

He became a Prisoner of War and dispatched with many others to Canada, Vancouver, British Columbia, and a POW camp. In a few months, the war ended and he was able to return to the fatherland. What he found there was devastation everywhere. He married a pretty blonde girl and they returned to Canada where they have resided ever since. I offered to find a writer to do his part of the book, but it didn't happen. For an extended period, my own efforts were on hold. Then I found that when I spoke to various groups, there were often some that would tell me I should put my stories on paper.

Later, in an enjoyable golf game with the legendary General Bob Scott who wrote, "God is My Co-pilot" and at least 15 other books. I mentioned what I had started and he said, "Doc, everybody has at least one book inside them. Do it. Finish what you've started." I went back to work.

Pressure of a busy dental practice and many outside distractions have delayed me to this point. What we have here is a sincere effort to relate what happened in my life until the end of World War II. I have changed no names and embellished none of the stories with fantasy.

I love the people I flew with and hope those who happen to read this will say, "Yes that's the way it was." I told it "as it was" to the best of my ability. If you note transgressions against any of God's commandments, excuse them because of the pressure of war. I have long since atoned by prayer to the Creator himself.

*Clayton Kelly Gross*

CHAPTER 1

# THE BEGINNING

AN ORGANIZATION OF AMERICAN Aces was formed in 1960 in San Francisco and in conjunction with the AIR FORCE ASSOCIATION meeting. The letter I received from George Ceuleers announcing that the group would meet was the first notice since I separated from the service in 1945, that *anyone* remembered what I had done in the defeat of Hitler!

I was excited to make the trip. The excitement tripled when I arrived! Famous names from aviation history – old buddies, Eagle and Bradley – Gabby who was the leading living American Ace, Bud Mahurin, Tex Hill, Robert Scott and others I had only read about. And I am PART of this?

I made it a high point of every year to attend these gatherings. In 1976, I hosted the reunion in Portland, Oregon, and the following year – a miracle – I was elected the 16th President! Now more excitement, as President, I was invited to the 1977 meet of Gemeinshaft der Jagderflieger, the German fighter pilot association. I met and spent a pleasant hour with Sir Douglas Bader, the legless British hero and Ace of the Battle of Britain. I had a picture taken with Eric Hartman, Ace of all Aces with 358 allied victories. I gave a short speech 'in German' to almost 1000 people in formal attire at the Munich Beer Hall where Hitler started the damn war. I danced with General Adolph Galland's beautiful 'wingman', later wife.

How could all of this happen to little old me? The more I spoke to the big-name Aces, both theirs and ours, the more I made good friends among these people, the more I realized we are much the same – forget the numbers. We are true fighter pilots – the hunters, not the hunted!

I do try to avoid any semblance of self-grandizement, but still admit that I have been better at everything I ever did than most (with the exception of my too-late-in-life golf career,) and even there I have tallied five 'Holes in One', to make me an Ace of Aces. Yet, with all of my accomplishments, I firmly believe that from 1941 to 1945, I did what I was destined to do – to fly and to fight and to win. I was born to be a fighter pilot.

I might not be here to say that if a certain Guardian Angel assigned to me, had not deflected, steered or stopped various machines or objects which might have ended my life 99 or more times from birth to present. But he/she did and this is what happened.

At 11:00 a.m. on the eleventh day of the eleventh month of the year 1918, the war to end all wars was over. With the Armistice signed, an infantry officer climbed out of the trenches in France and headed back home to Walla Walla, Washington. He was a hero! Exactly one year later to the hour, the former soldier, Orien Wilford Gross married beautiful Irish lass, Elizabeth Theresa Kelly. Fast forward one more year and 19 days, their first born son entered the world and it is possible that at that moment, Adolph Hitler, already planning for rejuvenation of Germany and of world domination, was doomed to fail. You see, nobody knew, especially me who knew nothing at that time, Clayton Kelly Gross was born to be a fighter pilot. Now I know that.

I was born to privilege – not into monetary type, but into a family I would not change if offered the entire world. I had love and care unsurpassed and I had education, both books and practical to prepare me for whatever I might choose.

My father was handsome and athletic. Raised on a wheat ranch in Walla Walla, he was instilled with values to accompany and compliment those talents. After completing high school, he decided the dust of wheat farming was not for him and headed to Alaska where the discovery of gold was drawing many of the more adventurous young men. There he worked for a mining company with time to be part of the 1913 Champion basketball team of Southeast Alaska, one of the 15-member Treadwell, Alaska football team and the middleweight boxing champion of Alaska.

In 1916, his brother Jim left home to join the Army and was posted to the Mexican border problem – much to his family's distress. Orien, known to friends and family as 'Ode', decided to chase after him and also joined to magnify the family woes. Thus it was that my dear father was in uniform when we entered World War I.

Mother on the other hand, was a lovely teenager in the midst of the metropolis of Walla Walla, population a few thousand souls. Grandfather Kelly was an Irish policeman who had a few of the foibles particular to that race. He would drink a bit and he would gamble a bit more, which characteristics did little to endure him to Grandmother Kelly. She had borne him 5 daughters, Elizabeth Theresa Kelly being number three. Both French-Irish grandmother, Mary Janice Huguenot and son of the old sod, John B. Kelly were staunch Catholics. Returning war hero Orien was from a strict religious family in which Grandfather Gross had not allowed alcohol or playing cards. When he was killed in an unfortunate fall from a horse, grandmother Mary Theresa Gross and her boys returning from the world travel courtesy of our military forces, negated those rules.

In 1919, my mother, still in her late teens and never suffering from lack of suitors, pledged to and married the dashing young

Lieutenant and my gene complex was thereby in the making. So taken by his beautiful bride, my father soon adopted Catholicism and so it was on November 30, 1920, I entered the world and was baptized Clayton Kelly 'Aloysious Anthony' (two saints just to be safe) Gross by Father Cronin.

You know of my father's makeup...my mother was a complete opposite except in handsome physical makeup – the one item I apparently failed to inherit from either of them. Mother was deeply religious, seldom, if ever, had more than a sip of alcohol, was not only not daring, but maybe even overly cautious. She worried about everything. Later in life, she asked how things were going and I reported, "Just fine, Mother!" Her response was "Oh, I worry so when things seem to be going fine." To cover the worries imagined or real, she prayed and that seemed to work for my well being since I went from danger to danger with my guardian angel steering me past trouble and trouble by me.

My father had a best friend who continued his education into college and on to medical school. His name was Harry Clayton Cowan and, on the occasion of my birth, Dad announced my name would be Harry. "Over my dead body," said mother, and hers was a good decision for I was probably 25 before I had to shave daily. Harry didn't fit well and to compromise and keep harmony in the family, they settled on the doctor's middle name after he delivered me. Their second son came three years later and was given my father's name, Orien W. Jr. which fact irritated me, once he got old enough for sibling rivalry. I out-grew it eventually.

My education began at St. Augustine's school in Spokane where the family had migrated when I was between two and three years old. Dad, an insurance company executive, had accepted a transfer for better opportunities. My class had four boys and 22 girls – which scared me. In those early days, girls scared me more than Messerschmidts did later. Fortunately, I overcame fear of 'LaFemme' almost to the point that it interfered with my mission in life – to fly and to fight. But that's another story!

CHAPTER 2
# SCHOOL DAYS

**S**EPTEMBER **1926**
I don't consider my schooling start, as indicative of what they say is courageous behavior that I would exhibit and be decorated for. I went home from my first day in the first grade in tears. As a matter of fact, I was that way all day long as I recall. In my defense, I must say that I was only 5 years 9 months old and, in public schools, I would not have started until the following year. The Catholic Archdiocese, however, decreed that if you would be six before the years mid-point, you could start. Maybe my mother, with my little brother just two, couldn't wait to get me out of the house. At any rate, on the first Monday after labor day in 1926 she led (pulled) me by the hand to the door of the first grade room at St. Augustine's School where a black-robed Nun towered over me, smiled and forcibly separated me from my mother. There were sobs, but no tears – yet. Sister Mary understood and comforted me with tender head pats. "Just find a seat and relax – we'll be starting soon."

There were about a dozen other children already seated – all girls I noticed. I selected the second row seat in the first aisle, close to the door in case I decided to bolt. Another boy came in and I felt a little better... almost relaxed. Then it happened. Another boy arrived, about my size, but for some reason, quite self-assured. After he passed Sister in the entry, he marched straight to my desk and in a very authoritative voice for a little guy announced, "that's my desk – get out!" The tears started.

Sister Mary hustled back and ushered him to another desk in another row, but every time I stole a glance in his direction, he was glowering at me. Although they wouldn't let me leave, I decided to quit school forever as soon as I could escape. I never forgot that guy's name – 'Dickie Driscoll'. Eventually his family moved away a few years later, but we had became 'friends' and during that time I discovered I could whip his butt in a fair fight. So I forgave him for that first day.

I learned to exist and even enjoy schooling under the Nuns. Our class stabilized at 30, four boys and 26 girls that brought the four of us guys closer together for protection. Who needs girls at this age?

I did suffer one indignity around the fourth grade year. It was a singing class and although all voices were in the "squeaky" range, some were higher than others and mine evidently one of them. Sister Mary Ellen decided I matched some of the young ladies and so placed me on their side of the room. I could imagine the ribbing I would get from Bill Bradley, Mike Sullivan and Bill Olson when this was over!

Now Sister had to follow the music and wave one hand as a director and so could not watch us closely. I got out of the desk with the girl and crawled on my hands and knees down the aisle to the back, across and then up the right hand row where I took a seat with the guys. I sensed her presence before she rapped on my desk to halt the singing, then asked; "Just what voice are you singing?"

"My reply was brilliant, "Oh, I have a voice all of my own!"

I took an open hand slap to my cheek that knocked me out of the desk to roll across the floor to the wall. I dared not cry, but I wanted to. Then she raised me to my feet by an earlobe and marched me back to my designated area. The class went on.

And so did my education. I learned to be an Altar Boy and a favorite of Father Cronin and his assistant. I was a Boy Scout. We played some pretty rough make up football games and I learned to take a good blow with the best of them.

I finished the seventh grade – one to go before high school when, now in the depths of the great depression, my father's company moved us to Boise, Idaho. I left my buddies and I missed them. I made new ones in Boise.

Once moved, the family found an apartment in a duplex on State Street. The Idaho State Capitol was clearly visible a dozen blocks down the street.

While the family unpacked, little brother Orien, and I decided to scout the neighborhood and began a walk around the block. We found the local Cathedral only one block away. About that time, we saw something else. Four kids were coming toward us. Two placed themselves in front of me – two behind. The significance of that did not immediately sink in. "Hi." I said.

The answer was ominous. "This is our neighborhood. What the hell are you doing here?" I was shoved in the chest. The two in the rear did the same to Orien. We placed ourselves back to back in defense. About that time a fifth smaller kid came in from the side and jumped to plant a blow to the side of my head. I caught his shirt before he got away and gave him a return he would not soon forget. He ran...crying.

The battle, two against four, raged for a few minutes until an adult voice intervened and they disappeared as fast as they had arrived.

Orien and I were bruised, but unbowed. We ran home to tell the tale. A week later, the attacking boys made a 'kinda' apology and said they had only wanted to 'test us'. Eventually, we became part of the neighborhood.

I learned to like Boise. After that initial confrontation with the neighborhood kids, we were accepted. My eighth grade class had some good guys that lived nearby and we became close.

The Army Cavalry unit was based only a few blocks away and I spent time with the horses – and even got to ride occasionally. The polo field was also next door to that and I was allowed to walk their mounts when they changed to a fresh horse.

Mother always had help in the form of a young farm girl who traded work for residence while going to school. When Grandmother Gross visited, Junior and I had to surrender our bedroom and move to the screened porch. I thought that was O.K. – even neat because I got to see my first naked woman when our pretty "school girl" left the bathroom shade partly open while bathing.

I got a job delivering the "Press" starting with the worst route in town and being rewarded later with one of the best when I doubled the size of the first one. I earned enough to buy a new bike with balloon tires. I started high school in 1934 and immediately fell madly in love with a beautiful Basque girl. She dropped her hair ribbon in the school yard one day and I had a "knockdown fight" with another guy for the privilege of retrieving and returning it to the girl. I won. To no avail – my father's company transferred us back to Spokane.

In Spokane, I enrolled in Lewis & Clark High School, a large public school on the South side, which we all knew was the "best" side of Spokane.

I got a shock when my first report card arrived. I had an 'F'! At St. Mary's Academy under the Nuns, my freshman year had been nearly straight 'A's. Maybe the distraction of girls (which by now did interest me) or maybe overconfidence led to the failure. I did not let it happen again.

Outside activities consisted mostly of bowling and shooting. I was part of LCHS rifle team that ranked in the top three in the country. I even became a 'letterman' through the rifle team.

In my junior year, I got my first 'steady', a romance that endured for a year until I was 'dropped'. Will I get over it? It took awhile, but I did and moved on.

I settled in to a very different high school life at Lewis and Clark – a public and very large high school on the South side of Spokane. For the first time, I experienced lay teachers after my first nine years under Nuns. It took a *lot* of adaptation, but I learned. For outside classroom activities, I participated in the German Club. Why not, one of my great grandfathers was from Germany! Also tried the Thespians, probably feeling I would join that other Spokanite, Bing Crosby, someday. I was a failure in my only role, pure panic as the 'second bell-boy'.

I continued to bowl at every opportunity and improved. I started a high school bowling league.

I developed some good friendships and friends, Hank Moore and Jim Lyons and I joined the school rifle team. Under Coach McMacken, we were part of one of the top three teams in the country (the best we thought). And then there were girls. I noticed them early, but shyness thwarted any dreams I might have had – for awhile that is.

One day I got up the nerve to ask one of the beautiful Day sisters, Angionette, to a dance and she accepted. In one of our first trips onto the floor and dancing cheek to cheek, the proper mood for the music, I found my chewing gum stuck in her beautifully styled hair. End of that relationship.

Early in my junior year, I took Mr. Teakles' American History class. Pretty Lenora Allin sat at the desk in front of me. Mr. Teakle excused himself for a moment and left the room. Lenora stretched and over her shoulder said, "Darn, I wish I had a date for the dance tonight." For the first ten seconds I was paralyzed. Then quietly, "Would you go with me?" She turned and said, "Really?" "Okay."

I finished that class but skipped the next two to hurry to my

Dad's office. "Dad, I have to have the car tonight!" He wasn't happy, but did agree. Next, I stopped at his secretary's desk and borrowed two dollars. Then I hurried back to school to quiz everybody who might know Lenora.

"What is she like? What does she like?" My best information was that she smoked. I didn't, but I wanted to be prepared so went to the store and bought four different brands of cigarettes so I would have the right one. After bathing and preening to the best of my ability with what I had to work with, I was parked in front of her home – early.

That date led to a steady relationship for almost the rest of my days at Lewis and Clark and ended only when she broke my heart – she dropped me. It took time, but I healed.

Finally! Excitement! We are nearly finished with high school. The senior class of Lewis & Clark High School assembled in Mrs. Stubblefield's study hall – all 338 of us – the largest class in school history at that time. Truman Reed, our Principal had a Graduation message about our future, which involved use of the 'Law of Averages'. A lot of it was funny, but one thing got my attention.

"Nothing is certain in life. It's possible one of you may not live until graduation". Who is he kidding? We graduate in three weeks!

Two days before the big finale of our high school days, we went three hundred strong, to Liberty Lake for the traditional Senior Sneak. We had fun...to a point. A friend and I rented a rowboat and headed out. Even alternating the rowing, we had enough after a half an hour and headed back to shore. A sideshow began as we headed in. There were two boats, one with six of the Tiger football team and the other with five of the round ball team. Whoever started it, I cannot say, but we saw a little jousting with oars. That caused one boat to take on a little water that caused several to jump for the second boat to avoid a cold dip. In minutes, both of them were capsized and eleven were in the water wearing their heavy clothing.

Jack had the oars of our boat and headed for the melee. "We gotta' help."

"Are you kidding. We'll be pulled in next." He kept rowing and in the middle of it, hands were grabbing us from all sides, and as I predicted, we went under. Now there were three boats and 13 guys struggling. I was a strong swimmer but had never tried it with clothes and shoes weighing me down. It wasn't easy, but I managed to climb aboard a capsized boat, riding it like a cowboy – cold and thoroughly soaked. I could still see the humor of the affair. That ended quickly. On my left side about five feet in front of me, a boy came to the surface. His right hand rose straight up. I will never forget the panic on his face. If he had reached toward my boat about one foot away, he could have grabbed it. Instead he slid straight back down.

Several more boats had left shore 100 feet away and at least two guys were in swimming suits. I screamed at them. "Right here. A guy just went under here," pointing to where John Paulson had slid below the surface. They started diving. In the meantime, those of us pulled from the water and shivering in May's 50-degree weather were taken to shore and gathered around a welcome bonfire. Hundreds of classmates were shouting questions.

I told the story of Paulson going down a dozen times to those around the fire. Within a half an hour some news from the divers brought new horror. They found a body but it wasn't Paulson. It was Patterson, one of our star basketball players. That doubles the tragedy. No one knew he was missing.

Before we left for home, a low-flying plane summoned from Felts Field located Paulson's body, and divers brought him up. Now I had a strange feeling. I was probably – no surely – I was the last person to see him alive. I can never forget the look on his face.

Our graduation was a few days later, and yes, Mr. Reed was right. Some of us didn't live that long.

CHAPTER 3

# THE FIRST DRAW TO THE SKY

I LOST MY FIRST LOVE. A tough thing for anybody but being seventeen helped a little. I started my college career at Gonzaga University. That's when I met a new girl at a 'carhop' at Hires Root Beer and we had a yearlong relationship. One bad part was she worked nights on Friday and Saturday and those were the action times for people our age. All the dances and other goodies fell on those nights. We had been 'steadies' for a goodly time when a friend had a temporary solution. He knew of a girl whose steady boyfriend played in a band. She had the same problem I did. The band had 'gigs' on weekend nights.

It was arranged. One date only wouldn't really be cheating. I met the young lady who would change my life. Her name was Gwendolyn Yeo. She was a majorette for my old high school and beautiful. We did enjoy each other on that date and soon had sneaked several more before we decided to tell our 'steadies' the news and create a new one.

Not everyone was happy – my old girlfriend, her boyfriend *and* Gwen's mother! It seemed that Mrs. Yeo thought I was too old (three years), too experienced (I wasn't), and Catholic. We persevered through all of that and formed what would later be a life-long union – until death did us part.

Gwen was so pretty. I would have pursued her even if she could not boil water, but that wasn't the case I discovered, to my delight. A few months into our relationship on one of my drop-by visits, she surprised me with a plate of delicious fudge, one of my weaknesses. "Who did this?" I asked on the second or third sampling, "your mother?"

"No, I did!" she said smiling sweetly.

I was in heaven. All that beauty and she can cook, too!

A few weeks later, digging into a batch of out-of-this-world divinity, I knew I would marry her. When she baked me a chocolate cake for my twentieth birthday, I announced my intentions to the whole world.

It wasn't until we had tied the knot officially that I discovered that fudge, divinity and chocolate cake were the entire extent of her culinary talents. Outside of these, she really had trouble boiling water.

Besides Gwen, another love was in the making for me – flying! My calendar always seemed filled with those things which kept teenagers busy; school, girls, bowling, just monkeying around and probably, although I don't remember much of it, studying. The social side included dance dates, movie dates, an ice cream soda to follow either and of course, 'parking'.

When it came to movie choice, I was the same guy then as I am today, the one I picked had to have action, the more the better. So it came to pass that on one balmy evening in

Spokane, I talked my sweetheart into seeing a great movie, "I Wanted Wings" instead of the more romantic-type she wished to choose.

I thought it was a really great movie! I could visualize myself as one of the cadets and it looked to me like all those glamour guys would get a sultry girlfriend like Veronica Lake, with hair down over one eye. I am sure that at that moment I resolved to try to join them.

The government had come up with a new program called "Civil Pilot Training" and it was made available at Gonzaga University. I was one of the first to sign up. The first section was ground school only but as we progressed, real flying was a part of the course and my dreams of being a glamorous aviator began to come true. Up 'til then, as real as my desires to fly were, I don't think I believed they could come true. Flying was too expensive to privately afford, according to my father and way too dangerous, according to mom. Now I could do it. My classes at Gonzaga University ran from 9:00 A.M. until 3:00 P.M., at which time I darted for the bowling alley. After dinner I went back across town to Gonzaga for the night school, the ground school part of CPT and then on a beeline to Gwen's house for a few hours with my sweetie. If I got home by midnight, I was lucky. My assigned flight time was 7:00 A.M. and so I was up at 5:00 A.M. for a quick breakfast and the trip to Felts Field. I finished in time to get dad's car home so he could drop me off to start another day of the same. It was tiring, but I loved it.

Long before CPT, I had already had one experience in flight. My father was an Infantry officer in the Washington National Guard, 161st Infantry after his service in WWI. At the time of their summer encampment in 1928, the pilot of the ages, Charles Lindberg was scheduled to fly his "Spirit of St. Louis" into Spokane's Felts Field and the infantry moved there as an Honor Guard. An entrepreneur offered a 15-minute flight in a Ford Tri-motor for $15.00 and my Dad decided that at 7 years old, I should experience that. Brother Orien Jr. was too young and the family didn't have the funds for all to go. I was it!

While I was excited, I must admit I was scared silly once that monster started its engines and began to roll. I was seated about mid-ship on the right aisle. There is only one row on each side. When I was strapped in, I clutched the wooden seat handles until my knuckles turned white. I don't think my head turned more than one degree from straight-ahead until I heard my fellow passengers scream, "There he is! There he is!"

I turned long enough to see the familiar silver form of that famous aircraft along side our plane. I looked long enough to plant that image in my mind, then made the mistake of looking down at the far away earth. Immediately, I went back to staring at the bulkhead until I felt the wheels bump down on the dirt of Felts Field. Back with the family, I had only praise for the great experience, with no mention of white knuckles.

I think every pilot remembers his first trip aloft with nobody else aboard! Maybe from the moment *after* my first solo in the Porterfield at Felts Field in Spokane on that eventful March day in 1941, I always felt supremely confident of myself in control of an aircraft, with maybe just a few exceptions. But I have to confess I wasn't too sure when Don Jones, my first instructor, told me to roll to a stop after about the sixth practice landing of the day. I didn't dream why until I came to a complete stop and with engine idling. He opened the door and got out, then turned and put his hand on my shoulder and shouted over the engine noise, "Take it around a few times. I want to watch from here." Then closed the door!

The thought very definitely entered my mind, 'am I ready for this?' I hoped so because I was alone when I pushed the throttle forward and started my roll. My heart was pounding. I tried to be super-precise, pushed the stick forward, tail off the ground, not too far! Air speed? I have enough? The Porterfield answered for me when I had enough that it wanted to fly off the ground without my effort. Pull up. Not too steep! Now turn 90 degrees left, continue to climb to 800 feet, turn left onto downwind leg. I looked left down at the field and could see Don following my efforts. When I looked back, then ahead, I was shocked to find a yellow cub entering the downwind leg ahead of me. My first thought and reaction was to hit the brakes. I nearly pushed them through the floorboard before it sank in; brakes don't work in the air! I throttled back a little. Watch the air speed. In between parts of a prayer, I was shouting at the Cub to hurry. He turned onto his base leg and then onto final. By this time I was satisfied I wouldn't over-run him and his pattern gave me a reminder of what I should do. I followed him in. When I touched down, it was like a feather. I let the tail drop, ecstatic because I had done it. Soloed! Flown all by myself.

I wanted to stop and get Don but he was smiling, applauding and waiving me around again, then again and again. By the time he let me stop, I may have been over-confident. "But as happened all through my flying career, whenever I got that feeling, God brought me back to earth with something to remind me. This time it was a crash two weeks later that killed dear Don Jones and another of his students, Warren Brooks. It happened in the same plane that I had flown in my first solo and which I flew that day just thirty minutes before they took it up and spun in.

In 1940, recruiting boards for both Army Air Corps and Naval Flying Corps made trips into Spokane. I took both tests, probably because I wanted to double my chances of being accepted. When I passed both, I was told to make up my mind. I think I reasoned something like this, 'If we ever fought a war and I flew back after a battle and if my army field had been hit, it might have holes in it, but at least it would be there! If the same thing happened in the Navy, it would be possible the landing field wouldn't be there and no place to land! What then?' I chose Army.

Instead of taking me immediately to my Veronica Lake, the Army notified me that I was on a waiting list and they would call me. I had almost forgotten it when the Japanese bombed Pearl Harbor and a telegram reminded me. My CPT program had progressed through both Primary and Secondary Phases. I had a private license and had graduated into the powerful 225 horsepower, Waco UPF-7 biplanes with their open cockpits, helmets and goggles and everything! I was already a pilot.

My first ever passenger was my brother Orien Jr. In the Porterfield I decided to show him my full bag of tricks that at that time was limited to steep turns and S turns across a road. In less that ten minutes he was airsick and lost everything he had eaten that day. I started to land immediately, but he was too embarrassed. He used both our handkerchiefs to clean up the mess, but they weren't enough. So still in the air, we both took off our undershirts. That pretty well got it cleaned up. Then, I'm sure against all regulations; he threw all the soiled clothes out a window and into some farmer's field.

Only then would he let me land. I was pretty sure his first ride would be his last, but rules were changed after Pearl Harbor and one class after I was commissioned and got my Army Air Corps Wings, he did the same. His assignments were to the Air Transport Command and as a fighter pilot, I took great joy in singing that classic, "Mother, take down your service star, your son's in the ATC" every time we were able to get together. In flying those monsters, however, his total flying time went by mine like I was standing still.

CHAPTER 4

# AIR CORPS CAREER

BEFORE LEAVING FOR THE service, I had been one of Spokane's better bowlers. Bowling at the Bolero in 1941 I had attracted the attention of General John B. Brooks who had arrived in Spokane in command of the Second Air Force. He was a bowling fanatic and when I made my usual stop at the Bolero after Gonzaga classes, more often than not, he was there or would be before I finished a few games. After a while he didn't ask me, probably because of a lifetime in the military, he would "order" me to be there at 1600 the next afternoon to bowl with him. I didn't mind. In fact, got a kick out of it. His bowling was hopeless with a thousand bad habits ingrained so hints were useless.

When I mentioned a few weeks into our friendship that I had been accepted for flight training by the Army Air Corps. He got excited and told me, "If you don't go through Randolph Field, known as the 'West Point of the Air', you aren't a real pilot," and then stated simply that he would 'fix it'. I thought no more of it until that day shortly after Pearl Harbor when my orders to report arrived.

With at least a bakers dozen of other young Spokanites, I was sworn in and assigned a serial number. When orders arrived a day or so after that, all the others went to the West Coast Training Command in California. My orders alone read, Kelly Field, Texas, the Gulf Coast Training Command. A few eyebrows were raised at the unusual assignment but I knew why. General Brooks had remembered his promise.

The Japanese dropped the bomb that started the war on December 7. My swearing in and departure for training came only weeks later. Everybody knew we weren't prepared for war as far as planes and other weapons of war were concerned. I can tell you, they didn't even have uniforms available for the great influx of young men reporting for duty.

Everybody was at the depot to see me off. Mother was crying. Dad's jowls were flexing, but dry-eyed, a hug and a final very firm handshake. Did I see his eyes glistening? Orien junior or just 'Junior' as we called him from birth, was grim-faced, but managed a slight curling of lips to nearly smile. He also hugged and pumped my hand. After Pearl Harbor, the requirements for Aviation Cadet Training had changed and he had applied – 18 years old. Little Roger pushed his way to my side and grasped me tightly about the waist. I was pretty choked up by all the emotion, which embarrassed me to a degree. "Hey, no big deal. I'll be writing and I'll get a leave." I noticed I was a little choked up myself.

Then as gently as possible, I suggested my family get out of there. I had to say goodbye to Gwendolyn. Finally, after the engineer had already tooted the whistles a couple times, they got the idea and reluctantly moved away, all waiving but mother was bawling into her handkerchief.

I looked down at my sweetheart. I don't think I had ever seen her look prettier. Absences must truly make the heart grow fonder... and I hadn't even left yet! For a moment, I held her shoulders and stared trying to memorize those beautiful features. Then I covered her face with kisses saving the last for a long, long buzz on ruby lips. We held each other tightly and I whispered "I love you. I love you," over and over again. "Promise me you'll wait! Promise!" "I will. I will." A few more whistle 'toots' and a 'chug' let me know I had to step onto the step or maybe miss the war. While we slowly gained speed, I stayed on the bottom step waiving and she ran a few steps alongside. A few other guys behind me also with good-byes were about to push me off my step. So it ended, the young guy off to fight a war, although it seemed ages off in the future. I was headed for training.

We were picking up speed, swaying, as I soon found out, trains do in motion. It was not a troop train, just a common Pullman, but I can't recall a single female, at least in my car. I was assigned an upper berth and I tossed up my new leather bag, which Dad had had them stamp with a gold C.K.G. Then I climbed in to 'reconnoiter'. Kind of cramped, but certainly enough room for my five foot eleven inches and a half and 142 pounds. I liked the little net hammock for storing some items, so I delved into my bag to see what mother had packed. I found an envelope with letters from both my folks full of love and admonishments. And, an extra ten-dollar bill from Dad.

Travel for the next week was routine. Three times a day I wound my way through rocking Pullman cars to reach the diner. The food was fine and I decided I could become accustomed to linen tablecloths, silver and liveried waiters to cater to me.

Because General Brooks had 'fixed it' so that I went to the Gulf Coast Training Area to reach Randolph Field, the West Point of the Air, I left Spokane without knowing a single soul on this journey. I met and spent time with a lot of young people, but made no alliances and when I had reached San Antonio, Texas, a week later, I was as alone as when I left.

I disembarked with the apprehension that comes with meeting the unknown. Very quickly, I saw a sign saying Aviation Cadets and it gave some security. Slowly, more young men gathered until we had two dozen, half-hour later. Then we were herded by several-uniformed non-COM's out the door and to an olive drab coach.

Now I was not a 'zootsuiter' by any means but I was 'up to date'. Assigned to a temporary 'tent-city' on the edge of Kelly Field, Texas. My wardrobe consisted of Camel Hair tan sport coat, slacks and brown and white saddle shoes. Blessed with a full head of wavy hair courtesy of my father's genes, I wore it quite full with the sides dovetailed in back. One thing they did have ready was a barbershop and we were marched in almost immediately after arrival. A few, who didn't know what came next, patiently explained to one of the barbers, just how they would like it cut. With a smile, they might listen to the instructions, then proceed to give the same 'buzz' cut to each of us. The one I was assigned to gleefully clapped his hands. "Oh boy. Look what I have here!" Then he cut it as short as could be done without a razor. With my civilian get-up, I looked absolutely ridiculous!

One of my tent mates, who had become a buddy, was Corporal John J. Martin, Jr. from Berwick, Pennsylvania. He was already in the army when the war started and had asked for transfer to flight training. His temporary wearing apparel was already army uniforms and he felt sorry enough for me to loan me a floppy blue 'fatigue hat' to cover my bald pate.

The next morning we fell out for roll call in the gray light of dawn. As a Sergeant called each name in order, I sang out "Here" when he got to me. After Zimmerman, when all were accounted for, I heard "Aviation Cadet Clayton K. Gross, two paces forward." I did. "About Face!" I did. "Gentlemen, I want you all to see a great haircut. Uncover mister."

I felt the temperature of my face rise 10 instant degrees in the morning air as the rest of the troops burst out in hilarious laughter. Don't argue, I had been told. Just say, "Yes sir." I did.

A week later we were all uniformed, out of our tents and into wooden barracks. I learned a lesson quickly. The non-commissioned officer in charge of our particular building called us together near his room.

"All right," he said. "I want three men who can type. Sing out!" Now I could, using two fingers. Maybe I could get a 'cushy' job. I was too late. Three hands were already up.

"You, you and you," Sarge said. "Get those mops and buckets and swab this place so clean we could eat off the floor! And *let* that be a lesson to you. Never volunteer for anything in the Army." We settled into routine. Not an airplane in sight except overhead we spent our days in -'close order drill', lengthy marching and inspections – lots of them. We were assigned a designation – Aviation Cadet Class 42-H, the first to enter the service after Pearl Harbor.

CHAPTER 5

# WHERE ARE THE AIRPLANES?

THE WEEKS OF PRE-FLIGHT were designed to let us know we were "in the Army now – not behind the plow" and they pretty well did that. Of course, I felt I didn't need it after a summer of Citizens Military Training Corps and a three-year 'hitch' in the 161st infantry. It was of little matter and I suffered those weeks with all the neophytes.

Then came the great day. We headed to a flight school! My group boarded buses for a small town toward the Texas panhandle, Coleman. Where we went didn't make any difference to most, now that we would be flying. We were met by a joyful group, – 42-G members who could hardly wait to exercise "upper class" privileges. They started as we disembarked and didn't stop until lights out.

Young and strong, it's a good thing! Life under our upperclassmen and the indoctrination kind of wears a guy out by the end of the day. The playing of 'TAPS' was a fitting finish and restful. I found out that it had words and it helped to contemplate them:

*DAY IS DONE. Gone the Sun.*
*From the Lake. From the Hill.*
*From the Sky. All is well.*
*Safely Rest. God is nigh.*

*Thanks and Praise for our Days*
*' Neath the Sun. ' Neath the Stars.*
*' Neath the Sky. As we go.*
*This we know. God is nigh.*

All the frivolity and horseplay of minutes earlier ceased at lights out and gave a chance to lay quietly, reflect on all that had happened, and wonder of the future.

Before sleep came, my mind would flit from thought to thought. 'I know what I'll do next to my upperclassman. I love flying – I hope I'm on tomorrow. What the hell good is knowing the 'principle of the gasoline engine' going to do for me? The war news: will it be over before I get there? Not likely! The Japs are still pushing us around. I wonder what Gwen is doing? Some guys lay awake worrying about flying the PT-19A. Not me, thanks to a near hundred-hour head start, I'm a hot pilot!' Eventually I would fall asleep.

The days meld together. We find we must busy ourselves with books as well as flying –"Principles of the Gasoline Engine", "Meteorology". Hey! That might help! I now know what pretty clouds to avoid. As far as the gas engines were concerned, I didn't intend to get out and fix one – but I learned anyway.

I had my introduction to discipline training in pre-flight – certainly learning what a "brace" was and how to always draw 'one more chin' to please an upper classman. When we got to Coleman for primary flight training, we were introduced to real "hazing" for the first time. They used the pair system. Fortunately for me my upperclassman whose duty was to whip me into line was a great guy. The scion of a well-to-do bakery family from the East, he acted gruff as hell, but really couldn't bring himself to do any more than pretend to be mad at me. The net result was that he took as much punishment from me as I got from him. At graduation for his class, I was sorry to see him go, although I looked forward to moving up myself.

We got 'racked back' for a hundred different offenses, real or imagined. For a certain number of 'demerits' you walked tours of the quadrangle in full dress, sometimes with rifles. Each evening we entertained 42-G with their project of the evening. One more memorable example was a demonstration of the firing sequence of the 16-cylinder radial engine. Sixteen of us in skivvies formed a circle arched with hands and feet on the floor. We counted off so you knew which number cylinder you were. Then when it was your turn to "fire" kicked both legs out straight. Woe was to the cylinder that miss-fired or did so out of order. When that happened, and it always did, the engine shut down and we got a lecture on how stupid we were. When we did get a good rhythm going in proper sequence, the bad guys would 'rev' up the speed until we blew it – then the lecture.

The underclass also was responsible for such menial tasks as making beds, shining shoes all at the whim of the privileged one. Our time to get even came with this. I routinely short-sheeted John and he would just as routinely roar at me to come do it over. That meant two jobs instead of one, but it was worth it. One night he crawled in expecting to find a blockade as usual and was pleased to find a normal extension of the sheet envelope. What he didn't find out till the following morning was that I had emptied the fine soot from a stovepipe into the foot area of his bed. His feet and legs were absolutely coal-black when he got up. Of course, I had to use an hour of my leisure time hand-scrubbing sheets, but again, it was worth it!

At another time, John was headed for one of our weekend dances and was impeccable in his Class 'A' uniform. I, of course, had to put a final shine on the oxfords. He put one foot on the bench, hiking the trouser leg up for access and in doing so, exposed a spotless white stocking. I couldn't resist it. While he was in distracting conversation with a friend, I gently painted a one-inch ring around the white sock with my little Shinola brush. It wasn't until I tried to do the same on the other foot that he noticed and for a moment, I thought I had pushed too far. When I traded a clean pair of my own and accepted my ten demerits, we were, thankfully, back to normal.

Funny that later my being 'hazed' was the most memorable part of primary, except for flying, of course.

Admittedly I was over-confident when I finally reached primary flight school. Eighty-two hours of flight time and fresh from secondary CPT training in the 220-horsepower Waco UPF-7, the pretty low-winged monoplane PT-19A held no fear for me! Then another miracle occurred which accentuated my already swelled ego. On arrival at Coleman, Texas, near the panhandle of that huge state, we spent two days moving in and attending required orientation lectures, with the usual formations, braces and other hazing by our upper class. Finally the big day arrived. Instead of the usual Class A dress, we were told to don flight suits, helmets and goggles and march in formation to the flight line. Each barracks was a squadron and each was divided into flights of seven for assignment to a flight instructor. Each group of seven marched single file to an assigned position, in front of a PT-19, where our instructors waited.

As my flight reached it's position we were halted by command, told "left face" and "at ease," all of which we did. Our civilian instructor had his back turned with a clipboard and roster of his students positioned on the wing of a PT-19.

Over his shoulder he shouted instructions, "As I call your name, sing out." And he started, "Green," "Here!" "Groendahl,"

"Here!" "Gross," "Here!" Before he went on, he stopped as if to study the roster, then turned and looked at me. "Gross, how the hell did you get down here?" It was Sam Porath, my instructor from Spokane, Washington, the guy who taught me to fly the Waco UPF-7, the last instructor I had flown with who had accepted a civilian flight instructor job with the Army as if to prove the small world syndrome. After he came over to shake hands with me, he went back to the roster. Then he selected me to take the first ride in the PT-19. I was relaxed. He was a friend and he wasn't military. After formalities concluded including a lengthy lecture by the military commander, I got a short bit of orientation and then we did a few snap rolls and after one landing, he let me try one. This was our introduction to military flying and I got out, feeling like Rickenbacker himself. I felt very sorry for my classmates who had never been in an aircraft before. I was definitely over-confident. After our first ride, I was assigned a new instructor, a D. K. Gibb who might have been assigned to calm me down. After a shaky start when he pointed out the local mountain and I didn't see anything bigger than an ant hill, compared to mountains in the Northwest, we got along fine.

And Shirley…It's strange that I was so much in love with Gwen that I was almost led astray. Every time I could raise the price of a long distance call, I spent it for a few minutes on the horn with my sweetie. That happened several times a week.

Now Coleman, Texas, site of the flying school up in the panhandle, was not that big a town and so if you placed a call in the evening, the only time we had free time and could afford the lower rates, you got the same operator every night. At first Shirley was all business, but after a dozen times she began to make comments and eventually began to tease me, "Maybe you could save a lot of money if you had a local girl." She made other suggestions, too. By the time I was an upperclassman, we found a day when I could get off base, she had a night off, and we had a blind date. I didn't think she was as pretty as Gwen was, but she wasn't bad and she was there. We went to a carnival, had a good time, smooched a little in her car before she dropped me back to the base. I'm glad we couldn't get another day clear together before I moved on, or who knows what would have happened.

She gave me a bad time putting calls through to Gwen, but did do it. That was the end of my Texas romance.

Here we go again! I lost Don Jones, my instructor with student Warren Brooks in their fatal crash in the early part of my CPT training. Now a week into Primary flight school and déjà vu! In a morning training flight, Cadet Stanley Howe and Instructor Halbert flew a PT-19A straight into the ground. Halbert had lots of experience. Howe was on his third time aloft.

Conjecture in the barracks is Howe had to freeze on the controls and Halbert couldn't overpower him. Too bad, but having had it happen twice in my first year of aviating, I guess this business can be deadly. My confidence is not shaken. I can hardly wait for my next flight, but I had to. All flights were canceled for that day while an inspection of our fleet of PT-19's was conducted. Back to the war, the next day.

The class of 42-H at Coleman was made up of guys from 29 different states at graduation time. It just seemed like most were Texans because they composed 40% of the group and they never let you forget where we were and what we were. I took it personally, the first few times I was called a 'damned Yankee'. I hung out more with my buddy John Martin (from Pennsylvania) and Green and Groendal (from Illinois and Michigan) and after the first few dozen times, I didn't notice it anymore. So, I'm a damn Yankee!

Here also began a habit that has remained for all my life. Without even noticing it myself, I mimic speech of people I talk to, southern, foreign, anything. If I talk to you long enough; I'll have your accent! Thus, it didn't take long before you couldn't tell me from a Texan. I was in a soda shop in Coleman one day and the young lady asked, "Where y'all from?" I said, "I ain't from Texas. I'm from Washington, y'all." She answered, "Oh, you're another one of them!" "Yup!"

The days became routine. Hours in the air accumulated. We became "Upper Class" when 42-I arrived. The Primary Flight Course was 75 hours. A half dozen classmates did not make it – washed out and sent to Bombardier or Navigator training. Not me. This damn Yankee made it and was through with Primary and headed to the next test – BASIC FLYING SCHOOL.

CHAPTER 6

# BASIC AND ADVANCED TRAINING

As PRIMARY TRAINING WOUND down in the latter part of April, everybody was guessing where we would go for Basic, I knew of course, that General Brooks had arranged it so I casually bet my entire $75.00 monthly pay check that we would go to Randolph. A few days later, orders were posted, we were headed for Waco, Texas, and I was the most destitute guy in the class.

We arrived in Waco in 2½ ton trucks and from the moment we touched ground, the upper class had us in a perpetual 'brace". I remember the first four hours very well, marched into a barracks, assigned a cot and locker; we were told to have bed made and gear properly stowed in thirty minutes to stand inspection. At that time an upper-class group promptly tore up every bed and told us to do better in 15 minutes for re-inspection. The second time, half of the beds survived including mine, but the locker contents were unceremoniously dumped on the floor and after a lecture about how raunchy we were, we got another 15 minutes to do it again. At the time of the third inspection, lunchtime saved further destruction of our efforts. We were lined up at attention and then in a fast double-time herded by column to the mess hall. If we thought there would be a moment of relaxation here, forget it. The lunch lasted fifteen minutes and we were harassed continually, eating a square, square meal, eyes riveted straight ahead; fork or spoon from plate, straight up to mouth level, straight to mouth and then just as squarely reversing the trip. I never saw a thing I ate. Really under the stress. I didn't taste it either, so still don't know what it was. Unfortunately many trips of the utensil reached the mouth with nothing on or in it. When the 15 minutes elapsed, a whistle blew and we were back in formation double-timing back to the barracks. I can't say what the hell my fellow classmates underwent for the balance of the day because at that moment the loudspeaker crackled to life and I was startled to hear, "Aviation Cadet Clayton K. Gross, report to the Officer of the Day". I trembled when I asked a nearby upperclassman where it was, wondering, "What in hell could I have done now?" Reminded never to walk outdoors, go on the double, I hurried to find my fate.

Ushered into the OD's office at rigid attention I found a young First Lieutenant holding a telegram. He let me sweat for a moment then in measured tones said, "I don't know who you know, Gross, but I have orders to send you on to Randolph Field."

"Yes, Sir!"

"You will find it's not who you know but what you do that will get you ahead in the service" "Yes, Sir"

"Dismiss."

I did a picture perfect about face and went out the door. I did know "who I knew". General Brooks had kept his promise. The problem was I had already lost all my bets and was completely broke. My buddy Martin loaned me $10.00 until payday. It was probably my $10.00.

As I started out the door of the OD's office, I checked hat position and prepared for a double time trip back to the barracks.

Then it suddenly struck me, what could they do to me now? I walked back at a leisurely pace unchallenged by anyone. I felt like I had a measure of revenge at Waco Texas Flying School.

My buddies were frantically readying themselves for another inspection but took time to wish me well as I repacked everything and moved out, alone again and probably the loneliest cadet in the Corps.

Randolph Field! The very name was exciting! This was where the cadets met Veronica Lake. The drive down the entry road with the famous tower anchoring the end was enough to raise my blood pressure to new heights.

It was another gift of God that I was alphabetically placed with Gunter, Hale and Hamilton. Although all were Texans and again I was a "damn Yankee", we hit it off from the start.

Boy-the rules! Our dress was dictated down to the last garter. The white glove inspections of our four-man room were brutal. Woe to the four of us should the inspector find dust on the sash over the door.

We added new dimensions to our physical fitness routine and we ran a mile or played touch football on alternate days. The first day of the mile run nearly did me in – six minutes or under required. I was immediately sorry I was a smoker, but everyone else was as well and I learned to live through it. I loved the football. I had tried to play in high school, but Coach always said my 112 pounds was a little light and the uniforms were too big for me. Now, weighing in the 160's, the result of proper diet and regular hours, I still had speed. I fit in!

These were war years and many good athletes were in the service – quite a few at Randolph Field. Roommate Gean Hale played at Rice University and on our alternate day team, was the quarterback. I still remember the huddle when he said, "Gross, go down the sideline and cut across the end zone." I flew! Didn't look until I broke sharp right across the end zone. The ball was coming in. I extended my arms to the ultimate and felt the ball settle gently on my fingertips. I held it! Call me a player, among other things.

The confidence in my flying abilities persisted – for awhile! That's another story.....

Randolph had rules for everything, mostly designed to make us look as if we 'belonged' at the West Point of the Air. Nothing, not even a scrap of paper was to be carried in shirt pockets, which incidentally had to be buttoned at all times. Metal collar stays were required to keep the collars fully extended, stiffer than a triple dose of starch. Shirts and pants were, of course, spotless and well creased. Garters were worn at all times and subject to 'snapping' to prove their presence. Shoes, of course, were maintained at a high shine capable of image reflection. There was never a dull moment, which eased the loneliness of my solitary transfer.

My introduction to the 450 HP North American BT-14 went smoothly and within a few hours in the air I was again smugly confident of my ability. Unfortunately it must have showed. I found that out when Lt. Berg, our flight commander, gave me my 20-hour check ride. I lifted the BT off cleanly, precisely making each turn at the right altitude and angle. We went through the routine of turns, rolls, and other required exercises. Each, I felt, completed as well as the Lieutenant himself could have done. When he suddenly cut the throttle and shouted, "Forced Landing", I quickly selected a flat open field and properly glided to within a few hundred feet of the area before he poured the coal on again and ordered me back to Randolph. My landing was a thing of beauty. You simply could not even feel the touchdown. As I rolled toward our parking area, I was grinning from ear to ear and still was when I climbed out of the cockpit. Then he cut me down...

He stood silently for two or three minutes while I waited for a compliment, then without the slightest semblance of a smile said, "Not very good, Mister." "I'll give you one more chance before I wash you out. If I were you I would work very hard on everything. That's all!" I saluted silently, absolutely stunned!

That night I lay in bed, staring at the darkened ceiling wondering what I would tell my father who was so proud of my accomplishments. I just would not be able to face him. My feelings about Lt. Berg varied from disbelief to hatred to...God only knows what. I turned cold and clammy whenever I saw or passed him. My hours in the BT-14 continued to pile up until I was within ten of completing the basic course and he had not said another word to me. I almost began to relax knowing in my own mind that the check ride had really been good, not what he claimed! June 12th I passed him on the flight line and he stopped me. "Did I ever give you another check ride? No? Get your parachute and meet me here in five minutes."

I was panicked. I got my parachute with eyes so bleary I had trouble seeing the chest strap to fasten it. When we reached the assigned plane, my knees were shaking so badly I had great difficulty climbing into the cockpit. I prayed fervently as I started the engine. My taxiing was jerky. It seemed to me the brakes were extra sensitive and the more I tried to smooth it out, the worse it got. Finally I completed warm up, got clearance for takeoff and with heart in mouth, finally lifted off the runway. Still proceeding straight ahead as instructed I was probably 200 feet in the air when he suddenly chopped the throttle and said, "Forced Landing."

I could not believe it...on takeoff? I put the nose down and turned one way and then the other. I couldn't find anything suitable. At about 50 feet he put the power back on and patiently said, "All right. Forget it." The rest of the ride was very much the same. Hardly anything went right and each failure deepened my concern and raised my blood pressure. When directed back to the field I was sure it was all over. This would probably be my last landing for the Army Air Corps.

Naturally, it was a lousy one. I slightly misjudged it and hit the landing gear roughly on the cement surface so we bounded two or three feet in the air. I tried to catch it by pouring on power, but it was too late.

We literally crunched down on all three points and then rolled ahead. By the time I parked, I was as low in spirits as it is possible to be. I had head down when I faced Lt. Berg. Then I heard him say, "Well, that was better. Keep working on it." And he turned and walked away leaving me with mouth open, in disbelief. I knew then that the whole charade was to cut me down a notch or two but I was so happy and relieved, I didn't care. I was going to be a pilot!

Leaving Randolph was as unforgettable as my arrival, maybe more so. The schedule after completion of Basic Training allowed three days travel time, but for those of us assigned to Kelly Field on the other side of San Antonio, we had two days vacation, not needed for travel. My Texas roommates used it for a quick trip home. I took my time staying at Randolph, a little bowling, swimming and whatever. At Randolph, each Cadet was issued two sets of printed nametags upon arrival. Red ones to be worn as an underclassman and blue ones for the great mid-point day when you became the upper class and can get even for all the hazing you had undergone those six or seven weeks as the lowest of the low. The upper class in our barracks had already donned their 'blue' and was busy making plans for the incoming plebes.

As I packed my footlocker one evening, I found my saved red tags. I don't know why except that just like my mother, I seldom threw anything away that still looked good. I got a fiendish idea! The men of Class 42-I in our barracks knew me, but down the line a little, they didn't. I replaced my blue tags with underclass red. I took garters off and rolled my socks down until they actually showed at the shoe tops. I found shirt and pants that had been rolled up in my dirty clothes bag for several days and were hopelessly filled with a thousand wrinkles. I left the collar button open, loosely tied a tie, unevenly and not tucked in. Two buttons above the belt line were left open. I put a pack of cigarettes in each shirt pocket and another bulging out a pants pocket. I got a hand full of dirt from the garden area and sprinkled both shoes with a layer of dust. I lit a cigarette and jammed the other hand in a side pocket. With cap tipped back until it was nearly falling off, I started out. Walking down the inner hall of the second building down the line, I found exactly what I was searching for, four new upper classmen laying plans for newcomers. I listened outside the open door, chuckling at my little joke, then with a raunchy slouch, stuck my grinning face into the room.

"Hi, ya guys, anybody want to go bowling?"

I could tell from their unbelieving, mouth-open gapes, they could not believe what they were seeing.

One of them, probably a born leader, took the initiative, "You drive in here, Mister?" He didn't say it. He shouted it.

For maybe five minutes I played the rube. And the more I did, the redder his face got and the tighter he clenched his fists. He put me in a brace, which I went along with for a minute, then broke out, which changed his color from red to purple. Plainly he and the others to a lesser degree were not fooling and since I didn't want anyone hurt, especially me, I thought I would explain my little joke. I couldn't do it. Every time I tried, they got madder. I heard a fifteen-minute lecture on how slim my chances were to make it three days let alone three months at Randolph. I was told there had NEVER been anybody as raunchy as me at Randolph. I'm sure they were right. My little joke had backfired completely! I was in ramrod straight brace against the wall and when I showed fifteen chins, he wanted twenty. I was having trouble breathing and so was he, for different reasons. After a half-hour, he let me go. We were both limp. I didn't try to give him the truth, first because I wanted out of there – way out! And if he had believed me, then he would have had the satisfaction of knowing he got even with his upper class. Best to just get out of there and I packed and I did.

Kelly Field and the finish of flight training lay ahead and I rode the next transportation the forty miles into San Antonio and twenty out the other side to get there.

A great deal of Kelly Field was temporary that is, the hangars were wood, built for World War I and were still in service. Our quarters, however, were nice, a permanent multi-storied structure in Southwestern style architecture. Each room housed four cadets, alphabetically, of course. Mine again held Gross, Ed Gunter, Gean Hale and John Hamilton. We got along fine. I didn't have an opportunity to become over-confident. As we had progressed through primary, then basic flight training, my advantage of 80 previous hours in the air dwindled in importance. Besides my first ride in the AT-6 was memorable. It happened on July 7, the second day at Kelly, marched to the flight line, alphabetically divided into flights and sections, we gathered in the ready room of our WWI hangar and listened to a no-nonsense lecture by Capt. Briley, our squadron commander. At the conclusion, he announced that because Lt. Burton, my assigned instructor, was on vacation and that he, the Captain, would handle our section until his return. My name was the first on the list.

"I'm not sure the weather is flyable today. I'll take the first student and we'll go check it. If it's okay, we'll radio back. Otherwise, we'll wait until it is. Gross, Clayton K., get your parachute and let's go!"

"Yes, Sir!" I couldn't believe he couldn't look up as I had done and see the ceiling was about two or three hundred feet with slight drizzle, definitely not flyable, but then cadets don't make such decisions. I grabbed my gear and followed him. The AT-6 was not a frightening bird. It was built by North American as was the BT-14 cleaner looking, more horsepower, and of course, for the first time, retractable landing gear.

The Captain told me he would ride in the front cockpit, normally the student's position, for this first ride. I climbed in the rear and studied the newness while he proceeded with checks and start up. Most noticeable to me was the absence of a control stick, an empty socket moved as he checked control surfaces. The rear seat stick was in brackets on the right side. "Well," I said to myself, "If he wanted me to have one, he would say so."

Kelly had no runways – one huge flat field, much as I had seen in WW I movies. We reached position and with tower permission, roared to a take off and began a smooth climb toward the low ceiling. I felt a thrill as I heard the "Thunk" of the landing gear tucking into the belly. As I could have told him, we were in the clouds before we reached 300 feet. He put the nose down and over the radio said, "No good. We won't fly today." Then on the intercom to me, "As long as we're up here, we'll try it a little, you've got it." I panicked not knowing if I should grab the stick and try to insert it; grab the microphone and tell him I had no control or what." As a consequence, I tried to do everything and got nothing done. The left wing dipped and we started to slowly dive left and down. After a second, the Captain took control again and righted us, and obviously perturbed, said "I said, you have it!" By this time I had the stick in my hand, but not in place and the wing dipped again. I decided I better explain quickly, so abandoned my effort with the stick and grabbed the mike. "Sir, I don't have a stick back here." He looked back over his shoulder incredulously and I waived the loose stick to him. He shook his head and took over to land without further effort to test me.

When we got out, he stood menacingly in front of me, hands on hips. "How the hell did you expect to fly without controls?" "Sir, I thought it was purposely out for this ride."

LIVE BAIT | 39

He shook his head and walked away. There wasn't a chance I could be overconfident in advanced flight training!

Routine set in and the hours aloft piled up.

Then the word got out, first by scuttlebutt and then officially, you don't graduate without night flying orientation. Like everything else new, it made for some concerned moments and accelerated pulse along with other symptoms but nothing out of reason. Besides that beautiful night in August had clear skies and lots of moonlight, insured that I could see a little. A piece of cake, I decided.

We split into sections for aircraft assignment *and area* assignment. The sky around Kelly was divided into quadrants much to my relief so that we wouldn't have dozens of novice aviators flying blindly around in the dark and running into each other. Each quadrant would have two trainers, but at different levels by at least two thousand feet. Each of us was to fly for one hour, then return for two practice landings, then taxi back to our squadron area. The first student assigned to each plane was to park and leave the engine running. The second would turn it off so that it might be refueled for the next pair. That system came as close to killing me as anything else that would happen in my flying career!

I was the first to fly in my assigned craft. Over the past few months of flight school I had developed a unique, maybe kind of hot pilot exit from my bird once a flight was finished. I would make a normal exit from the left side of the cockpit onto the "cat-walk" designed for that, then rather than walk down to the lowest part of the wing to jump to the ground I stepped off the leading edge and would bounce off the tire and onto the ground. I did it all the time. When I finished my required hour from about 11:30 until just after midnight, I was elated at both the beauty of the night from the air and my successful flight. Smiling from ear to ear I shucked my seat belt and shoulder straps and climbed out. Because I was first, I left the engine running per instructions. I put my right foot on the front of the wing and stepped off into space. At that split second, I realized the whirling propeller was inches in front of my face. I could not stop, but my right hand instinctively shot back and by miracle, caught the radio antenna positioned in front of the windshield. Grasping it, I swung my body against the engine cowling inches from the metal Hamilton propeller. I was able to draw back to the walk and exit posterior with heart pounding and knees shaking. I said a prayer of thanks.

I didn't completely quit the front exit habit, but believe me; I made sure the engine was off for the rest of my career.

Only a little over three more weeks to go! If I don't screw up some way, I'll be a pilot and an officer in the Army Air Corps. A dream comes true!

On the way to my room after dinner, I stopped by the bulletin board; a new order was prominently posted...

> "Within the next few days, two officers will visit this base. They are black. All personnel are notified that they shall be afforded all courtesies and respect due anyone wearing the uniform of a commissioned officer. All personnel are cautioned that any violation will be dealt with quickly and severely.
>
> By order of the Commander-in-Chief
> Franklin Delano Roosevelt, President"

I shrugged and headed for my quarters. I asked my roomies if they had seen the order. They had. "Why did they need that kind of thing?" You damn Yankees just don't understand that there are a lot of people in this part of the country likely not to accept them if they aren't threatened before hand.

"Oh!" I remembered all three of them were Texans. I hadn't been exposed to that feeling in the Northwest. "I see." In the next couple days, the warning was repeated on the intercom several times.

They did come and go and I didn't even see them. I have no idea what was the purpose of their visit. I do know I would have saluted if I had seen them.

As time went quickly by and the 65 hours of advanced flying school neared an end, my roomies and I had many things to prepare. We were measured for officers' uniforms. Even more important to us – all four were to be married on Graduation Day!

---

FOOTNOTE: Sorting through my mother's belongings – long after the war, I discovered copies of the correspondence initiated by General Brooks to ensure my attendance at Randolph and Kelly Fields for basic and advanced training. I can guess that no other cadet in the system had all this brass working on their behalf.

CHAPTER 7

# TWO HUGE STEPS... GRADUATION AND MARRIAGE

**G**WEN WAS EIGHTEEN AND that was not very old and as I matured, I began to understand her mother's reluctance to lose her daughter to marriage at that age. The fact that we were at war and I was in the somewhat risky business of piloting further strengthened her opposition to the union. She confessed years later that she had visions of Gwen being widowed and pregnant long before she ever had time to teach her all she meant to tell her before the important step of marriage. Nevertheless, we were in love and against all opposition, we steamed full speed ahead.

Gwen had not traveled any more than I had when we finalized plans to marry on my graduation day from flying school. She began the scary trip from Spokane alone heading into the unknown. My father pulled strings to at least get her a berth for the four-day trip. I was in the frantic final days before the end of training. It was with reluctance the 'wheels' at Kelly Field granted me a four-hour pass to meet her train. I was absolutely tingling with the excitement of seeing my intended after nine months of separation and when the train pulled in two hours late, I was running up and down the length of the Pullman section trying to spot everybody alighting. It seemed to me that half of the civilian population was aboard. The end result was that I did not find her. Some time was wasted trying to find out if more trains were expected – they weren't.

I went to the Plaza Hotel where my three roommates and I had reserved rooms for our fiancée's. She wasn't there. I tried other downtown hotels and finally was told by the desk of the second, "Yes, she is in room 721." I trembled as I knocked on the door and when it opened, I gathered her into my arms. – Whoops! She was an attractive young lady, newly arrived and looking for her fiancé'. It wasn't me and she wasn't mine. An hour later, I found Gwen sitting on a suitcase in the lobby of the Gunter Hotel – in tears. The reunion wiped away those and the anxiety I felt in my search.

In the remaining hour of my leave, we became reacquainted. Installed in the proper "honeymoon" hotel and introduced to some of my roommates wives-to-be, I left her and went back to Kelly Field to become an officer.

The AC class of 42-H, Kelly Field had been called to convocation a week earlier. As we entered the hall, each was handed a slip of paper with name, rank and serial number and four numbered lines. The instructions were…"In a few days you will become officers of the United States Army Air Corps and rated pilots. (Heart thumping!) We ask each of you to list your preference, in type of aircraft you would like to fly. One restriction, if you are five foot eleven or over, you may not request fighters."

Damn, I was five foot eleven and one half inches! At the same time, another thought entered my mind. 'I am getting married to a beautiful girl in a few days and after a nine-month separation, it would be nice not to head to a war zone immediately'. I listed:

1. Instructor
2. Light bombardment
3. Medium bombardment
4. Heavy bombardment.

The results were not to be known for some time but I planned to not worry – to enjoy life as a married officer.

All four fiancée's were finally installed in adjacent rooms awaiting the great day.

We would take turns standing up for each other. We asked Gean and Judy Hale to be Best Man and Maid of Honor for our union. Their room was adjacent to ours and before our wedding night – doors were usually left open.

Gwen had been shopping and returned to hear Judy on the phone with somebody and saying, "Oh, she's alright – just like all the other damn Yankees – she talks so fast you can't understand her." Welcome to the South, Gwennie. You'll get used to it.

At another time, Judy stuck her head into Gwen's room. "Hey, Hoss! Ya' want to go to a movie show?" Definitely the first time she had been called Hoss.

One last day of duties, we had to undergo a physical and get shots. Then we were herded to a dental clinic where each would have a cursory exam and cleaning by 'dental hygienists'. As usual, we were lined up – this time in three lines with each entering a separate door. Once inside, it was found to be a single room with three chairs. Two were 'manned' by attractive young ladies and one by an elderly Chinese male. A lot of guessing about which door would give you which of the three. My line, of course, drew the Chinese man.

He was very much into his job and after thirty or forty minutes of scaling and polishing during which time he was continually lecturing me about care and I was continually trying to look at the young ladies I had been denied. He asked if I had any questions. Not really. I don't think I had heard a word he said.

On the eve of graduation day, the Hamiltons jumped the gun and were married in a private home. We were all there. Half way through the ceremony, my knees weakened and I had to sit down. If I can't get through their marriage, how will I get through mine?

September 6, 1942. Class 42-H met that morning in the auditorium for the 10:00 o'clock commissioning ceremony. There was a speech by the Commandant about our future. He mentioned a few negatives, but I did not notice an effect on any of our class – we were ready.

By noon, we had changed into our new uniforms complete with silver wings and gold bars. The eight of us set sail for Randolph Field. Gwen and I chose that chapel for our wedding. It was a permanent building unlike Kelly. I had arranged for Father Ryan, a Catholic Chaplain to meet us there. I also remembered a floral corsage for Gwen and a photographer. I had purchased diamond rings and picked them up. I got a gold wedding band for myself. The ceremony took all of twenty minutes and my knees did not knock or weaken. The photographer had not appeared when we entered, but as we turned to leave as newly married, I spotted him in the aisle and immediately nudged Gwen to alert her. The flash, of course, caught me talking out of the corner of my mouth. We did get a formal portrait on the front steps – four new officers and their new brides!

There was a formal dinner dance honoring 42-H that evening at the Gunter Hotel, but we had a few hours – what to do. Straight ahead of the Chapel was the PX and we decided to go have a milkshake. Not until we had ordered some and been served did it occur to any of us that the base Officers Club was to our left as we headed to the PX. While we were cadets we were not allowed to even look at it. Now we could have used it but had forgotten our new rank.

That night the 129 new officers and their dates sat for a sumptuous dinner, followed by a dance. As a new married on my wedding night, I was not interested in the food or dancing. After two or three dances and a few introductions of my bride to friends, I suggested we head for our room. There was no objection from Gwen.

I thought we would be the first out, but over fifty classmates had also married that day and I found myself in a long line at the coat check counter to get my cap. It would be a memorable day from start to finish, but I had to remember a couple things. I am an officer now and we could have gone to the 'O' Club. Secondly, the first time I introduced Gwen I said, "I want you to meet my wife, Miss Gwen Yeo. Oops, she is Mrs. Gross!"

We headed for the hotel.

CHAPTER 8

# A FIGHTER PILOT!

**H**ONEYMOONS FOR THE NEW pilots lasted three days when we each received orders.

Mine lifted me to cloud nine level – I was assigned to Fighters! What happened to the "nobody 5'11" or over?" I didn't care. Robert Pittard, Jr. and I were headed to Hamilton Field, California and the 328th Fighter Group.

Strange, I thought – two only of the 129 graduates of 42-H Kelly Field were to be fighter pilots. Were we that good or were we expendable?

Gwen and I boarded a train the following day. We had a week to report. We would need to find a place to live. It would be our first home!

We arrived in San Francisco with a day or so to spare and used it to visit my father's sister, Aunt Elsie Lowrie, and her family. I had to show off my new uniform!

After a night with them, we headed north of the Bay Bridge to search for quarters of our own. In the nice community of San Rafael, we found an apartment overlooking a body of water – a slew. Nice enough. All apartments in that two-story wooden structure were occupied by officers stationed at Hamilton. I liked that.

When the war started, the Roosevelt Administration had imposed a freeze on rents. The owner had previously resided in the largest unit and because it had never been rented, he could charge whatever he wanted. We took that unit and its exorbitant fees, and, to be able to afford it, shared it with the Pittards. That also posed a problem, it only had one bedroom and we were both newly married. To make it work, we pledged privacy as much as possible and we alternated nights in the bedroom – the other couple on the couch in the living room.

Nobody called us 'damn Yankees' here, but Gwen found a new one. All the other officers were 1st Lt. or Captains and their somewhat stuffy wives always introduced her as Mrs. 2nd Lt. Gross. Despite these problems, my excitement for the future kept me in a state of euphoria.

Orders on September 21st, 1942, from HQ. 328th Fighter Group said in part:

> 1. Pursuant to auth cont in Paragraph #2, SO #253, HQ IV AF, San Francisco, California, dated September 17, 1942, the following named 2nd Lts. AC, are reld fr. atchd Sqdns. As indic and asgd thereto:
> 
>    329th FIGHTER SQUADRON
>    Clayton K. Gross 0-663512
>    Robert S. Pittard, Jr. 0-663554

The 329th Fighter Squadron flew the sleek-looking P-39, a tricycle landing gear plane that was something new, but had many advantages. I met my flight leader, Harry May and more confusion. Harry was a former Stanford basketball player and was 6'7" tall. If I thought my one-half inch was over the limit for

LIVE BAIT | 49

fighters was strange, how did he get his assignment? Anyway, we began our own orientation.

One disadvantage we were warned about was the engine is behind the pilot and it gives the aircraft slightly different characteristics.

This stage of my career would be a little different. There is one seat only in the P-39. Nobody will fly with you on your first trip up! You better know as much about it as you can before you go there. We spent hours in the cockpit on the ground – memorizing the instrument panel and various control systems. There would be a blindfold test to make sure you could find everything. No objection from me.

I talked with every pilot who had time for me about the new, unknown characteristics. We started the engine and had taxi tests! No problem here. Every aircraft I had previously flown was a 'tail dragger'. The visibility in the P-39 was outstanding.

On the 19th and 20th of September, I flew several hours in an L-2 Cub – good to get back in the air. On September 22, 1942, sixteen days after graduation at Kelly, I was deemed ready to take the P-39 into the blue. "Oh," I was told, "It's best to circle Hamilton after take off to fix the location in mind. It's been camouflaged."

"Okay, I'm ready. I hope my P-39D1 is as well."

Gulp!

It was another beautiful California day when I received clearance and taxied to the north end of the runway at Hamilton Field. In position and headed south, I began the normal pre-take-off procedures – feet firmly holding the toe brakes, I pushed the throttle forward to check the magnetos. I felt a sudden vibration set in on both legs and the P-39 began to inch forward. I pulled the throttle back and patted my thighs – "Calm down legs. Everything will be alright."

I again pressured the toe brakes and advanced the throttle – same vibration – same result. No way could I check mags. Normally one would hold the brakes and then with full power, and turn the switch first to left, then right, then back to both. I shut power down and calmly asked myself how often you found a mag problem anyway. To hell with it! I'll take off without the check and I again put power on. This time, no brakes.

I began the run smoothly; finally feeling like this bird wanted to fly. Easing back on the stick, the nose wheel came free and then I was airborne and climbing.

Wow! I was over the bay and then headed over the Bay Bridge. I continued to climb and fly straight-ahead until minutes later I realized I had reached the south end of the San Francisco bay and still hadn't made a turn! The Airacobra handled very nicely as I experimented with several degrees of turning, climbing, diving and anything else I could think of.

Suddenly I remembered that Hamilton was camaflouged and I had not made the recommended circle to fix the location in my mind. I headed to the north end of the bay and spent most of my first hour in this war bird looking for my home roost. When I did locate it with some difficulty, I managed quite a nice landing, thank you! I did not mention to anyone of the magneto check problem.

The next day I flew it again. This time my legs behaved and I did check mags. Then I neatly lifted off and circled looking for the landmarks after which I headed out over the Golden Gate Bridge and the Pacific Ocean. There I began to carefully learn the capabilities of the aircraft. I climbed to six or seven thousand feet and tried a 'peel off' to a dive that put me near or over 300-MPH. Wow! A new record for me! I lazed from the dive into a steep climb – not quite ready to try an "Immelman' yet.

I leveled out and searched the sea to the horizon for an invasion fleet. By God, the Japanese will not make a sneak attack while I am up here defending the coast! When I rolled out straight and level, I caressed the gun handle switch – I would have charged them, but I wasn't sure how to un-charge them. I flew back to make what I thought was another perfect landing. I was sure that the powers that gave me this job had made the right decision. This is where I belong.

CHAPTER 9

# TRAINING TO FIGHT

**W**HEN I BEGAN TRAINING in fighters, I had completed over 200 hours in military training and with my CPT time, had amassed over 300 hours in the air. I really never experienced a problem in flying the P-39s. A lot of people did. It was truly said that the first 100 hours in the Airacobra were dangerous because it had characteristics unlike any other plane. We did lose a lot of pilots in training. I still loved the aircraft.

My hours in the air climbed. After my third transition flight, we were into formation flying. Four weeks and about 30 hours in the air after that first ride, I did find out about firing airborne machine guns. We began ground gunnery training. Now I am ready for the 'Jap attack!' Hours piled up in my logbook.

There were a number of Navy bases in the Bay area and we began mock dogfights with their F4-Fs and F4-Us. This is the life!

On one sunny day, 50 air hours later, I recall a training flight like it was yesterday.

I had fun! Airborne by myself on a gorgeous California day in the Bay area, I cruised out to the ocean, staying away from downtown San Francisco. There was a large flock of Seagulls below me...tempting, but I left them alone. From about 1500 feet, I spotted a fisherman with waders standing in the surf and casting into incoming waves.

Ooh...I'm a dirty guy! I circled south and then inland until I was well away from him, but watching. Then I added power and nosed down to pick up speed. I can't beat the speed of sound, but I can go fast enough that I will be on him before he can react to the roar. I came from directly behind him - maybe ten feet over his head and pulled up in a lazy left turn to look back. He was sitting in the surf and looking at me. Better not stick around where he or somebody could get my I.D. I climbed to 5,000 feet over the bay. I love this bird!

As I turned south toward San Mateo. From the corner of my eye, a damn Navy Fighter was boring in from about 8 o'clock. You S.O.B. I mouthed to myself and I rolled into him and down forcing him to go over me. That meant he lost me for a moment and in that split second, I wracked back hard right and climbed. Not finding me there, he rolled out. "Too late friend". Now I chopped power and dropped onto his tail and for the next few minutes I hung there and we put on a grand show for anybody watching from below. I got me a Wildcat! If my guns were charged, he is 'meat'! My little P-39 can whip an F4-F any day – anytime.

Eventually he signaled surrender with a 'wing rock' and I pulled out and waved.

I had been in the air for the better part of an hour and at full power for part of it. I headed for home before I would have to settle for a ditch in the bay.

I feel great! I am definitely a Fighter Pilot!

There was the war being fought in two theatres – Pacific and Europe. We had to be in this training for use somewhere. Protecting the West Coast gets a little boring. And if I thought that was a bore, I found my next assignment worse. I was sent to San Francisco for detached duty at 4th AF Defense Center.

My work area was a room with a large table on which there were images of the coastline and expanse of the Pacific Ocean. Around the table were eight women, each with a long pole to position models or identification signs of any offshore activity. Their information was relayed from our primitive radar or visual sightings to a control center which then directed the ladies through earphones of what to place and where to place it on the board.

I sat in a high chair at the end of the table for an overview of the activity, I understood, although hard to believe that this 2nd Lt. was then to decide whether or not to scramble fighters to investigate. There would be no Pearl Harbor here!

As usual, nothing occurred on my watch. The ladies fought boredom by knitting. I twiddled my thumbs. After a few days of this, I asked them how to knit. They got a kick out of that and produced spare needles and yarn and gave me instructions. Soon we had eight ladies and a fighter pilot quietly clicking plastic needles. Before the week ended, I had nearly completed a woolen, olive drab head cover to be sent to a soldier in a cold climate area. Yes, I put holes in for eyes and mouth.

My first month anniversary rolled around during that week and I stopped for a dozen long-stemmed Roses for my bride. I was desperately in love.

I can't remember but we might have eaten them later. Gwen was having trouble cooking. She bought a series of pamphlet-style cookbooks – each named something like 500 Tasty Snacks or 250 Ways of Serving Potatoes and 2000 Useful Facts about

Food. She had at least two dozen of them and in preparing a meal, three or four would be open in various areas of the apartment and she had to run from book to book to keep up.

We ate out a lot.

P-39 hours piled up and battles against the Navy were daily occurrences. I found that I could win a dogfight with the Wildcats or Corsairs if we stayed below 5000 feet. If we climbed above that, I lost some advantage.

The 328th Fighter Group was an RTU (Replacement Training Unit) and occasionally a few pilots were dispatched to other units. I began to get a little 'antsy' – what and where is my future?

More changes… The 329th Fighter Squadron moved to Oakland Army Air Base, which was shared by and known as Oakland Municipal Airport. It was basically a single runway we must share with an occasional DC-3. On the other hand, from the flight line to the Dike, which held the San Francisco Bay out, the land was flat and if properly done, a P-39 could be airborne before getting there. We did it on scrambles.

Several planes were on alert in all daylight hours – can't trust those Japanese you know. Crew chiefs would start and warm them up occasionally so they would be ready to go instantly. Pilots were assigned for that duty and when on alert, stayed in the ready room in flight suits and with MAE WESTS. Parachutes were in the cockpit and ready. It was a game when the alert siren blew to set a new record to get in the air. You were to get instructions by radio when airborne. I assume there was another new second lieutenant sitting in a high chair in San Francisco that would activate the procedure.

Most of our scrambles were practice.

We also took off in pairs. Pilots not on duty would invariably be out to watch the procedure. On one particular day, two planes answered the call and within a minute, were roaring toward the Dike. It didn't look to me like they had enough speed and dike collision looked imminent. They did mush into the air enough to clear the seven or eight foot Dike and then both disappeared. We saw splashes and knew they had gone in so began to run toward the area. Before we had gone far – both planes reappeared – airborne! They had slapped the belly (or propeller) on the surface, but came free. Can't blame the wingman – he had to follow the lead!

An announcement one day caused much excitement. Half the Squadron would be transferred to an active fighter group flying P-38 Lightnings. When the USA entered the war, we had only three so-called "modern" fighters – the P-38, P-39 and P-40 and none of those were really that up-to-date. The government couldn't tell people that because morale would be damaged, so they picked what they thought was the best, the P-38, and they put a great PR program on. I believed them and pleaded to go to the 20th Fighter Group. They didn't take me – thank God! I stayed in the 329th until some time later when twelve of us were dispatched to a newly formed unit – the 354th Fighter Group. It would be my assignment for the rest of the war.

CHAPTER 10

# THE 354TH FIGHTER GROUP

FINALLY OUT OF A training unit and assigned to a tactical group. I had flown fighters for 65 hours. The 354th was also flying the P-39 so no transition problems. I was one of four pilots assigned to the 355th Fighter Squadron. We had individual interviews with our new Squadron Commander, Capt. George R. Bickell.

"You" he said, will be 'C' Flight Commander. That calls for rank of Captain, but you will have to wait until I get my Oak Leaves before I can give you that. I am recommending promotion to 1st Lt. This date." Hey! Two and a half months out of flying school and I'm to be a 1st Lt. I'll probably be a General before this war ends!

In the next few weeks, Gwen and George's wife, Peggy, became close friends, and that couldn't hurt my career. This is a Great War! A few weeks later, the Group headed for Tonapah, Nevada, where we would get more pilots, more P-39s and concentrated bombing and gunnery training.

I was assigned a crew of great guys who would crew all Fighters I would fly for the rest of the war. C. E. Smith was the Chief and he proved, to my thinking, to be the best in the Air Corps. I would from this point on trust him for hundreds of single engine trips into the blue – many over water and enemy territory.

In my last week in the 328th Fighter Group, I had drawn duty as Officer of the Day. That required me to spend 24 hours on base and on duty. I had a room in the BOQ and poor Gwennie would be alone for that night.

I made my rounds after supper and returned to the BOQ where a poker game was in progress. I wanted desperately to get in the game, but I had less than $2 in my pocket. A friend, Ohman, loaned me ten dollars and I took a seat. Good poker games are not short-term affairs and this one did not end until breakfast time. When we adjourned to go eat, Ohman was broke and I was the big winner. He was one of six pilots to be assigned to a tactical unit in Africa and was due to leave within 24 hours. He offered me his '37 Chevy Coupe for $100 and I took it. Poor guy! It was his stake that got me in the game. I proudly drove home to show Gwen our first car. I hoped Ohman's combat tour would be better than his poker playing. Anyway, the Group headed to Tonapah by train and I left the car for Gwen.

It was one thing to out-maneuver a Navy Wildcat or Corsair in a mock dogfight, but if we were to use our skills for real, we better learn how to shoot something besides a camera at our opponent. We got the chance when we went to Tonapah, Nevada, for bombing and gunnery training.

The Airacobra had a 20-mm. cannon that fired through the hub of the propeller, two 30-calibre machine guns firing through the propeller and two more in each wing. That seemed like a lot of firepower at the time. The nose machine guns were calibrated to fire just after a propeller blade passed, so that you wouldn't shoot your own propeller off. That made sense!

LIVE BAIT | 59

The training began with ground targets. Big...maybe 10x10-foot screens were erected at 45-degree angles. "Bullseye" circles were there to say..."Shoot here dummy." It was great sport. I actually began to feel more and more like a "fighter" pilot.

Shooting at the ground targets went well if you got a little closer to the ground to put more shells in the target, but I could handle that and my scores were tops or close. The 30-calibre ammunition was color coded so the 'hits' could be properly credited to each pilot. This was great! At least it was until my buddy, Bob Weissinger; 'A' flight commander flew a little too close, flew into the ground and 'pranged' his kite but good, not to mention himself. I went to the hospital to see him and found him still wearing his flight suit, on his back over a half-barrel type of apparatus. Spine injury they told me. I said goodbye because his war was over, and a good part of his life. I saw him next about 30 years later – paralyzed from the waist down and in a wheelchair.

Besides the ground gunnery, we practiced dive-bombing. One hundred-pound 'dud' bombs were hung under each wing and the problem was to deposit them in painted white circles on the dessert. We started 'runs' by peeling off at 5000 feet and releasing the bombs at 1500 to 1000 feet. More fun and we didn't lose any planes and pilots in this task, at least to my knowledge. We did lose plenty of both to other causes. The word of the day during our Tonapah stay was "to find the landing strip after your training flight". Look around to spot the column of smoke rising from the latest crash. The P-39 was a fine aircraft once you became accustomed to its idiosyncrasies, different because of the engine behind the pilot. If you did crash, the engine gave the pilot a huge nudge in the back and few survived with just paralysis like Weissinger.

I vividly remember two incidents in my early years that could have been an indication that I would be successful in aerial gunnery. First, an incident in the winter of '29... Three buddies and I were encamped in a vacant lot with a supply of snowballs, ready for the next vehicle to venture into our territory. Not many of these missiles would hit their mark, but mine did! My target approached – I took aim, estimating his speed and leading him the icy ball arched perfectly to strike the driver's side window at head level. He swerved, skidded and stopped and before I realized my danger, he exited and started after me. Unfortunately, his legs were much longer than mine were so, despite my speed, he had me by the collar and proceeded to lecture me – me with hanging head, promising to never do that again. My friends snickered as I suffered. After he released me and left, I did point out that I was the best shot of our gang.

Another, around my eleventh year, I was into slingshots – a big homemade one that was capable of shattering a street light. I remember one other experience and nobody chased and caught me this time. Our store, same one that sold penny candy, had some small ones made of wire and perfect for launching BB's. We were practicing in the lot by Frank's home when a sparrow flew into my range. With no time to think I instinctively turned and fired. Direct hit! The bird fell like a rock from the sky. I picked up his still warm body with remorse, but at the same time in awe of my skill. Maybe it's inborn. I had no idea how I would use that skill in another ten years!

Tonapah was a nothing community…one casino/hotel called the "Tonapah Club." The pilots used it as a gathering place when off duty – not because of the lure of gambling, but for the generous bar. They had a policy of buy two drinks and the third is on us. The first two cost 50 cents each and were measured about three fingers whisky and one mix. Few made it past the free drink in sober condition.

We had moved to Tonapah, Nevada, for the bombing and gunnery range training. There we filled out our roster and began to develop our unit personality. Because it was short-term duty and Tonapah had no facilities, the wives had been left in California. It was the first separation of my married life and I felt I couldn't tolerate that if there was any way to avoid it. Within two weeks I did find a way. Earl Wulff and I located the only available, adequate motel room in town and tied it up for the duration. It was small. The bathroom was five foot square and that included a tin shower stall. There was a table that could seat four, a hot plate with two burners, an old couch and best of all, two bedrooms. The walls were thin which required a degree of decorum, but there was visual privacy. We immediately sent for our wives who drove over in the 1937 Chevy coupe I won in the Oakland poker game. We were the only two in the group with our wives available and private transportation. It was an enviable position.

Gwen and I were in bed one evening when there was a scream from the adjoining room. Ever the brave type, I bounded out of bed and into the Wulff's room. He was roaring with laughter and Barbara was pounding him with her fists. It turned out that he told her "Better duck under the covers. I'm going to spit straight up." After she did, he farted and she was one mad lady!

I flew a total of 30 plus P-39 hours in the four and one half weeks of Tonapah training. I had three hours as co-pilot in a B-34. The loss of P-39's to crashes had caused a shortage. We flew ten pilots back to Hamilton to pick up replacements. It wasn't a long ride, but we did set down in Reno on return and called requesting permission to RON that Saturday night.

"No soap," was Bickell's answer. "Get your asses back here!" It was worth a try.

It was in these flatlands that I discovered a fun game that might have killed somebody. I hadn't considered that. The country was so open and traffic (gas rationing you know) so sparse, that from altitude you could spot a car from a mile away. When I saw one, I went a couple miles ahead and dropped to road level, toward the poor victim. I could only imagine their feeling when a 200-mph aircraft suddenly appeared head on. Fun!

My scores on gunnery were as good as anyone else's. The same for dive-bombing. My ego was rising again. I flew my last training mission there on February 28 and we were ordered to head for our new station at Hayward, California

When we left for California on March 1, Barbara and Earl Wulff went back by train because the Chevy wouldn't hold four of us. It would hold three, however, and Squadron C.O. Bickell asked if he could ride back with us. Of course, we were buddies! The first hundred miles from Tonapah were great. With me driving, Gwen in the middle; we sang songs, told stories and had an uproarious time. Just outside of Reno, I approached a railroad crossing. In plain view I saw a train approaching from the right. I sat there for a minute and it suddenly occurred to me that I had time to get across before it got there, so I crossed. I wouldn't have tried that if I had not been sure I could make it and I did. The train was going a little faster than I anticipated however, and from George's point of view, I guess it looked like it was coming through his door. After the train passed, George had one question, "What the hell were you thinking of?" When we got to Reno he got out, and probably took that same train the rest of the group was on to California. He rarely spoke a civil word to me in the next two years.

I loved the camaraderie of the men around me. I was raised with a family of military with my father, a WWI infantry officer, my uncle Clarence who commanded the 161st Infantry

Regiment of the Washington National Guard during my three year enlistment in that outfit, my CMTC training. It was for me and I would have been happy in that environment forever!

My assignment to the 354th Fighter Group from the 328th RTU Group had convinced me it was my future. My friend George went from Captain to full Colonel before I got my railroad tracks. Who needed it as a career anyway?

CHAPTER II
# HAYWARD, CALIFORNIA

For the first, but not the last time, the group split. The 353rd squadron went to San Francisco, our 355th across the bay in Hayward, and the 356th north of the bay in Santa Rosa. The Hayward Army Airdrome facility suited us just fine. Hayward was East Bay and South of Oakland far enough to be out of the big traffic area. The field was a single runway, north to south, very adequate for P-39's. Best of all, we did not have to share the field with anyone else unlike my previous experience in Oakland where commercial aviation traffic limited what we could do. And the people of Hayward took us into their hearts and their homes.

Since housing was limited, it was a chore to find suitable quarters for those of us married and wishing to co-habit. Gwen found an ad in the local paper offering room with kitchen privileges for one or two couples. Together with Pete and Marion Nacy we investigated and found an attractive California-style home, red tile roof, quite close to the base, owned by Mr. and Mrs. Grover Boyd, who we soon renamed Mom and Pop Boyd. Mrs. Boyd showed the two bedrooms and we four decided this would be our temporary home. One room came with a double bed and the other with twins. When she bluntly asked which of us wanted the double, Pete and Marion stopped to blush and that hesitation gave Gwen and me the double. It's a good thing, too, because one night soon after the Nacys experienced an embarrassing collapse of one twin that woke the entire household. It would have happened to us in the same manner probably.

The Boyds soon became like real family and we corresponded for years after that 1943 assignment. I found that on take off South to North, I could adjust my flight a few degrees right and skim the red tile roof by a few feet. That insured that no one else in the family was sleeping in while I had arisen early to go to my 'office' in the sky. Although I probably loosened a few tiles on the roof, the Boyds and our wives never complained. In fact, insisted I continue to salute in that manner.

The 'Officers Club' in Hayward, California, came to be by chance. Our assignment to Hayward followed our return from the Tonapah, Nevada stint where we had formed the group and undergone several months of bombing and gunnery training.

Just as friendly as the Boyds, were the few business people we had contact with in Hayward. I said the 'Officers Club' came about by chance and it did in this manner. Most of us enjoyed the relaxation of an alcoholic beverage from time to time and we sampled several establishments in the area to do that. As will happen, the pilots tried one here, one there and eventually most of us gravitated to a bistro on the main highway through Hayward named the "Shalimar Club". The owner, Al, was no dummy and encouraged us to use the Shalimar as our squadron hangout and we kept the barstools and tables warm on most late afternoons and evenings. When we asked Al a few weeks down the road where we might find a place to hold a party, he immediately came up with the offer to close the club to the public and use it. It worked just fine and from that time on, anytime we wanted it shut down for private use, it was done. The back bar was decorated with our pictures, short snorters and other memorabilia. We were a private 'Officers Club'.

Gwen was 19 and I was a young 22 and neither of us had a great deal of experience with alcohol at the time. Not wishing to be left out of any fun, we experimented with various drinks until we found that we both could stomach "Whiskey Sours." They were sweet enough to go down without our needing to make faces and besides, we liked the Marachino Cherries that lay on the bottom. Also, one could sip them over a long period that meant we didn't need to buy or drink a lot of them. Unless, of course, there was a party, and there often was.

On a spring evening in 1943, we scheduled such an event. The occasion that has long since slipped my mind, but not the events of the evening. As usual, Al locked the doors and hung out the 'private party' sign. The joint was very soon jumping with about 32 officers of the 355th, wives and dates. Gwen and I, in the seventh month of our honeymoon, were very much a part of it. Late in the evening and with my sixth or seventh Sour clutched in my right hand, I found and decided to join a group stationed in front of the lounge arranged in a circle and loudly singing some of those familiar group melodies, a favorite pastime of mine. I temporarily lost track of Gwen as I forced my way into the singing circle, lending my untrained but melodious tenor voice to the current refrains. My right hand waved my drink in perfect time to the melody and my left arm went around whoever happened to be standing to my left. It turned out to be an attractive blonde. I really hadn't noticed her until a tapping on my shoulder caused me to turn to see who wanted my attention. What I saw as I turned was the blur of Gwen's right hand that landed glancingly on my chin and bounced off to strike the glass in my right hand.

The glass flew to the wall behind us where it crashed in a thousand pieces and wasted the Marachino Cherry. Not because of the strength of Gwen's 105 pounds, but more from the surprise of the attack, I staggered back into the venetian blind. As I fell, a dozen of the wooden slats shattered and I swear I felt the plate glass window behind them give, but fortunately not break. I wound up in a heap on the floor sitting in the debris. I could see Gwen, her nose tilted in the air heading back to our table for her purse and then striding out the front door. I was on my feet and after her in an instant.

"What did you do that for?" I said catching her as she reached our car.

"If you don't know. I'm not going to tell you!"

"What! I wasn't doing anything. Just singing!"

The rest of the ride home was in silence, her choice. I got the same treatment as we got ready for bed, but thanks to our getting the room with the double bed, we made up before we went to sleep. The honeymoon was on again.

The next day I went by our 'Officers Club' and tried to pay Al for the blind that was already replaced. He wouldn't take it. "Hey, it could happen to anybody!"

He probably could afford it.

I logged over 100 hours in P-39 time in the three months. Much of that was in valuable mock dogfights with each other or more often, the Navy who also maintained a large presence in the Bay Area. I also got myself into more trouble with Bickell by twice being caught buzzing the field. Nothing thrilled me more than clipping the grass with my propeller before a near loop approach to land. I had understood George was not on base the first time – he was. Confined to Base for 24 hours.

The second time I knew he was absent. Guess what? He returned early! – Another confinement.

My flight mate and still dear friend, Lowell K. Brueland, who would later be known as Callender, Iowa's only Ace with 14½ victories, got himself in a little hot water one Spring day. We discovered a new sport. Fly to five or six thousand feet, roll down the window and toss out a roll of toilet paper. It would unfurl as it dropped, leaving a thin line of paper trailing toward the earth. The object was to cut it as many times as possible as it descended.

Unfortunately for Brue, it didn't work that way. The P-39 engine is behind the pilot and the air-intake is directly behind the canopy. When Brue tossed the roll out the window, air current sucked it into that in-take and before long; the power plant gave up the ghost. P-39s are an all-metal aircraft and they didn't glide well at all. He was over the Bay and didn't relish a dip by parachuting. He thus was left with the alternative of heading for the nearest dry land that happened to be Redwood City, California. With great skill, he landed on an empty street with wheels up, of course, skidded into an intersection without hitting anything! Ever cool under stressful conditions, he calmly filled out the form one – "Emergency landing – Fourth and Page, Redwood City, California".

The P.A. announcement said, "All pilots to the ready room immediately! – Repeat, – All pilots to the ready room immediately!" "What's this about?" "How the hell would I know!"

From the look on George Bickell's face as we seated ourselves, it was not about a fun thing. The Major strutted back and forth for a moment and then let it fly. "Early this afternoon, someone in a P-39 flew under the San Mateo Bridge. There was a painting crew working on the bridge and one worker fell into the Bay. Fortunately, he was retrieved or one of you might have been charged with murder. I want to know *right now*, who did it?"

There was silence. I had flown that day and so had most of the squadron. I hadn't gone near the bridge, but I would at the first opportunity to see how in the world it could be done. The bridge, southern most on the bay was billed as the worlds longest, but 99.9% of it was on pilings only a few feet apart. There was a small drawbridge section which, when raised, couldn't have been 25 feet high. In normal position, it was no more than a dozen feet above the water – maybe less. Somebody was both a great pilot and stupid to do it.

Bickell spoke again. "I'm telling you. If we find out later, it will go twice as hard on you than if you admit it now."

Nobody spoke.

Then he gave us a re-run of the lecture we got after Brueland had his little accident in Redwood City. "You're going to pay for every penny of the cost of these P-39's if you 'prang' one while fooling around. That is if you're unlucky enough to live. Dismiss!"

We filed out silently but soon were chattering all at once. "Who?" "You?" "Not me, but I'd like to shake his hand!"

Flying under the bay bridge was strictly forbidden, but was done many times. I went under the Golden Gate that was big enough to fly a squadron of B-17's under in formation. I did it alone and was careful to not go near anybody who might be able to see identifying markings. I started at 5000 feet over the bay and dove to gain speed, then went under at near water level and immediately headed North along the coast that was not heavily populated.

"Hey, no big thrill! I can do lots of things more fun than that!" I never went under one again, especially the San Mateo.

There was a time when I tried to become a more sophisticated drinker, more than Whiskey Sours. Two of our pilots who were inseparable buddies usually stopped at the Shalimar on the way home from the flight line, and more often than not, could be found holding down two stools in the evening. I noticed them because 90% of the time they simply sat and talked, each with two shot glasses in front of them filled with clear liquids. About every 15 to 20 minutes, they would take one glass in each hand in the space of three seconds, chug-a-lug both. Out of curiosity, I asked what they were drinking and found they were a shot of Vodka and one of Tequila.

I had never tried either one, but one afternoon on the way home, I decided to give it a try and ordered the pair. More from cowardice than trying to mimic the originators, I let them sit for awhile in front of me, then with a deep breath, picked up both. I didn't try to down them in a gulp; I simply took a sip only of the first. My God! It was liquid fire! I decided the other must be the chaser that put out the fire, so I sipped that one too. It was WORSE! I put both down and stared at them and the thought occurred to me that I could possibly salvage some of my investment because either one would probably work in my Zippo cigarette lighter. When nobody was looking, I walked away from the bar.

Here was a new and exciting mission – a night solo in the San Francisco Bay area. The object was to give the searchlight people a workout and test of their abilities.

I volunteered myself. On the night of March 20, 1943 I lifted off the Hayward runway around 2100 and climbed quickly to 10,000 feet. The night was quite dark but quickly lit up a little when about four fingers of light stabbed through the sky, swaying back and forth trying to find me. It really didn't take too long as I maintained a steady course. When one did find me, the others quickly joined and I was amazed at their intensity. I didn't stay there long. I quickly rolled left and down and when they started to follow – reversed in a tight spiral right and found darkness again. I climbed back up – set a course and waited for them to find me again with similar results following. It was a fun game and was repeated a couple more times before I headed back to Hayward and home.

To lose them had not been a problem, but if I had been an enemy bomber, I would probably not have been able to use the quick evasive maneuvers I had at my command.

A fun flight!

I didn't win my second car in a poker game. I might have won a few extra dollars in those endeavors, which accumulated as surplus funds that gave me the idea that we could afford something better than the Chevy. At a San Jose used car dealer, we found a pretty gray 1941 two-door Buick Special that caught our eye. We took the offered test drive and it purred like the 34,000 indicated miles had just properly broken it in. He wanted $900 for it and offered $300 for the Chevy. We decided on a scientific test to decide as we cruised down the road. If the cigarette lighter works, we'll buy it. It did.

I felt better when we were transferred to Portland, Oregon, because I had to fly up and Gwen drove the Buick with Marion Nacy. The new car had a better chance through the mountains than the old one. They made it without a hitch!

Every time we got settled – we moved. That's war. At the end of May we had orders to move again. The 353rd and the 355th would be stationed at Portland (Oregon) Army Air Base and the 356th to Salem, Oregon. The wives drove and we flew.

It was a long flight for a P-39. Belly tanks were added. There were mountains, which would require us to stay above 12,000 feet enroute. Probably dumb, but I took a kitten we had adopted for the ride. Maybe for lack of oxygen, she was very quiet riding behind my head on my backpack parachute.

After an uneventful three hours and 48 minutes, we landed gracefully in Portland and she was out of the cockpit when I opened the door. Gone, never to be found. Portland gains one California cat.

CHAPTER 12

# LIFE AND TRAINING IN THE GREAT NORTHWEST

I GOT A NEW JOB – Deputy Operations Officer. I was still a 1st Lt. I still flew with 'C' Flight on operations involving flights. In addition, I was investigating crashes. And we had plenty of those.

People got killed and occasionally it was not a pilot. Planes returned from a practice aerial gunnery mission and the crews went to work on them. An Armorer drew a wheeled stand in front of a parked Airacobra and standing on it, turned the propeller a partial turn. The P-39 with forward firing 30-mm guns through the propeller had a mechanism to coordinate the shell ejection so we wouldn't shoot our own propellers off. Very smart.

The pilot who parked this bird and the Armorer weren't that smart. The pilot had not switched off his guns and the crewman had not checked it. When he turned the propeller, a round fired and struck him directly in the chest from a foot away. He was blown off the stand and lay on his back – probably never knowing what hit him. I was nearby and ran to the area.

He was carried to a room and Doc Start, 355th Flight Surgeon got there to examine him. I went in with Doc.

He was the first dead man I had seen at close range. Oddly enough, after the initial shock at the size of the hole and the quantity of blood, the thing that impressed my memory was his face. His eyes were wide open, eyeballs rolled back and his mouth was gaping. Doc lowered his lids and that made it better, but his mouth would not stay closed. They fashioned a cloth sling under his chin and over the top of his head to close it.

I have now seen death, close up – very close up and it does not seem to affect me all that much. I think my faith in God has a lot to do with that. Nobody lives forever. Life is a test. You're dead. You finished your test before I did.

We were losing pilots at an alarming rate. The P-39 with engine behind the pilot had an altered, very different center of gravity and new pilots often learned it the hard way. A lot spun in on the turn from base leg to final approach.

Preaching that to neophytes over and over again had to help, but still it happened. One stuck in mind. I sat in the Ops office one afternoon when the door burst open and somebody hollered, "Somebody went down on final…" I ran out, saw a column of smoke starting to rise near the end runway 15. I roared out toward it in my Jeep. The plane hit going pretty straight in, about fifty feet off a green at Broadmoor Golf Club. Golfers were on the green when it happened. There was fire, pretty hot by the time I got there and the pilot's body was about twenty feet away. Although his face was for the most part unrecognizable, his body seemed intact. Ammunition started exploding and every time it did, I instinctively ducked. That made concentration difficult. A man, undoubtedly one of the golfers tugged at my sleeve. Bang! I ducked. "Sir, this is Mike," and he told me the man's name who stood beside him. Bang! We all ducked again. "He pulled the pilot out after the crash". Bang! Bang! We all ducked. "Yes," I said, "I'll be right with you." The meat wagon, pardon me – the ambulance pulled into the field and two medics jumped out.

Bang! Bang! One took the pilot by his shoulders and the other his feet to place him on a stretcher. He sagged about two feet down in the middle! All that held him together was his flight suit. Bang! They put him on the stretcher and carried it to the rear of the ambulance. When they put the stretcher handles into the canvas straps to hold it, one side came free and the earthly remains of that poor pilot took another blow. It fell about three feet to the ambulance floor and it made a squish sound when it hit, not a thud. In the meantime, the golfers told me again about the heroism of the one who risked life and limb to get the pilot out. "He burned his hands pretty good."

"I'll get to you in a minute," I said and ducked another half dozen times as more ammo went off.

When the ambulance left, I turned to find them. They were gone. I wrote it in my report, but we never located him. An unsung hero!

Another crash off the side of the airport showed me what happens when a P-39 strikes the ground going straight in. Debris was scattered over a fifty-yard circle – much of it difficult to identify. I wandered through the site and found the cannon, bent but this I recognized and picked up one end to look at it. And dropped it! It appeared the pilot had been pushed through it. The end looked like my mother's old meat grinder – hamburger.

A little later I picked up a glove and dropped it even faster. The pilot's hand as still in it!

One of our pilots made Ripley's "Believe it or Not" column. With his plane in distress, he bailed out and landed on the roof of a local hospital where a Doctor and a Nurse were conveniently sun bathing. It's lucky the plane didn't land there instead.

Housing was not as nice as the Boyd's in Hayward. We took a one-room apartment that was minimal to say the least. Gwen kept looking and eventually found a newer, better one on Sandy Boulevard. We moved from the first one after only two weeks and little use. The cranky landlady refused to return our security deposit. "You didn't take care of it," she said. So we left.

We were fighter pilots and somebody decided we needed to hone our abilities to judge moving targets. They scheduled us for skeet. Now I had been a member of arguably the top high school rifle team in the country. I had won the Tyro award with the 30-06 rifle in the 161st Infantry Washington National Guard, and qualified as alternate for their Camp Perry Rifle Team. I was expert with machine gun and every other weapon they offered me. I had never fired a shotgun. Although I didn't like the shoulder jolt, it was really a fun game.

The range was actually in the center portion of Portland Army Air Base toward the East End. There were five or six evenly spaced stations with a single post holding a small waist-high platform that held our shells. There were two launching houses, one right, one left. The shooter, standing at ready, called "Pull" and a clay pigeon would fly from one side or the other, sometimes both. One needed to quickly sight, lead and fire as the bird traversed in front of you. Changing stations gave you a change of problem and we did that as well. On this particular autumn day, I was at a center position and ready. I called "Pull" and the clay target flew from my right to left. As I swung my weapon to follow, a Chinese Pheasant rose from the weed area in front of the range flying in the opposite direction. Instinctively, I swung back and fired. The pheasant dropped. I got him! "Hold your fire! Hold your fire!" I shouted. When everyone had lowered their guns, I charged down a slight bank, keeping my eyes on the spot I saw him drop. Five feet into the weed patch I was startled when another one rose in front of me. I used the other barrel and hit him as well. Now with a couple buddies helping, we located both warm bodies. I recalled pheasant dinners my mother had prepared when my father brought home trophies from his hunting. That sounded like a good idea. I took both birds to the mess sergeant and asked him to clean them. I detected a bit of reluctance, but he did it.

Then I called Gwen and told her to 'bone up' on pheasant dinners and told her why. Then I asked Pete Nacy if he and Marion would like to join us for a gourmet dinner.

Our small apartment had a miniature "Pullman" kitchen and we had dishes and utensils for two – that's all. Also, Gwen's culinary experience was mainly for chocolate cakes and hot dogs. What followed that night was a disaster, but we had fun. The birds were either 50 years old or the preparation was lacking because I have never tried fowl that tough! To be nice to guests, we gave them the plates and forks; we used saucers and spoons. The serving dish was the lid of a pan. Each couple had one knife and we had a community paring knife, sorely needed. The good part was I had enough of a booze bottle left that we were all laughing, even Gwen who was ready to cry earlier.

This much remains, I am a good shot and I am never to ask people to dinner again without prior authorization!

Portland did have clear summer days on occasion and on one of these, I had an hour in a P-39 alone – a 'slow time' for a new engine.

With nothing to do, I went sightseeing. Majestic Mount Hood lay east of the city and on this particular day was more beautiful than ever. It still had a snowcap. The sky was a deep blue color and cloudless – if you didn't count the wisp of white that trailed from the very peak of the mountain toward the south.

I decided to see how close I could fly to the 11,235-foot peak. Then I would forevermore be able to tell people – "Oh, I got within ten feet of the peak." I wouldn't say from above it – or climbing by foot.

I approached from the north. As I passed the very top by just a few feet, I was hit by a violent downdraft that may have included the hand of God. I pulled the stick into my belly and poured on full power, to hell with 'slow time'. I am sure my tail surface was in snow or inches from it before I finally escaped the power that rushed me down. My heart was pounding. "Never underestimate the power of nature," someone had said. Believe me, I never will again.

Only later did it occur to me that I might have started an avalanche. I hope no skiers or climbers paid for my excursion to the mountaintop.

On Sunday, July 23, I was in for real excitement. I took a flight of four for a scheduled mock dogfight twenty miles south of Portland. We engaged P-39s from the Salem-based 356th Squadron in a grand and glorious mock dogfight. For fifteen minutes, we ranged from 1,000 to 5,000 feet and back with some probable wins and maybe some the other way as well. I think I was ahead.

About that time I was in a duel I know I was winning. The situation required a nearly inverted very tight turn to bring me under his belly. Just then I heard an explosion in the engine and silence. It quit. I rolled out immediately.

I was about 1500 feet – no power and dropping at an alarming rate. What to do? I switched gas tanks – nothing. I looked at the area – completely forested. I switched tanks again, and then again.

By now I decided I had dropped too low to attempt a bailout so after maybe trying one more switch position, I began searching for the best possible crash area. I found an opening of maybe 100 feet by 100 feet where trees had been cut. The stumps were still there. I would die, of course, but it was all I had and better than the middle of the forest, I felt. At about 250 feet, I saw a two-lane, paved road and immediately rolled right to use it. It had traffic, not much, but some cars going in both directions. I felt I had no other choice. It was them or me – maybe both, or hopefully they would get out of the way.

At that last moment, I spotted a field, slightly east of the road. It was open and flat. The only remaining obstacles were several tall pines I would have to clear. How many times have P-39s spun in landing under-powered? I prayed.

I could not have cleared the last tree by more than a foot or two, but I did. There was a bulldozer working at leveling the very dusty field. I went by him by 20 feet – no more. With wheels up, I gently touched down and nearly immediately spun in a 180-degree half-circle. Just as immediately I had the door open and sprinted away – to safety should there be fire. There wasn't and I went back.

The dozer operator had stopped and appeared paralyzed. He had not seen or heard me until I hit the ground beside him. I could get no response or conversation from him though I tried.

By this time, cars had stopped on that road and curious people were gathering to gawk at my downed bird. I waved to my circling flight to indicate I was okay and they left.

In the next two hours I entertained up to 100 Sunday drivers who had gathered. It swelled to several hundred by the end of the day. At least two dozen times I told a questioner, "Yes, it has wheels. No, I couldn't put them down because I didn't know what I would be landing on. Yes, there are guns."

Maybe an hour later a very nice lady from a nearby farmhouse brought me a sandwich with homemade bread slices over a half-inch thick. She also thoughtfully brought a huge glass of milk – nothing too good for our fighting men! I sat on the cowling and answered more questions and ate.

The bulldozer operator never moved in all the time I was there. I wondered if he had had an accident in his pants.

I spent most of the day waiting for relief and transportation, which finally got there in late afternoon.

Gwen and I had invited another couple to have dinner at the club and she was irritated that I was late getting home. She called 355th operations to ask where I was and why. Sgt. Cahill answered, "He's down at the crash." Knowing our pilots, she was concerned.

"Who crashed?"

"He did," was the answer with no explanation?

She said she had to ask, "Is he okay?" Then Cahill told her "Yes." She met our guests and went to the club.

I came in sometime later, still in my dusty flying suit and found them at the bar laughing and having a good time.

"Hey, don't I deserve some sympathy?"

"Well, I was told you were alright." So I joined them.

A month later Col. Martin wrote a commendation letter for my file…

"(G-3)

HEADQUARTERS
354th Fighter Group Army Air Forces
Army Air Base
Portland 19, Oregon

27 August 1943.

SUBJECT: Commendation.

TO: 1ST Lt. Clayton K. Gross, 355th Fighter Squadron, Army Air Base, Portland 19, Oregon.

1. It is the desire of this headquarters to commend 1st Lt. Clayton K. Gross for cool and level-headed action when his airplane was forced down July 23, 1943.

2. Lt. Gross was on an individual combat mission when the

engine of his P-39 airplane failed. After taking all possible measures to start the engine, he chose a partially completed runway on the Aurora airport and made a forced landing. Using the correct procedure for an emergency power off landing, he skillfully landed wheels up on the flight strip which was under construction. Although there were men and equipment on the runway, the landing as effected without injury to personnel or damage to private property, and with a minimum damage to the airplane. Lt. Gross then acted as guard to protect his airplane from curious bystanders until relieved by proper authority.

3. This type of action in such an emergency is a credit to Lt. Gross and his organization.

> S/ Kenneth R. Martin
> KENNETH R. MARTIN,
> Lt. Colonel, Air Corps,
> Commanding."

We continued to log hours in the air. New replacements arrived to swell the ranks or quite often, replace those lost in accidents. 'C' Flight got three assigned and they were great ones; alphabetically, as usual with the Army Air Corps, RADOJITS, RHING and RYAN. Three talented young men who would all eventually fail to live through the war. In practice dogfights after their transitions, each proved to be above average. Probably because of my many hours in the aircraft, I could best all, but they gave me a real workout.

The north border of the Portland Army Air Base was the mighty Columbia River and to keep it from flowing over the field, a dike about 12 to 15 feet high kept the river in check. During one of our many 'war games' one smart ass pilot had the brilliant idea of using the wall of the dike to hide his approach of the dike in his assigned task of an attack on the base. It was a pretty good idea actually worthy of me, but the way he did it was not the best. The span of the P-39 propeller was 9 feet 8 inches and since nothing extended beyond that, with gear retracted, he reasoned that flying up the river about a foot off the water. He would be completely hidden by the 12 feet of dike and so he would have been, if the water had been as low on his side of the dike as the field was on our side.

As he neared the field and readied himself to come over the dike for a complete surprise attack, he pushed his bird just a little lower and that was a mistake. The first sign of his presence, besides the somewhat muffled roar of his engine, was the geyser of water put up by his propeller when it hit the first wave. That impact slowed and pulled him down and the main body hit the water with a giant splash, readily visible above the dike to anyone who looked! The pilot went from 200 MPH to 0 in about fifty feet and he found out quickly that the P-39 doesn't float worth a damn.

Long before the first Jeep could reach the splash area, he and his bird had settled to the bottom of the Columbia. The crowd of a hundred or so gathered on top of the dike anxiously waiting for a sign of life to come to the surface. We had an ambulance waiting which was about as useful as a Sherman tank. All stared at the river. Somebody ran toward some rowboats anchored not too far away. Most of us stood and smoked and stared. After five minutes, we knew he was in big trouble. After fifteen, we knew he was gone. About a half-hour later with a diver getting ready to go after his remains, a few of us still standing and staring glumly, a miracle happened. He bobbed to the surface, all by himself and obviously alive, soaked and sputtering, but definitely alive. Cheers rang out that could be heard back in our hangar area.

We got his story later. He was stunned by the sudden stop

but safely belted in, he was unhurt. When he finally settled to the dark bottom, he took stock of the situation and decided he was all right. The cockpit was dry – almost. It took a few minutes to calm down and plan his escape. Take off all heavy clothing and shoes, hard to swim with shoes on. Make sure all belts were undone so he was completely free and practice breathing. He didn't know how deep he was, but figured he better have a full capacity of air to get to the surface. Now, all was ready! Open the door and leave. He took several deep breaths and tried the door. It wouldn't open! The pressure of the water against it wouldn't let him open it! After a short panic, he found an answer, he could open the window and let the water in to equalize the pressure. Then open the door! But after? Going under water, what if it still wouldn't open? It took a while to get up the nerve to try it, but finally fearing his limited air supply was diminishing, he went ahead. No problem. The door opened and half-hour after he went in, he bobbed to the top. Even the P-39 was eventually raised and with some part replacement, got back in the air. Dried out, of course.

CHAPTER 13

# TRAINING MISSIONS TILL READY

ALL OF OUR TRAINING was fun, purely because all flying was fun. Maybe one exception was a low-level mission 'Uncle George' Bickell led from Portland to Salem –the purpose – to surprise the 356th with an 'attack'. We put sixteen P-39s in the air (barely) from our squadron. I led "'C' flight. George flew a ground-hugging route and the rest of us followed in tight formation. At altitude that would have been no problem but 20 to 25 feet off the ground, with rolling terrain down the Willamette Valley and our fearless leader adjusting his altitude constantly to follow it, meant that each of us magnified his movements in waves which increased in relationship to the distance from George. 'A' flight was the lead flight, 'B' on his left and we were on the first flight on his right with 'D' on our right and slightly behind us as we were to the lead flight. I had to watch George's flight, but could not resist looking ahead to make sure we weren't running into anything because I wasn't positive he was making sure of that for us. I could see my wingman and element leader and the 'B' flight planes on the other side of George bouncing perilously close to treetops from time to time. Or sliding close to me or others until ten minutes into the mission, I was fairly sure all sixteen of us weren't going to make it in one piece and that thought worked me into a cold sweat.

About that time it began to roll down my neck though, low and behold, we rose over the last hill and before us was the Salem strip that we proceeded to beat up in goodly fashion. The 356th was wiped out! And all 16 of us lived! Thank God George felt that with the enemy destroyed, we could fly home at a safer altitude which we did. Good training, I suppose.

We were to find out many times in combat that it wouldn't be that easy when the real enemy put up walls of flak to fly through once we got to the field. More on that later.

On Friday the 13th of August 1943, I was given a job, which sounded like real sport. A B-17 from Geiger in my hometown of Spokane was on its way to 'Bomb' Portland. Our job – intercept and shoot it down before it could accomplish that. It was 'C' flight's project and I led the four-plane mission with Vern Rhing on my wing. Al Johnson – such a great guy – but such a sloppy pilot, led the second element and Tony Radojits was his wingman.

I say Al was a sloppy pilot pointedly. For years after this particular day, I asked myself the same question over and over – should I have done something to get him out of the air and into something or some job where his apparent lack of coordination wouldn't hurt him or somebody else? He came to me when we were stationed in Hayward, California flying the P-39; a brand new 2nd Lt. rated pilot – with shiny new silver wings. As was custom, I flew with him on my wing after his initial check out in the airplane. Before I got into any kind of real workout to test his skills on that first flight, I rolled out of a simple turn and watched him slide toward me so violently that I had to pop the stick forward to avoid him. I put that down to a little nervousness on his part, but a few simple maneuvers later, it was repeated and he just plain scared me. We landed and I had a heart-to-heart talk about controlling his airplane in flight. I don't think I ever met a nicer guy, a big infectious grin and a very good attitude to my criticism of his efforts. He promised that he would be more careful and over the next few months, he did improve, but never to the level I thought he should be. I asked myself how he ever got through flying school. That is where he should have been eliminated – not when he is a commissioned officer with those cherished wings.

I had to visualize the answer. Everybody liked Al and probably his Primary Flight Instructor would have experienced his shortcomings and said, "He's such a nice guy. I'll let them wash him out in Basic." And in Basic, I envisioned the same thing, "Let them do it in Advanced!" And I would guess the Advanced School Instructor would have said, "Hell, he's gone this far. I can't do it to him!"

And so Al graduated and was posted to 'C' Flight 355th Fighter Squadron, 354th Fighter Group where we did everything we could to teach him to fly. He was the only pilot of the many I flew with that I reported to our Squadron Commander. George liked him also and said we would watch him. And as I said, he was better by the time this weird Friday the 13th came around.

We met for a briefing at 0730. Takeoff was scheduled for 0815 but at that hour, Portland Army Air Base was socked in with a fog so thick we had trouble finding the flight line in a creeping Jeep – no flying until it lifted. Hopefully, Spokane was the same so their bomber couldn't get here before we got off. (It was.)

We waited in the pilots' ready room for an hour with no improvement. At about nine o'clock Al checked with Base Weather to determine the possibility of a sudden clearing and when they said no possibility, he told us he would be right back and left.

What happened next was a scenario that is designed for today's "Twilight Zone."

Al was married to a sweet little girl – Peggy, a childhood sweetheart who was as much in love with him as he was with her. They had a quick breakfast that morning because Al had to leave at 0645 to make our briefing. Peggy then went back to bed for a couple hours. At 0930 she was up and washing the breakfast dishes at the kitchen sink. With the water running, she did not hear Al unlock the front door and enter the house. When he appeared at her side in the kitchen, she was understandably startled. "What are you doing here?"

Al did not answer, but instead kissed her tenderly on the neck and cheek, she told us later. Then not having said one word since his entry, he turned and walked out the front door again. He was gone. It was a 25-minute drive each way from their house to the Airbase and he stayed in the house less than two minutes – never saying one word.

Peggy was still talking as he left as quickly as he had arrived. "What's going on? Why are you home?" and then as he left, she said she smiled and commented to herself – "You nut!"

A little over an hour later he was dead.

Al was back in the ready room by 1000. The weather was breaking and by 1030, we were taking off by elements of two. I climbed out to the north and leveled the flight off at 12,000 feet. A Controller thought he had picked up the 'bandit' and vectored us to the west. A few minutes later, I spotted the lone B-17 about 2,000 feet below us on a due south course. I placed my flight in an echelon right formation and circled over the B-17 position about 1:00 o'clock for an overhead pass at the target. With a 'tally-ho' that would have made "G-8 and His Battle Aces" proud. I peeled off for the dive. Vern on my wing followed and Al, the #3 man, was to follow him and Tony to bring up the rear. My eyes were riveted on the target until I heard Tony scream "Lookout!" and then, "My God!"

I looked back over my right shoulder to see the wreckage of Vern and Al's planes locked together and then falling apart in hundreds of pieces. I totally forgot the bomber and swung in a circle around still fluttering debris. I found two parachutes in the air with bodies dangling from both, but neither was fully deployed; one in fact appeared shredded and trailed behind the pilot in a line. There might be a chance one survived, I remember thinking as I watched both go to the ground on an island of the Columbia River where it turns north toward Washington before going west to the sea. I called PAAB for emergency landing and dove for the field to report the crash area.

Tony told me what had happened. When I initiated the attack – Vern followed, as he should – in trail. Al peeled off and either forgot to watch Vern or simply misjudged his turn – at any rate, he flew directly into Vern's cockpit. Rescue reached the general area and found both pilots battered and long gone. Probably neither knew what hit him.

I was stunned, but my own bride was shook, probably more than I was. Uncle George sent his wife, also named Peggy, and she told Gwen who was six weeks short of her twentieth birthday, that it was her duty as wife of the flight leader to go along to tell Peggy Johnson the news. Gwen said it was the hardest thing she had ever had to do. Peggy Johnson who was no older than Gwen would not believe them. "You're lying. You're lying. It's not true!" She said that over and over. They were all crying and she told of Al's strange, short silent visit just a short time before.

Could a story such as that have happened on any other day than Friday the thirteenth?

Our ground transportation was fine with the Buick – the one with the working cigarette lighter. Gwen now had enough driving experience to be considered accomplished but a new problem surfaced. Gasoline was rationed and the Buick used more precious stamps than we had needed before. When I complained out loud, one of our pilots privately gave me the answer. "Drive down to the flight line after dark and see Sgt. X." That evening

I tried it. I was not alone. Four or five pilots were in line ahead of me at the aviation fuel truck. I was a little concerned about the effects of 100-octane fuel on the engine, but was assured it would be fine. It was. I never worried about the fuel shortage again. When we shipped out for combat a few months later, Gwen now thoroughly spoiled, had to go back to ration stamps. I wonder if it was legal? Probably not.

A lot of activity in our last month in Portland and much of it had to do with parties. Parties, of course, require liquid refreshments and whiskey was rationed in both Oregon and Washington. To alleviate the shortage that followed rationing, all personnel or at least most got liquor licenses in both states. Vancouver was just across the Columbia River.

One more solution was tried – once! A pilot in an AT-6 was dispatched to California where there was no rationing. He bought two cases of assorted goodies and stowed them in the back seat, well strapped in. All was well until he had an engine failure on the return trip. Fortunately for all, he had cleared the mountainous area that borders California and Oregon and was able to land without incident on a little traveled highway. He then found a phone, courtesy of a nearby farmhouse and called 355th headquarters. Major George Bickell was there.

He related his story – rather proud of his accomplishment.

"Oh, my God!" said Bickell.

"Don't worry, Sir. I'm okay and so is the aircraft."

"I don't care about you or the '6'. If an inspector gets there and finds any whisky in it, you are automatically on K.P. for the duration. Get back to the plane and bury every bottle if necessary – GET THEM OUT OF THERE!

No more California expeditions were scheduled.

The 355th Squadron officers held one party in a rented hall, just a week or so prior to our departure. Wives and/or girlfriends were there. One pilot did bring a girlfriend who managed to antagonize every other female in attendance.

She was attractive. Kind of the "real dish" type. In the course of the evening, she went to every table and told the pilots, "I'm with the Civil Air Patrol. We're based at The Dalles up the river. I'll be there next weekend if you'd like to fly up and see me."

Gwen, as I suppose all other wives did said, "Don't even think about it."

The following Friday, I arranged a short trip to Spokane to see my family once again. I had completely forgotten the young lady since I had a prettier one of my own. I stayed overnight, had some tearful good-byes and took off for PAAB. The weather was bad. I tried twice to let down without success and then, being slightly low on fuel, asked to be directed to an alternate field. They directed me to THE DALLES. Please believe me – I had completely forgotten the lady's invite. Forgot it, that is, until I set down there and saw her running to my parking area. Man! How will I explain this?

The Dalles Airport is North of the river and the city. This very friendly girl had a car and offered to take me into town "– where we can have lunch – and talk." I had to accept. A ferry takes cars across the Columbia to town.

I wasn't very good company for the girl. I bought her lunch and noted her disappointment in me. We ferried back to the landing strip. Just before we docked, she spotted another P-39 circling to land and her demeanor jumped a few notches. The new Airacobra parked next to mine. The plane was not from our group and I didn't find where he had come from. He was a Major and knew my erstwhile date and she knew him. There was a hug before they got into her car. Before their car doors closed, I hollered at him, "Major, I'm very low on fuel. Can you spare some?"

"Yeah – yeah!" and they left.

I siphoned every drop I could get from his tanks to mine – don't know how far he had to go, but I had an idea that he wouldn't mind if he had to RON.

I kept getting the same answer –"Still solid with 300 to 500 feet max ceiling." I decided to try to fly down the Columbia at water level – Portland was right on the river. I took off to try it.

I've made a lot of dumb decisions in life, but this had to be one of the worst. From The Dalles, the Columbia winds, not bad at first. I flew at maybe 50 to 100 feet and had no trouble for the first 15 river bends, although I noted the turns were getting closer and closer, almost requiring 90 degree banks to make them.

Then I went around another corner and found the clouds clear down to the water. I straightened out – poured on full power and pulled the stick into my gut. There are mountains bordering the river and I had no idea if I would be flying into one or not. I prayed. I came out on top unscathed and very appreciative.

I flew over Portland AB and since I had no desire to fly elsewhere, followed tower directions on an instrument let down. This time I made it. Combat couldn't be more dangerous than this – could it?

Maybe the worst part of the experience was explaining The Dalles stop to Gwen!

The government had invested over one year in my fighter training. I had logged 500 hours in P-39s. When do I fight the war? I soon found out!

THIS IS IT!

Do we need anything else to illustrate what is to be? We are issued War Department 'change of address postcards' to be completed and mailed that date:

"Previous address:
    355th Fighter Squadron
    Portland Army Air Base
    Portland 19, Oregon.

New Address:
    1st Lt. Clayton K. Gross, O-663512
    355th Fighter Sq., 354th Fighter Group
    APO No. 4952, %Postmaster
    New York, N. Y."

Signed and mailed to all likely to write. This is it!

We are scheduled to board a train to the East on October 6, 1943.

Gwen left for Spokane in the Buick and our war time separation began.

Very sad day!

CHAPTER 14

# ON THE WAY TO WAR

THE 354th FIGHTER GROUP boarded a train in Portland, Oregon on the 6th. On the third of October, wives had been sent home. Sadly Gwen had left me for God only knows how long. This fighter pilot admits to choking up but when we passed through Spokane, I avoided the teary part. We were off to somewhere to do our part in the war.

Trains in 1943 didn't go very fast – that is, it seems like they stop every two hours night and day. If we looked out or got out to stretch, there was often nothing to see but fields. We saw a lot of America in the next three or four days. A lot of 'bull' sessions passed time. On October 10th we reached our destination, Camp Kilmer, New Jersey, – a port of debarkation.

Settling in filled our time for a day or so. One night Red Emerson and I went to the late movie that wasn't all that good. It was over just before 2200. With cloud cover the night was quite dark, but for October, really very mild. We were in no hurry but decided to shortcut between barracks to save steps on the way back to our own area. Most lights were out except for bulbs lighting entrance doors.

We had slowly sauntered along the way for several minutes when a shrill female scream froze us momentarily in our tracks. It had come from the opposite side (Northern end) of the building we were passing at the time. Several more times the screams rent the air as we double-timed around the corner. In a dim light from a distant bulb, I could see a fatigued-uniformed soldier on his knees over the screamer. Both Red and I shouted as we saw the circumstances and the attacker jumped up and took off. On the ground was a very hysterical WAC, her blouse torn open and her skirt and other clothes in disarray. We stopped only for a moment to determine her well being, and then Red stayed with her while I took off after the attacker. For awhile, I could hear retreating footsteps, then silence. In the dark, I had no idea where he had gone, and neither Red nor I got a look at him for identification.

I retraced my steps to Red and the young lady who was still sobbing violently. She wanted to go to her barracks, but we firmly led her to base M.P. Headquarters where we left her in the care of several of their personnel, including two WAC's. They were calling for Doc when we left. Both of us felt very good. We had broken up a rape attempt.

Most of us went to New York City. It was an amazing experience for those of us who qualified as small town 'hicks'. Ten pilots from 355 banded together. The train stopped at Penn Station – next to the famous Ambassador Hotel. We decided to live it up at dinner there. I can't remember what we ate, but it was good and it was expensive. The bill came to $50 – five dollars each. Measured against the usual per diem for sustenance of $1.25, we were definitely living it up. The waiter dressed in Tuxedo-type livery had pretty well decided that military officers in uniform didn't belong here. I collected from each guy and added $5 for the 10% tip. I got a frown.

"Isn't that enough?" I asked.

"It is for the bill." And he wheeled around and left. If I could have grabbed the tip back, I would have.

We left to go have a few drinks.

I visited the PX on an afternoon a week before we left Camp Kilmer. Joined by a fellow officer, we were sauntering back to our living area when I found myself the object of an attack by a small Terrier-type dog who came from between two barracks away at half the speed of a fighter plane. Close behind were several GIs shouting at the mutt to stop. Their screams stopped him before he actually hit me, but he was a foot or two away with a mouth full of teeth anchored by two dangerous looking fangs and he was snarling.

One of the enlisted men gathered him up quickly and clamped his mouth closed. With a nervous laugh, he tried to explain. "Sorry Lieutenant. Ha! Ha! He doesn't seem to like officers. We'll take care of him," and they left for the closest barracks.

We talked about it on the way to our quarters. How does he tell an officer from a GI? We have similar facilities – it couldn't be the smell. Somebody must have trained him to look for rank insignia —not much else to go by.

Oh well, nobody hurt.

On October 17, we were put on alert and all leaves and passes cancelled – great anticipation followed by several more days of nothing – typical Army!

On the 20th, we got an early call and boarded a train for a short ride – then trucked to a dock where an ocean liner awaited us – the HMS Athlone Castle. Bands were playing and Red Cross girls were there to give out goodies. My anticipation level was sky high!

I will never forget the trip overseas from the minute we got out of the truck dockside. Following orders that officers would carry *all* their own luggage, I staggered up the inclined gangplank with my B-4 bag and duffel bag, especially the damn duffel bag. Again on orders, I had shipped the footlocker home to Gwen and as I had moved nearly all the contents into the duffel bag afraid to leave anything I might possibly need in the next few years. The last few feet of that trip uphill I resolved to re-evaluate everything and jettison half of it at sea. I didn't, of course.

We were assigned a room – Brue, Red, Virgil Dietrick and me. It measured about 8x10 feet and included two double-decker bunks with a wash basin and mirror. At first glance, we were disappointed, but not after we found out what everybody else had for quarters. The ship according to printed specs posted on the bridge had a capacity of 1,020, emergency capacity 2,500. We had 7,000 on board! Although the A. Castle had been a luxury liner, our 'cabin' had no private bath. There was a 'head' not far down the hall and a bath, with a huge tub also within reach and available if you didn't mind waiting in line.

We reconnoitered most of the vessel before it finally tooted a horn a few times and steamed out of port. It was jammed! The PX or whatever the English crew called it, had most of the necessities but huge lines, maybe two hours long at some times of the day. I tried it once because I learned that cigarettes were without tax on board ship and cost a nickel a pack. When I finally got to the store, I bought ten cartons for $5 and a few dozen candy bars. I didn't go back the rest of the trip. All the cigarettes were Phillip Morris, the only brand available. By the end of the first carton, I couldn't stand the taste of them. I kept the rest for barter.

Everybody on board was assigned two meal periods a day. For the troops that meant standing in a chow line at their assigned hour and eating from a mess kit once finally served. It was brutal. Before the trip was over, an Infantry Commander armed his troops and forced their way into the kitchen after a few hours wait. He was put in the brig and probably had a career end for that episode.

The officers had it a little easier. We also had two meals a day, but they were scheduled sit down affairs in the very proper dining rooms complete with linen and English waiters in livery yet, with printed menus! Quite nice if you didn't starve in between and providing you could get used to fish for breakfast. My sitting was the third and last, both breakfast and dinner. That was ten in the morning and seven for the evening meal. I liked that because at eight, after our sitting, the dining room closed for a short period and re-opened for use as an Officers lounge until 2200 hours.

The ship sat in harbor for full day and finally got underway around noon on the 21st. We slowly made our way out of the harbor and to open sea. Shortly after that, announcements were made to secure all portholes – no lights to be shown on deck –

U-boats you know. That's comforting. In the morning, we found our ship to be part of the huge armada. It was difficult to count the number of ships since there was a great deal of shifting position. Several Navy destroyers weaved back and forth on our flanks.

About two days out we were startled by the unmistakable sound of cannon fire. All of us moved from whatever we were doing and headed for the deck to see what was happening. There were several shots before I got on top. We had a five-inch cannon mounted on the fantail and they were practicing. It happened every day or so and it was no big deal.

Morale among the men was not good. We had crowded living space, but it was ours 24 hours a day. The enlisted were housed in holds and bunk style, five or six bunks deep. What really hurt was each bunk was assigned to three men – each had it for eight hours, then vacate!

The two meals a day didn't help. Lines to the PX could be hours long. Throw in a fair percentage of seasick men and you could guess the results.

I was Officer of the Day about six days at sea. My station was on the ship's bridge. Other than interest in all the goings on in that Command Post and the best view I had had of the fleet accompanying us, the only thing I remember was the chart posted on one wall (or is it a bulkhead?) which stated:

```
HMS Athlone Castle
Capacity              1200
Emergency Capacity    2500
```

We had 7000! Little wonder we felt crowded.

On day one of the trip, the nearly two hours in the lounge produced about thirty poker games and I went quickly from table to table until I got a chair. Some games were fair, some terrible if you happened into one that featured limits and wild card games. By the end of the third evening, the more serious players had gravitated to one game and by the fourth, an infantry Colonel had taken command and made arrangements that altered the rest of the trip for me.

The little bribery did wonders for the eight of us who had formed the 'big' game. A table was reserved in a corner near the kitchen and out of sight of anyone peering through the windows. The dinner finished by eight and the lounge opened. We left with the others at the ten o'clock closing. After 15 minutes away, we proceeded to the side door and gave a secret rap. We were back inside and playing in a few minutes. We took 50 cents to $1.00 from every pot for the kitty, depending on the size of the pot. In the all-night game, which every poker player knows is necessary; the kitty could grow to $60 to $70. It was split with the eight to ten people who took care of us. Around midnight, they placed a platter of extra-ordinary sandwiches on the table and we took a five-minute break to wolf those down. Then back to business! Coffee was available always. At 0600, they announced; deal once more around please, and after that, the game is closed. When finished and the table cleared, we were served a huge American-type breakfast; ham, eggs (fresh and as many as you wanted, potatoes, toast and the works. With that we tiptoed out and to bed. I climbed in my sack by seven-thirty a.m.; usually an hour before the rest started getting up. When our ten o'clock breakfast hour was approaching, the gang would try to wake me, after all, with only two meals a day how could you skip one? It didn't work, I rolled over and after they left, got quality sack time. I tried to be up by two p.m. because at two-thirty with a secret knock at the side door, we were admitted to the lounge for a great lunch which actually made waiting for the seven p.m. dinner no problem. I went to dinner with my regular schedule and then started all over again. Instead of two meals a day, I ate four and by the time we reached Liverpool, England, had roughly $2,000 profit. A very interesting crossing, despite the everyday submarine alerts!

Someone had a copy of a 'racy' book called, "The Memoirs of Madame Madeline". It was in much demand. If you got it, you read from cover to cover and passed it on. I don't think it was idle during the entire voyage. I had put my name on the list and got it at mid-day. I climbed in a tub of hot salt water and read it to the end. My goodness! Are there really women like that?

No poker for one night at sea – I drew duty in one of the deep holds where hundreds of our GIs were quartered. There was really nothing for me to do but kill time.

It did give me time to reflect on the conditions the men were enduring. With multiple assignments to each bunk, there was always someone who needed quiet to sleep. The guys were aware of that and so things were quiet for the most part. In one cleared area, there was a poker game in progress on a blanket. Besides eight or nine players, a dozen kibitzers were ringing the players. I joined them.

For some time, I stood quietly with arms folded across my chest. It happened so fast, I didn't know what happened – I saw the blur of a small dog hurtling across the blanket at me. I instinctively raised my left arm in defense and found the dog locked on my wrist. It took three or four men to pry his jaws open and free me. I was bleeding pretty good and someone came up with a rag to stem it.

I heard many apologies as I left to go to the ship hospital and medics. Several men pleaded – "Don't tell on us, Lieutenant." I said I would consider that. Before I left I saw and recognized it was the same damn dog that had made a run at me at Camp Kilmer. He really doesn't like me!

England was rabies free and intended to stay that way and we had been warned before embarkation. Somebody hadn't listened.

The doctor cleaned and looked at my wounds – very obviously a canine bite.

"Where did this happen?" he asked.

"Doc, look at the duty roster and see where I was, but please don't tell them I ratted on them."

A day later the Captain ordered a shakedown of the ship until the dog was located. It was found and disposed of overboard.

A month or so later, The Saturday Evening Post ran a story of the incident – none of my doing. I was glad the men weren't 354th!

We are here! Land was seen on the last day of October and promptly disappeared again in a dense wall of English fog. That we would discover was standard in this country.

We dropped anchor in the harbor near Liverpool early the next morning. And we sat there for two more days waiting for the fog to lift. It finally did and our luxury liner was able to reach its berth in late afternoon. A band greeted us. Welcome to the war, Yanks! We did not debark until the following morning and the Red Cross was there with doughnuts and hot coffee. Could things be looking up?

I started my letter writing a day after Gwen left. I would write hundreds before I would see her again.

Oct. 4, 1943

"My dearest sweetheart,

Well, Dolly, my second big day on my own and I'm not very happy! No little wife to remind me of things and I can't remember anything. I hope I start improving soon or I'm going to be sunk!

I still haven't got your dress, as I have not been off the base as yet. And today we were confined to the post. I think that we get off for a bit tomorrow so I'll try to get it then. Don't worry anyway, Sweetheart. I did remember the bond finally today and got it. I'll have to figure out a way to send it now.

I also have a few clothes I want to send home. I can't even begin to get everything in my baggage and I don't know what I'm going to do.

Honey, the 355th luck is still holding out! Ha! Yesterday, Peters in "D" Flight came in to land without putting his wheels down. He had a belly tank full of gas on and when he hit, it caught fire. The plane burned but he got out o.k. The Major called off flying for good for our squadron and I don't blame him a bit! With our luck, we wouldn't have a plane or pilot left in 2 weeks. I didn't get in four hours to get my flight pay though, so that doesn't make me too happy.

Oh, Honey, I hope I get a letter or call from you soon or I'll go crazy. I love you so <u>very</u> much! Be a good girl like I know you are and I'll try to exist till I get with you again.

I love you,<br>Clayt"

CHAPTER 15

# THIS IS ENGLAND!

THERE WAS NO POKER the last 36 hours aboard the ship. There was much conversation, speculation, fog watching and re-packing bags. It took a lot of time to unload the ship.

The 354th debarkation began early on the morning of November 2. The solid feel of God's earth under foot felt very good after a dozen days at sea. More doughnuts, coffee and pretty Red Cross girls to look at and then we boarded what they called a train – much different than ours. There were compartments that would seat about six to eight. Each compartment had its own entry/exit door. The gauge of the tracks was very narrow compared to ours.

And so began what would escalate over the next couple years – our criticism of their goods and customs and they of us and ours. I heard a story later in my stay in England – not sure of the truth, but a good illustration of the situation...

'A very proper gentleman reading his paper while waiting for a train. An American GI standing nearby was looking at a line of British boxcars, called GOODS CAR by them. He sneered and nudged the Brit. "You call those boxcars! Ha." The gentleman glanced up and said "No" and gave him the proper name. Not satisfied, the GI retorted, "Ya know what we'd do with those in America?" Calmly lowering his paper, the gentleman said, "Well, from what I've seen, you would either eat it or make love to it." End of conversation'.

I boarded and claimed a corner seat by a window. A couple hours later we chugged out of the station and began a long, long and as I remember, very cold ride through the English countryside. I guess somebody knew where we were headed, but those in our compartment weren't in on it.

When we made a final stop and went from train to trucks, we found ourselves at an Air Base called Greenham Commons. No aircraft in sight and not just because of the blackout. We were fed and then assigned quarters in Quonset huts.

"C" Flight had one divided in two halves. Brueland, Emerson and I took the smaller section in front and the other five in the rear portion. There was a pot-bellied stove in each – colder than the cold damp weather outside. There were also three metal bed frames – not assembled. If we are to sleep, we had to correct both. In the light of a single bulb, we went to work. With my bed about half assembled, I stood up to stretch.

At that moment there was a single knock on the door and it opened to a strange officer who shook hands with me and announced, "Hi! I'm Pete Quesada."

"Hi. I'm Clayton Gross." I was about to ask if he knew how to assemble these damn beds when pumping his hand moved his jacket collar just enough to show a Star! I immediately 'popped to' and shouted, "TEN SHUN!"

Brue and Red were still on their knees and looked up like I was crazy. Before they could move, General Quesada stopped them with an, "As you were." Then he told us he had IXth Fighter Command and wanted to welcome us to the ETO. Then he left to go surprise somebody else. Nice touch I thought.

The following morning after a fitful sleep, we had a hot breakfast and then were gathered for a pep talk by the General. We were the first fighter group under his command and he had great expectations for us. Two things I remember most – he wanted us operational in as short a period as possible. Great! We don't have planes and have no idea what we will fly, but we'll try.

The other message was sobering. "You are a well-organized and well-trained group. We expect great things from you against the enemy. NOT ALL OF YOU WILL SURVIVE, but the job must be done. Good luck." My mind says I guess he's right, but it couldn't happen to me.

About the third day, with every person in the group antsy as hell, we wondered what would happen next. Headquarters and Col. Martin issued orders. Bob Stephens and I from 355 Squadron and Jack Bradley from 353 were to proceed immediately to an English Air Base, location unknown to us, but evidently plain enough to whoever cut the orders. Within an hour we were packed for a few days detached duty and into a Jeep, bravely heading into the countryside. The typed orders named a base in a general location on the other side of London. We decided to overnight there. The war grows more interesting by the day!

An hour later we roared into that huge metropolis. I was stretching my neck exactly like a rube in awe. Know that for the first 21 years of my life I had been as far west of Spokane as Seattle, as far south as my birthplace, Walla Walla, Washington, and as far east as Coeur d'Alene, Idaho, (34 miles) and as far north as Spokane's City Limits. London was pretty heady stuff for this young man!

We eventually found the very heart of the city and found a very nice downtown London hotel, Park Lane Hotel, where we secured a suite divided into two rooms. Steve and Jack took the double room; I had the single. All of us had noted the lobby sign with an arrow pointing to the "American Bar" so five minutes after arrival; we were following the arrows to find it. First lesson of wartime nightlife – it didn't open until 2000.

At that appointed hour we were back at the door of the joint. Five minutes after opening the place, it was packed with people – about 90% in uniform, and hardly any of our own "American" uniforms in the "American Bar." Not to worry. It wasn't our country. By this time in life I was a bourbon drinker and they didn't have that, but they did have scotch and we were told that it was not always available so enjoy while you can. I adjusted my tastes for the moment.

Meeting people was no problem. A dozen or so uniformed equivalents of our WAC's were there and more than interested in young 'Yank' officers with their rumored bankrolls. Three of them soon joined our group and I found myself in an interesting conversation with a buxom blonde who recounted most of the difficulties she was experiencing in this 'bloody war'. I bought her two scotches, as my sympathies grew warmer, already understanding the situation and grieving for the poor girl. Steve and Jack were likewise interested listeners to others. A while later the young lady (I can't remember her name) excused herself for the ladies room and in her absence, another WAAF slid onto the bench beside me.

"You're not going with her, are you? She has syphilis, you know!"

In all of my 22 years, I had never considered such a situation, although I knew the word in a very detached way. I was 'shook'. "Buy me a drink, Yank," the informer said and squeezed my hand in sort of a promise. I was shaking but I did as bidded and she had it by the time the blonde returned – looking daggers at my second friend.

"You've a lot of cheek," she said. "That's my seat" and practically pulled the second girl out. When she had regained her original place, I was flanked by both and our conversation was definitely strained. Finishing her scotch, the second girl shrugged her shoulders and left. Then the inquisition began.

"What did she say about me?"

"Nothing. We were just talking," I replied.

"Well. Stay away from her. She has syphilis, you know!"

I really didn't know but I did know the American Bar was out of scotch and I had lost my appetite for anything else. At the first opportunity, I slid next to Bradley and told him I was going to get the hell out of there, with or without my buddies. They didn't argue. We were in our room within a few minutes. I didn't know if I was ready for big cities, war zones and all that went with them!

At 0900 the next morning we were once again Jeeping through the English countryside to an English Air Base. We were escorted to basic quarters and briefed on our schedule. The object of our trip was to check out and fly a new aircraft that would eventually be the one our group would be equipped with. The afternoon was spent on technical manuals and our first look and cockpit check in the new bird. "These" they said, "are the attack dive-bomber version called the A-36. The ones you get will be fighters – built by North American in your country, called the P-51 Mustang." We had never heard of it.

By the middle of day two, I had spent several hours in the cockpit of this strange new beast and was beginning to like it. There were drawbacks. After over one year in the tricycle landing gear P-39 with it's ground visibility – it was not easy to get used to the large nose of this 'tail dragger' which required considerable essing back and forth to see anything while taxiing. I did like the purr of it's Allison engine from in front of me, rather than behind where it was guaranteed to give the pilot a large nudge in the back should you have the misfortune of running into anything.

The time came to get off the ground in my 'Mustang' called 'Apache' by the Brits; I did not experience the same panic of my first P-39 flight and soon was tooling over the English countryside. The craft responded very nicely to my every wish. I had been told *not* to lower the dive flaps, which would drastically alter flight characteristics. The control was plainly labeled and it was tempting, but I settled for a climb to 10,000 feet and a simulated target. I pulled out when speed built up to 300 plus MPH. Nobody had mentioned guns but there was a switch in front of me that I toggled on and off. I wondered if the guns were loaded. A stray German could wander into my area. I loved the aircraft already. After a fairly smooth landing and a critique of the flight I got a second ride, as did the others.

Two flights in the A-36 was deemed enough and we were directed back to Greenham Commons. We drove through London without a stop and got home in late afternoon. And what had the trip been for? We had been told that we would check the other pilots out. When we arrived, we found that many of them had been flying P-51As belonging to the 67th RECON Group at Maybury. Well that's the Army Air Corps. We did experience London before the rest of the gang.

I flew the "A" twice. It was really much like the A-36 without the dive brakes – a good aircraft. On the 11th of November, Ferry Command began delivering new P-51B1s. Much improved over the 'A'. It had a four-bladed prop instead of three. More important, the Allison engine had been replaced by Merlin built by the famous British automaker, Rolls Royce. Now we are talking *great* fighters!

On the 12th we were ordered to a new base, BOXTED near Colchester which would become our operational base. Things are heating up! We began training in these planes in earnest.

I have to admit that on every flight I would scan the sky for the enemy. After all, some of the world's biggest air battles had happened in these very skies. Alas! The Battle of Britain had ended before we got there.

Colchester was a quaint village and the scene of all leisure time. They did have a Red Cross center where one could get minor sustenance from nice ladies – some pretty. We were told the city derived its name from King Cole – "Old King Cole" of nursery rhyme fame.

There was a crumbling castle that we explored. It was old enough to convince me of its authenticity. Most impressive to me was the "bathroom" facility. Along one wall ran a trough two to three inches deep and slanted so that 'piss' would flow to one end and down a hole. That was bad enough – reminded me of the boys' room at St. Augustine's grade school. For more important evacuation one evidently placed their feet in prepared depressions, leaned back against the wall and dumped through a hole. My what a smelly place the old castle must have been and thank God for modern conveniences even if they must be shared with dozens of others in the Army.

For officers, a more sociable location was discovered in Hotel Rose & Crown.

It had a fine pub and here we were able to get pints of what they called beer. The brew itself was all right, but for some reason, they don't like it cold as we were used to. We still didn't avoid it. This venue became the party place for the group.

Don Blakeslee, an Ace and Commander of the 4th Fighter Group had arrived at BOXTED to train us in tactics. I attended the briefing and sat in the front row. What followed was a discourse of what might be expected and tactics when we engage the enemy. Most memorable to me was his discussion of a head-on pass.

"In this situation," he said, "the man who breaks first is at a disadvantage. We make the other guy break! If I see you break first, I'll shoot you down myself!"

My feeling was that it was a very melodramatic act. "What an ass" I said to myself. "What if the enemy gets the same lecture?" I will at least dip a wingtip to let him know which way I'm going – when I go. When Blakeslee finished his discourse, our own fearless leader took the stage and said, "If that's the way it's done, that's the way we'll do it". He would just barely live to rue that remark.

That afternoon Doc Start put me in the hospital with a strep throat infection. I was there for a week and missed much training.

It was probably a record. Exactly two weeks after receiving new aircraft, our P-51B's, the group flew its first mission. December 1, 1943, each squadron furnished eight planes – 24 all told scheduled. Three aborts lessened that. The time up was 1430 in typically bad English weather. They really just crossed the channel – flew over occupied territory and returned at 1530, a one-hour mission. I heard about it in the hospital while getting a penicillin shot.

Four days later they flew a second very similar mission, but put up 36 aircraft and had no aborts. It lasted an hour and fifty minutes. Two days later I was discharged from the hospital and back to the group.

On December 11, the Group's third mission, I had my initiation. The mission was more than a training flight – we were support for B-17's on a raid to Emden, Germany. We put 48 planes in the air at 1155 with our own Col. Martin leading.

I had known excitement before but I can truthfully state that my first combat mission taught me a new level of that emotion. After briefing, I had made a point to relieve myself before bussing to the fight line. To arrive at my plane, get strapped in, say goodbye to Smitty; then start the engine, and the taxi time before taking off, took no more than 30 to 40 minutes. The mission was in lousy weather, the 48-plane formation forming at low level under the 1000-foot overcast, then setting course for Europe. The blind formation flying in the soup, all went together to make my heart pound. After we broke out into scattered clouds with more above us and crossed the coast into enemy-held territory, one end of the formation suddenly called bogies, or bandits, in the area and that again tightened the nerves. I never saw a thing other than patches of ground under us occasionally and the mustang I was trying to follow, yet I was more than ready when our fearless leader finally re-formed us and we set course for 'home'. More instrument let downs and finally Boxted was below us. We were the second squadron in and I was the seventh plane in the 355$^{th}$; so I was number 23 to land. In that circling waiting for my turn, I suddenly realized that I had to 'pee' baaad!

In 1938 I had started Gonzaga University as a pre-med student. Because I had discovered girls a few years back and because I showed promise of becoming one of the world's great bowlers, I really didn't learn much of anything in my first year and a half at Gonzaga. Certainly pre-med. students didn't get into anatomy or bodily functions beyond pithing a frog in Zoology, so it remained for the excitement of combat to teach me the limitations and functions of kidneys and bladder.

To be a casualty would be tragic, but to come back with wet pants would be next on the list. By the time I set down, it was a crisis. There was no way in the world I was going to come home that way and yet I didn't feel that I had one spare second. As I rolled straight ahead on the runway, I unbuckled my seat belt and then opened the canopy. At the finish of my roll, I was out on the wing and urinating. My plane was not even off the runway! Fortunately, no one taxied into me. After that blessed relief, I got back in and taxied to my hard-spot parking area. I was no longer a virgin in the combat arena. Mission time: 2 hours 30 minutes. We suffered our first casualty. A friend, Norman E 'Stud' Hall was lost –later reported KIA. Quesada was right – this is serious.

As missions grew longer, so did my experience level. The nervous kidney syndrome diminished. Months later I would be able to brief for a mission, take off on a four-hour escort, land and participate in a thirty-minute debriefing with our S-2 (intelligence officer), Jeep to the bar and order my first pint of bitters before sauntering to the head. I always believed that besides calming down, the bladder must have stretched in time to aid that ability.

★ ☆ ★ ☆ ★

Relaxing in combat did not start immediately. I was scheduled on Group mission 5, another escort, this time to Bremen. Radio silence is always maintained initially and I noticed no problems until after rendezvous with the 'big friends'.

There was sudden activity and still no sound. I tried to call Red One, squadron leader Bickell without success. I had no radio. What the hell is going on? A few minutes later, Jim Dalglish peeled off and headed for home. I didn't know what his problem was, but it gave me company to go home. I aborted the mission landing two hours after take-off. The radio-less plane was not my own and so it could not be blamed on my crew.

To make me feel even worse, Chuck Gumm shot down an ME-109, the first group victory and in fact, the first-ever by a Mustang. I agonized! Could I have completed the mission without communication? For the first time in my life, I began to doubt myself.

★ ☆ ★ ☆ ★

December 1943 LOSSES:

| | |
|---|---|
| Norman 'Stud' Hall | KIA |
| Buford Eaves | POW |
| Jas. Kerley | KIA |
| Dick Payne | POW |

Bill Turner                            POW
Hayes Appel                        POW

354th AIR CLAIMS TO DATE
    8 destroyed
    3 probably destroyed
    6 damaged

★ ☆ ★ ☆ ★

CHAPTER 16
# I'M A PUBLIC SPEAKER?

THE 354${}^{TH}$ CONTRIBUTION TO the war continued to gain importance although, not without cost. On our sixth mission, a four and one-half hour support mission to the Kiel area, we met great fighter opposition. Four German fighters claimed destroyed, two probables and four damaged. Unfortunately, we lost three, including Owen Seaman, Squadron Commander of the 353${}^{rd}$ Squadron. He tried to coax a damaged Mustang back to England, only to go down in the frigid English Channel. His last words were, "It's a cold day for a swim." Air rescue could not locate him. The P-51 is not a good plane to belly into water. The air scoop will stand you on end and send you under in seconds.

By the end of 1943, the group had flown ten combat missions and claimed eight destroyed with seven losses. Unfortunately, none of the victories were mine, but on the plus side, I wasn't one of the losses either. I was frustrated by the nuances of aerial combat. One had to be in the right place at the right time. I listened to descriptions of the action by others. Surely my time will come! Then there was another interruption.

During my hospitalization in December, Eisenhower's headquarters, SHAEF, had requested a pilot from the group to go on detached duty to speak to the workers in English war factories – the theory being that it would pep up production. No one wanted to go. If I had a vote in the matter, I would have vehemently said, "No way." I was petrified by the idea. I had visions of another 'Second bellboy' panic in my high school play. Unfortunately, I wasn't there to protest.

My name was on orders and in March, I was off to the midlands, specifically Sheffield, a steel production area. I arrived by rail and was met by a distinguished and delightful man who introduced himself as Lord Thomas something, of the Ministry of Aircraft Production. I was truly impressed. He was in charge of my tour and gave me a thumbnail sketch of what we would be doing. I started shaking immediately. He then introduced me to a quite attractive WAAF in uniform who would be my driver for the week. That calmed me a little. I was installed in a comfortable hotel room and the titled gentleman came back to take me to supper in the evening. I began to think this might not be all that bad after all.

I was told to skip the formalities of Lord or Sir – "call me Thomas." Then I returned the favor – "call me Windy." In all my young life, I had been less than excited by the name Clayton, but it was mine. When my bowling prowess became evident, I was not reluctant to point that out to others. Somebody called me "Windjammer", eventually shortened to "Windy". I didn't use it much until we reached the war zone and then it sounded more like a fighter pilot than Clayton did. I was Windy then and for the rest of the war.

The next morning my driver was waiting as scheduled. We had time to talk as we drove to the first factory and I found she was married. Her husband was British Army and had not been home for over a year. I'm sure if I had thoughts of romance in the offing... but two things stopped me. I was married for just a year and a half to a very beautiful girl and I was very much in love. The other thing stopping me was my shyness.

I made it through my first speech. So nervous I could not hear what I was saying. I know it contained a lot of phrases such as "the dirty Bosche" and "we must all work together, in the skies and in the factories." My friend, the titled Lord, had introduced me. On being asked, I reported that I had the American "Air Medal with a cluster". In the introduction, he reported it as the "Air Force Cross, with bar". I didn't correct him because it sounded pretty good. I have no idea how the 50 or 60 workers felt about my talk, but I know they gave me a roaring round of applause. I began to think I would live through the week.

On another day, Thomas told me we would do dinner and the theater that night after our round of speeches. The play featured Dorothy Dickson, a very famous actress I was told. After they ironed the rough spots out in places like Sheffield, it would be in London. I enjoyed the play (can't remember what it was) and when it was over, Lord Thomas sent a note to Star Dickson's dressing room and presently she sent for us to come back. She was a lovely woman and friendly to me. I was thrilled. I got a letter from her later telling me to call her when they took the play to London.

The next day, I spoke at a small factory with about 30 workers. When finished, they lined up to shake hands. The owner stood at my side and introduced me to each worker in turn. The last man in line was certainly not a worker for he wore a very nice tweed suit, tie and a 'bowler'. The owner said, "Oh this is Mr. So-and-so." He owns the textile mill next door. That gentleman shook hands and told me that unfortunately, his mill and several others he owned in Great Britain and on the continent, were 'out of business' for the duration. Then he added, "I still have several operating in the States." Then he made a request. "My wife is an American and has not had an opportunity to speak to one for some time. Would your schedule allow you to come by my home and say 'hello' to her?" I looked at my driver, who said it was up to me, so I said we would be delighted. We followed his car to get there.

What I saw next I could hardly believe. We entered through a large gate and onto a vast estate. My host stopped twice, the first time to point out a hangar and an airstrip. "Can't fly now," he said, "Petrol you know." Again, we stopped at some stables and I was told to come back some day and we'll ride. Finally we arrived in front of a beautiful mansion, the closest thing to Tara of Gone with the Wind fame, that I had ever seen. We entered huge doors and I found a marble hallway with staircase directly ahead, also marble that split in two directions at the top. Coming down the stairs was an attractive woman with quite regal bearing. She extended a hand and I wasn't sure if I was to kiss it or shake it. I simply held it gently. Then she spoke. " I am from Vassar. Where you from?" I answered, "Gonzaga" and let it go at that. We had a cup of tea and cookies and made small talk. While her husband seemed like a very regular guy, she was the most affected female I had ever met. When we took our leave, the gentlemen presented me with a bottle of very rare scotch. On the way back to the hotel, I thought about the pretty driver, the scotch and wondered if an immoral proposal would be out of order. I did not do it.

A few months later, another pilot and I were in London and I saw an advertisement for the Sheffield play. I insisted we go and we did. I took a chance and sent a note backstage to Dorothy Dickson, the pretty lady star and low and behold, she invited my friend and me to join her at the end of the play. We did and she was as gracious as she had been when we met in Sheffield.

Not long after we had reached England a few of the guys began to grow mustaches. 'Cuz' Lasko had one about like Clark Gable and it looked good on him. I eventually decided to follow suit. I had inherited hair characteristics from my mother more than father and hadn't found it necessary to shave more than every other day. Because of that and the light blonde coloring, I had no illusions about instant results. Still I was quite discouraged when I could hardly see it a full month later. I continued to let it grow, hoping that eventually it would come into view, and it did, but not exactly as I had hoped.

Six months into the growing, it had the tremendous length of a quarter inch, trimmed of course. The color still made it difficult to notice from any distance at all except for a narrow band just to my right of center. As creatures of habit do, I seemed always to hold cigarettes in that area and the nicotine stained a yellow band where smoke filtered through the luxuriant growth. Even I had to admit it looked like hell, but who was I to care?

---

FOOTNOTE: I put up with it until I could get home to show Gwen who immediately wanted me to remove it. A few days later I did shave it off and she did not even know it was missing...until I told her!

CHAPTER 17

# COMBAT READINESS/ LIFE

WHILE THE MILITARY HAS a regimen to be followed for almost everything, we had a lot of personal leeway for our aerial combat. I don't mean every man for himself. Never is discipline, group and personal, more important than air combat, where life can be dependent upon your buddy and what he does.

The freedom came with weapons. The guns, four fixed, forward firing 50 caliber machine guns in the P-51B and C and six in the D model and later, were bore-sighted to come to a point at a certain yardage. The most common was 250 to 300 yards. I personally liked to do everything close and I had mine moved in to 150 yards and experimented with 100 and always thought 75 might be even better. I reasoned that firing from three football fields away would waste a great deal of ammunition, which might be of use later. Some pilots shot before getting in range and would hold it down until the barrels were burnt out and the tracers carved spiraling courses as they headed in directions other than the intended.

I never burned out a barrel and because I fired from close range, cannot remember emptying all guns, no matter how many targets I used them on in a mission.

The standard ammunition load was 2 – 2 – 1, that is two armor piercing, two incendiary and one tracer. I never changed that because it did a good job for me. Some of our pilots left out the tracer, reasoning that the point of light that visually showed you the path of your fire, would also give warning to your target when a missed burst went by him. Again, firing from close range eliminated that most of the time and I felt if he did get a warning, I could just chase him for another shot.

On ground targets where you had to pull out before contact, the tracers let me pin point the victim. Anyway, the way I did it, nobody complained, except the victims, that is.

Smitty came to our Ops office early one day to tell me that "LIVE BAIT" was back in commission with a new engine and needed 'slow time'. I scheduled the pilots and saw them off with the group for a deep escort mission. Then after another coffee with the Ops gang, I leisurely proceeded to our hardspot and after a proper pre-flight, lifted off into the broken clouds over Boxted.

There are few things I would rather do than fly a beautiful fighter plane, but nothing more boring than flying it straight and level when it was capable of doing so much. I leveled off just below the 3500-foot ceiling and decided on a sightseeing tour. First, I went South to the Thames, then turned West toward the barrage balloon fields of London. Before long on that course, I found company in the form of a B-24 cruising at the same altitude and crossing my course, left to right. Since it looked like something to do, I banked right and pulled along his right side. I really didn't want to frighten the bomber crew, so sat, oh maybe 50 feet off his wing tip, throttling back a little to match air speed. I could clearly see Pilot and Co-pilot not frightened, but grinning, ear to ear. They beckoned me in and now I grinned. They were speaking my language.

I moved in tight, like 10 feet, but they weren't satisfied. With more waving and what I thought might have been a mouthed word 'coward', they asked for it! I tucked "LIVE BAIT" in under the Lib wing, careful only that their #3 and #4 engines did not slice through my canopy. The Co-pilot gave me the universal 'OK – all right' sign and I smiled, not ready for what happened next. That bomber broke hard left and up like a fighter who suddenly discovered a covey of 109's on his tail. Blessed with pretty good reflexes that I had honed in two years of flying fighters, I tucked back in quickly, after the initial move left me just slightly.

For the next five minutes, I went for a ride following that guy in maneuvers I had no idea a B-24 could do! I knew several things for sure, they had to be empty and the pilot was no beginner! After five minutes or so, which left me in a fair sweat, they leveled off and still grinning waived me forward. I couldn't believe it, but he tucked in on me. Probably I could have lost him if I really wanted to, but I didn't. I took them through the rest of the maneuvers the Liberator tech manual said they couldn't do, and they did! If I hadn't been having so much fun in the air, I would have wished to be on the ground to watch the show. Unbelievable!

When I finally leveled out, my big friend was firmly on my wing, still grinning. He then motioned me to follow and, leading our tight formation flew North for 15 minutes. We gradually started a letdown until I could see trees at our level from the corner of my eye. Then we skipped over the last tree patch and let down to ground level, down a runway that I found was a B-24 base. I mean we beat that field up the full length of the runway and then chandelled left and up. I thought he would make a fighter approach and land from that position, but he leveled out again and signaled me to lead the same kind of buzz job. I sincerely hoped he was the Group C.O. of that outfit because what we were doing was one of my favorite pastimes and one that notoriously had me in trouble in the 355th Fighter Squadron. I didn't want them to suffer the same fate. In the meantime, I had the reputation of all fighter aviation to uphold, so from a mile or so out, I got my wingman in position, silently wished him well because I needed my concentration and would not be watching out for him. I gave that field a pass that may well have set a USAAF record for buzz jobs in which the participants survived. I know I cut grass and raised dust, and in the pullout, my friend was still there as always. This time, he did roll out, give me a giant wing waggle and made an approach and landing that would have made any fighter pilot proud. After his landing, I made one more pass, rocking wings in fond farewell.

I would love to shake hands with the crew, or at least know who they were. I flew home.

One of our 355 guys had a weekend pass to London and he came back with new insights into the English persona. When he got to our barracks, he was cussing, swearing and kicking his bunk and everything else that got in his way.

"Hey buddy, what's the problem?"

"Those bloody English are the coldest f------ fish in the world. They aren't human. They got no feelings. How the hell they keep populating this Island, I don't know!"

He ranted on, still very agitated until somebody sat him on his bunk and said, "Spill it. What happened?" He told us this story.

"Last night I was back to the American bar at the Park Lane Hotel and I see this WAAF babe who didn't seem to be attached, so I bought her a drink and we talked. You know small talk. Well, they still had some Gin and Orange available when we finished that, so I buy a second one and before we finish that one, the talk isn't small anymore. I tell her how lonely it is this far from home. She says she understands. Well, I tell her I have a room, would she like to go up for a bit. No hesitation, she is willing. We had held hands a bit in the bar. When I finally fumbled for the key into the room upstairs and we got in, we stopped in the doorway for a first kiss. Now it wasn't the best I've had, but I figured she just needed a little warming up. There was no objection when I started to unbutton her blouse. In fact, she started helping get mine off. Hey! This is going to be great! Before I pushed her back on the bed I had everything off. Those khaki panties they wear aren't exactly exciting, but when I got them off everything inside looked normal and exciting. Well, I didn't rush. I was gentle and I did everything I knew how, trying to warm her up. There in the good old missionary position, I went to work. I thought it was going just fine until I heard a crunching noise in my left ear. This you are not going to believe! I raised up and what do I see. She had taken an apple from her bag on the nightstand and she is *eating* it while I am making love. Can you believe that? Have these people got feelings?"

The barracks was roaring with laughter. One guy was on the floor holding his sides in uncontrollable hilarity!

"Hey. I may not be the greatest lover, but I am not the worst either. It's those cold English girls. You can have them!"

Two weeks later he was killed in action.

What a way to end a ball game! We had arranged a crude playing field in available space at Boxted. This was a rare dry day and a softball game was in progress – officers vs. E.M. One drawback – the field lay off the end of a main runway and any flight activity caused a game delay.

I had blooped a single over second base and went to third on a following hit. Headquarters picked that moment to send a full compliment of Mustangs out to fight the war. From third base, I had the best view of their take-off, but also had to suffer the ear-splitting roar and the dust with debris that accompanied every take-off. I hunkered down to watch.

All take-offs were in pairs. The signal officer would wave one element off – wait until they had proceeded above fifty yards and wave the next pair to follow. Because the 51's were 'tail draggers', the pilot had no visibility until he reached at around 80 to 90 MPH and raised the tail. All the element leader could do was watch and wait for the signal and then 'pour the coal on'. His wingman only watched him and followed him.

About four pairs were off the ground when the next element leader experienced a tire blow out before he had gone 100 yards and throttled back. The following pair had already begun their roll and had no way to see him. A hundred people screaming were to no avail. At full speed the propeller chewed up the tail of the unfortunate one until it hit the cockpit area. Many people began running toward the accident. The plane was rotating in circles left into the flat tire. Although the pilot had throttled back, his propeller was still wind milling and dangerous. The wing was at about a sixty-degree angle, but I was able to grab part of the exposed cockpit and pull myself up to reach in and shut the switch off.

The armor plate behind the pilot was bent at a ninety-degree angle and had delivered a fatal blow to the back of his head. No hope. With a half dozen people prying, we could not budge the steel plate even a millimeter. A truck arrived to tow the wreckage of the two planes off so the war might go on.

The game was over – no decision.

Who was responsible I can't say, but they found eight to ten people from among the Officers and men of the 354th and a dance band was formed. It really wasn't all that bad! Then the young ladies from Colchester and surrounding area were invited, so a dance was scheduled. The Officers Club and dining room was large enough to accommodate a passable dance floor on one end. Furniture was moved down toward the other end, which also housed the bar. Incidentally, the furniture included a 'crap table'.

I was a fairly good dancer and did enjoy several dances but my heart wasn't in it – probably because none followed me as well as Gwen always had. I sauntered down to the bar area. A few other non-dancers had initiated a 'crap' game and I joined in. I was winning a little and standing next to Gil Talbot at one end of the table when he got the dice.

The shooter would establish a 'bank' and the other players would cover a chosen amount starting at his left until the bank was 'tapped' or everyone had the bet they wanted. I offered to 'partner' with Gil and he accepted. What followed was one of the hottest runs of dice I had ever witnessed!

Gil shot the dice and I managed the bank. We eventually had English Pound notes piled as high as the ten-inch railing on the table and wide enough that I could hardly encompass them with both arms. The roar that went up with each 'natural' eventually drew many of the girls who probably didn't know that much money existed outside the Bank of England. The guys who wanted to dance were less than enthused by our distraction. The run finally ended. Talbot and I each had over 500 of those $4.12 bills – a $2,000 profit. Better than dancing, I thought!

★ ☆ ★ ☆ ★

January 1944 LOSSES
    John Nall                                                 KIA
    Nevatt Logan                                 KIA
    Robert Priser                                POW
    Joe Giltner, Jr.                            POW

354th AIR CLAIMS TO DATE
  53 destroyed
  17 probably destroyed
  47 damaged

CHAPTER 18

# GAINS & LOSSES FOR THE 354TH

**D**EAR FRIEND AND ROOMMATE Warren "Red" Emerson was in the hospital, wounded in action. Brueland and I made a visit. On January 5, the biggest day yet for Group claims, Red had destroyed an ME-110 and was after a second attacking the bombers when an unseen enemy had hit him with a rocket shell. You want luck – listen to this. The shell had exploded in or very near Red's cockpit. A fragment had passed through his neck entering on one side and exiting on the other. If he had had his head one-inch back, it would have severed his spinal column. Another fragment had crossed his chest, severing his parachute strap on his right shoulder – burned a path across his chest and cut the parachute strap on the other side. If he had been leaning a little forward it would have hit his heart. Talk about being in the right place at the right time – or was he?

He told us of his return. After being hit, he found himself alone and a long way from home. Stunned as he was, he probably would be a sitting duck for an enemy attack. His luck held. He nursed his wounded plane back towards home. Weakened and worried about blood loss, he set down on the first field he found after crossing the channel. He was met by a Jeep and helped from the cockpit and delivered to the infirmary where an orderly told him to wait. He held a handkerchief over his neck wounds sitting patiently while the Flight Surgeon finished treating somebody with a bad cold. Then he turned to Red..."What's your problem?"

"I've been hit." He got an apology and an ambulance ride to a field hospital. Brue and I found him in good spirits. He would return to get five more victories and Ace status before the war was over. By the end of February, the group had destroyed 121 and one-half enemy aircraft in the air, but at a cost of 21 of our own – a good ratio to be sure, but the cost is high. You could not help but notice this, but personally and with those close to me, there was the feeling that "it couldn't happen to me!"

In the first week of March, the 355th Squadron gained 17 new 2nd Lieutenants to fill the gaps. A couple would hardly last out the month.

March in England may be nearing spring, but one wouldn't know that from the weather we faced each day. We were able to fly fifteen missions; thirteen were of the usual nature since our arrival – escorting the big guys. Twice we did something a little different. On March 2 we were scheduled for an area patrol over Chautres, France.

On the 16th – another new one – dive bombing at a railroad marshalling yard at Criel, France.

The victories continued to climb – 36 more in the air in 13 escort missions. The losses climbed as well. The 355th lost three to ground fire in March, including Horace White on the second mission of the month.

The next was really unfair! Three new pilots assigned to the group were Tech Sergeant pilots. They had been through the same training we had, but the wise ones somewhere up the ladder had decided that not every one needed to be commissioned as air officer. Now they were flying the same missions we were but as enlisted personnel. That would be corrected by Group when they were all submitted for promotion to Flight Officer, but it had not come through yet when Don Dempsey went down and became a POW. There was a marked difference in treatment of officers and enlisted in the prison camps. Tough!

I felt very bad about the next loss. A tough mission, long-range escort to Berlin that I did not fly. Dick Kenyon was lost. He took a hit by a damn 88, the German anti-aircraft guns, very heavy this day and obviously accurate. He reported severe damage in both wings and engine and had to get out. He had not been wounded and the guys saw him safely in his chute.

'Bucky' Harris needled him when he reported his problem. "I know a certain redhead that's going to be damn mad." Handsome Dick had been dating an English lass with flaming tresses and he and 'Bucky' had arranged dates for the next day free. Bob Stephens, leading the mission, thought he would come down relatively safe in an area away from the target. We had been warned that the civilian population might not follow the rules of war, especially if they had lost kin to our attacks. Evade if you can. If not, get picked up by military was the suggestion.

Dick's plane was named 'BAD PENNY' but the old saying was incorrect – they don't "always turn up."

Only a few weeks before this mission, Gil Talbot, Dick and I had posed for a photo "Northwest men with the Pioneer Mustang Group in the ETO" and the picture was published in my hometown "Spokesman Review". It didn't make my family feel better when I reported the loss. Dick hailed from Walla Walla, Washington, and Gil was from Portland, Oregon.

Well, the war must go on.

★ ☆ ★ ☆ ★

You won't find Charles F. Gumm Jr.'s name on the casualty list, but he was as dead as any. Chuck was a friend from my hometown. It was he who flew a P-39 home from our Oakland base with me in a visit to Spokane. It was Chuck who used my plane during our visit to show off to family – and then would forget to tell me he had burned off part of my fuel – which nearly put me down on the return trip. It was also Chuck who shot down the first enemy aircraft with a P-51 and became the first Ace of the Group. He proved himself time and time again. Who knows what his record might have been, but for an unfortunate non-combat flying accident.

In early March he had taken off in his plane for a test hop after overhaul. He had cleared the ground and risen a few hundred feet from Boxted when the engine failed. It was determined that he could have safely bailed out to save himself, but the small English village of Nayland lay straight ahead and the pilotless plane might have caused death and destruction to the town and its populace. He decided to ride it down to prevent that. And he almost made it to a safe, open field when his wing caught a tree and cartwheeled him into a flaming end.

The people of Nayland held a special service for him and eventually erected a memorial bench and plaque.

When he died, his record read 6 confirmed victories, two and one-half probably destroyed and eight damaged – all by February 25$^{th}$.

What a loss!

CHAPTER 19

# MEMORABLE FEBRUARY MISSIONS...

I WAS BACK TO WORK with the group again – very disturbed by missed missions and opportunities. As a whole, we were beginning to establish the record that would make us number one in aerial wins for the war. From our early record of nearly trading one for one, we were building toward a five-to-one ratio of wins-to-losses. Still, the losses were there. And my wins weren't!

February 8th was a mission to remember! We were up at 0945 to take the heavies to Frankfurt – no fighter opposition, but plenty of flak.

We left our charges, the bombers, at 1205 on schedule, relieved by a P-38 unit. The orders were to proceed home seeking targets of opportunity. Tony Radojits and I were alone, but immediately joined another element, namely, Jim Dalglish and his wingman, Jack Turk. Proceeding in a westerly direction at 17,000 feet, we had little opportunity for detection of any target with a solid under-cast topping at about

2,000 feet. For self-preservation, we flew a mutual support formation with Tony and I on the right. Ten or fifteen minutes along the way, Jim and I spotted a lone ME-109 cruising in our direction just about 2,000 feet. Because he was about 2 o'clock to us, I had the shortest route to him although Dalglish tried to outrun me as the four of us screamed after him in a steep dive. Just before me came into range the 109 ducked into the clouds and we pulled up. Damn!

We reformed in mutual support and climbed again on course home, nevertheless watching the cloud area where he had disappeared. A few minutes later, he popped out again in the same leisurely straight-ahead course. Again, the mad race to get him, same result. He let down into the safety of the clouds just before we got to him. He must have seen our attack. In retrospect, I should have realized he was being advised when it was safe to come up again, real live bait for an attack!

We reformed again and once more started up watching for his reappearance as we climbed. I looked away from the target area long enough to check the other element. Four FW-190's were closing on them and already firing! I screamed at Jim, "Break left" which he immediately did. It was too late for Jack, however. His Mustang belched a great stream of smoke and he rolled over and fell from my view. The Focke-Wulfs turned tightly following Jim and I was turning to fall in behind them. I hollered at Tony, "Stick with me". No answer. I spun my head to check and found no Tony, but four more FW's sitting on my tail with cannon firing!

A decision took no time whatsoever. I was already in a tight left turn and simply continued to roll over on my back and pulled the stick back into my guts into a screaming dive, straight for the under-cast which had proved to be such a haven for the damn 109 we had been chasing. At the same time, I screamed at Jim of my actions so he would know he was on his own. He reported back that he had used an opposite tactic, pulling into a steep as possible climb for safety. We were both alone, far from home and each with a bunch of FW-190's in hot pursuit.

As I neared cloud cover, I pushed the throttle through the fragile wire gate into the sector labeled "WAR EMERGENCY" with its accompanying note "DO NOT EXCEED FOR MORE THAN FIVE MINUTES!"

The dive and that power got me out of range and away from my pursuers when entering the clouds. I had no idea where I was and prayed that these particular clouds did not contain a mountain. At about 1000 feet, I broke out over a strange, darkened countryside and checked my tail. Nobody back there. I decided that ground level would be the safest position and headed for the deck, setting a compass course of approximately due West. I was pretty sure that I needed some sort of miracle to get out of this situation alive and free. At full throttle, ten feet off the ground and following the contours, the countryside fairly flew by. Shortly I came up over a rise in terrain, to find a train, the engine in my sights and my fifties roared into action. At point blank range the engine's boiler blew and I flew through a huge cloud of steam or smoke. My first thought was "boy, are they going to be mad at me now!" I still had a sneaking suspicion that I would not get back.

At the speed I was traveling, I had really no decision time as new targets came into view over each hill. The next one available was a three-story building.

Over the next rise, I found real excitement. As I started down the far slope, I found a real live German fighter base spread before me. Worse yet, I was headed dead center across it and at least six ME-109's were circling at about 1000 feet. I knew if I altered course, they could cut me off. If I maintained straight ahead with speed, I might outrun them even with their altitude advantage. I was more than half-way across before anyone noticed me from the air, then I doubt if they recognized me immediately because they wavered in the flight pattern and did not immediately turn toward me. Nor did any anti-aircraft have time to fire, at least as far as I could see. By that time, I was across and still going like the proverbial 'bat out of hell'. They couldn't catch me! You can bet I kept my head on a swivel for a time to determine if they were trying. I still had no idea where I was or how far I had to go, but I maintained what I believed was a beeline for the Channel, continuing at ground level, firing at every available target.

The next rise held another surprise, and probably brought me as close to death as I would ever come, before or since..... I continued to keep a wary eye on my tail as I busted my way across the countryside. Now I was astonished, as I looked forward, to find my line of flight directly between two huge towers holding a dozen or so power lines. If I held course, I would have easily passed under them but instinctively; I sucked the stick back into my belly and tried to go over. There was a blinding flash and LIVE BAIT literally staggered, but stayed in the air! My three-inch thick 'bullet proof' windshield cracked completely through. I had lost considerable speed, but putting the nose down, although there were vibrations, I picked up speed again. Part of my left wing tip was missing. I wondered how in hell I was still flying, and more certain than ever, that getting home was a long shot.

Twenty minutes and a few more targets of opportunity later, my spirits rose as I saw the coastline straight ahead. I would make it! As I crossed the coast, I climbed to probably 25 feet and relaxed for half a minute, then my engine quit. I climbed a hundred feet or so before sighting the gas gauge on empty. I switched tanks and the Merlin caught again. "Thank God!"

Now I made another startling discovery. The throttle was still forward in WAR EMERGENCY, 40 plus minutes after I put it there! And the sign said, "Do not exceed for more than 5 minutes." Throttling back and climbing to a thousand feet, I started calling for a 'homing'. They heard and directed me slightly North of my present heading. Fifteen minutes later I was over Boxted. The landing was uneventful. The shock came when I got out and looked at that poor 'steed' that brought me through all of that. The air-scoop was completely missing from the belly.

The radiator, which had been enclosed, was out in the open and imbedded in it was a two-foot length of cable that had been torn from the power lines. That cable was built from 40, count them, 40 strands of copper wire – each at least a millimeter in diameter. The entire cable section was at least an inch thick! Every blade of the propeller was chewed up with nicks an inch deep in some areas. No wonder it ran a little rough. About six inches of the left wingtip was gone.

What an airplane! The factory had evidently never had WAR EMERGENCY abused to such an extent, because the next day they sent a number of reps over and they took the entire engine apart to look for damage. According to Popular Mechanics who soon published the story, they couldn't find anything wrong. The article was titled "Fighting at 425 M.P.H".

> "Recently North American was permitted to announce that the Mustang, with a published speed of 425 miles an hour, is the fastest aircraft on earth–capturing this rating from the twin-engine British Mosquito.
>
> "Various factors in the new version contribute to this speed. One of these is the exhaust ejectors at the side of the engine cowling, which are worth 200 or more horsepower in propulsive effect. Even more important is the redesigned cooling system, which gives the airplane its characteristically fat belly.
>
> "This radiator cowling is set far back, so that the entire front end of the airplane is very clean, striking undisturbed air. But especially important is the fact that this system is so designed that air passing over the radiator and expanded by heat is ejected through a much smaller flap opening at the rear. This use of the principle of jet propulsion recovers 80 percent of the power lost through drag of the cooling system.
>
> "As for the engine, which also has a lot to do with it, let me tell you the story of one of (Jim) Howard's flyers:
>
> "Lt. Clayton K. Gross of Spokane, Wash., has been shot at plenty, which is why his Mustang is called "Live Bait." But worst

of all was the day coming back from Frankfort, when suddenly his wing man was gone and there behind him were four Folke-Wulf 190's roaring in to complete the kill.

"Gross went right through the gate into the kitchen. He did a split S to the deck and stayed there, with his throttle on the firewall.

"He soon lost his pursuers. But the next 40 minutes – tearing through telephone wires, clipping the tops of trees, skimming housetops, dodging windmills at more than 400 miles an hour – were the loneliest of his life.

"The trip was eventful. At one point Gross was suddenly enveloped in a grinding, blinding flash and shower of sparks. His Mustang had ploughed through a set of high-tension wires. But it never faltered. Once he ran into six Focke-Wulfs and thanked fortune their wheels were down for landing.

"When he had gone into the kitchen–that is, into a turning dive with everything on – he had pushed the throttle as far as it would go, past the gate, the maximum military power. You are permitted to go to a "war emergency" manifold pressure for five minutes. But as Gross came in to circle his home airdrome, he realized he had been against the firewall all the way. This Packard-built Rolls-Royce Merlin engine had been pulling 'emergency' for all of 40 minutes. And she was still doing it like a sweetheart.

"This Mustang had come back with its air scoop, under the belly, half torn off, with a yard length of 3/8-inch high-tension cable embedded in the radiator. But what really made the ground crew bug-eyed was the engine and what it had stood.

"Lt. John Konopka, who mothers the Mustangs with passionate zeal, drained the oil and strained it, hunting for metal chips. He had the crew tear the engine down and reassemble it, gave it an hour's slow flying, drained and strained the oil again. Not a chip or sign of wear. Everything perfect.

"Boy!" said Konopka. "That Merlin may be English, but it sure is some engine!"

Brownie, our PR man, of course, had a different twist. The story he sent to the papers said I claimed 10,000 telephone conversations destroyed. Actually, I didn't even talk to him!

After an hour of winding down, the sad part of the mission began to sink in. I had lost Tony Radojits, the second of my three great "R" pilots. Dalglish had made it back, but Turk was gone, KIA. War *is* Hell!

On the 11th of February, Col. Ken Martin led a 48-plane escort mission to Frankfurt for our squadron. In horrible weather, we had ten aborts. It would have been better for him if he had been one of them. The same nearly was true for me.

I flew Red 3, the second element leader for him. We took 10 minutes to get off and form, and my take off should have warned me of trouble. It almost killed me. Taking off in pairs, Glenn Buer, my wingman, and I followed the colonel and Norm McDonald, waiting about 8 seconds for the 'flagman' to wave us off. I lifted 10 feet off the ground when I felt a sudden dip left and down. 'Prop wash', I thought. *Always*, we had to stand on the right rudder to overcome torque on takeoff. I immediately kicked harder and slapped the stick right and back. The response was slow, but it straightened out for me and I headed for the lead element to join up.

Leading a large group of high-speed fighters into a formation when it must be done under 1000 feet because of weather requires the leader to make very shallow turns while all get off and in formation. I had no problems holding my position in that mode. When the last flight was off, Martin set course toward our rendezvous point and began climbing on instruments, the rest of us in tight formation. The climb was uneventful and we broke out at 17,000 feet on course. We continued up to 20,000. As lead squadron, we were slightly ahead of the 353rd on our left and the 356th on our right. Shortly after crossing the channel, the weather opened up to where we could see the ground in places. We should have looked up instead of down. I heard a frantic call, "Bandits –12 o'clock high." I spotted a dozen FW-190's headed straight for our lead flight. What happened next confounded me. Martin broke hard left and I tried to follow. I slammed the stick hard left and nothing happened for awhile. Then I found myself spinning. We had belly tanks still quite full and I released mine as I spun. My controls didn't seem to work. Big movements brought very little response. How I finally recovered from the spin, I do not know. I do know I had dropped from over 20,000 feet to about five thousand and I was alone except for eight FW-190's who probably thought I was duck soup. I felt that way. I could see our formation cruising on course thousands of feet above me and I told of my predicament – shouting for help only to hear Col. Martin say, "Don't break formation. We have a job to do."

I couldn't believe that I was being sacrificed! I did the only thing I could do. I put LIVE BAIT into the steepest possible climb toward the formation under full power. The Focke-Wulfs were making 90 degree passes at me with cannons blinking and not one of them hit me. When I caught the formation still headed for the rendezvous, I reported that I had no belly tanks and no control and needed to go home. Buer answered and we headed back, with me fervently praying that no one would bounce us. Nobody did.

My approach and landing were accomplished with the shallowest turns I'd made in an aircraft since my first solo, and I made it! When Smitty got up on the wing, I demonstrated the control problem. He was devastated, but said the plane had just returned from its 100-hour check and they were responsible still, "I should have checked it closer. I should have!"

"Smitty, I made it. No problem. I know. It won't happen again."

"It won't. I promise." He didn't need to say that. He had kept me alive and he would always see that I had a flyable chariot. I knew that.

About 40 minutes later, the group returned but without our Group Commander and his wingman.

I remember in Don Blakeslee's first briefing before he led our first combat mission he said, "Whoever breaks first in a head on pass situation is at a disadvantage. We don't break first. Make the other guy do that." We wondered at the time what happens when the 'other guy' gets the same lecture? Martin, had agreed – that's the way we'll do it! Well, on this fateful day, Martin lived by his own orders and so did an ME-109. They went down together. No one saw McDonald go down, but he also failed to return. Definitely not a good day!

A few weeks later, we got good news from the Germans. Ken Martin and the 109 pilot had both survived the horrendous crash and although badly injured, were alive and in the same hospital. Jim Howard took over command of the group and I checked the sensitivity of my controls every time I climbed into my plane.

On February 22nd in an escort to Frankfurt, I saw my opportunity for an air victory. There was considerable fighter opposition from ME-110's, 410's, FW-190's and ME-109s. In a huge melee of friendly and enemy aircraft, I found a 109 in a hard turn left in front of me. I wracked left to follow. I had him – I knew it – must pull the nose through a little more to lead him. I was less than a hundred yards behind him – anticipation boiling over and he came apart – exploded! And, I had not fired a shot. When I rolled out, I found Glenn Eagleston and I had been nearly air-scoop to air-scoop. He nailed him before I could fire. There would be other days. At the bar that night, Eagle gloated and I sulked.

All this kill or be killed stuff we were doing each day was very, very serious business. Yet a little humor can find it's way into the mix at times. On February 29, Jack Bradley led the group out of Boxted on a long-range escort mission. As usual, we must maintain strict radio silence in order not to make the enemy's job any easier. Three squadrons of sixteen P-51s each and several spares formed up and set course across the channel to occupied Europe, Brunswick, Germany the eventual target.

Each pilot has a microphone in his oxygen mask and earphones in the helmet to receive. To transmit, a button on the throttle handle is depressed. While transmitting, you are unable to receive. Now it happens on this particular day, some junior birdman's 'mike button' had stuck in transmit position and whoever the culprit was, was in a good mood. As we proceeded to climb to altitude, this anything but melodious voice began a poor rendition of a silly ditty of the day, "Oh Mairzy Doats and Dozey Dotes and Little Lamzy Divey."

Bradley quickly reacted – "Okay – knock it off! – Radio silence!" Of course, the offender could not hear that and so he continued, "A kiddely Divey, too!"

Bradley's obviously irritated voice again screamed, "Knock it off!"

"Wouldn't you!" the song continued.

Now Jack got an idea. Obviously the singer can't hear so he ordered all who could, to rock their wings. Of course, that failed because when we did it – forty-seven strong – the other guy followed suit and compounded the thing by saying, "Bradley. What the hell are you doing now?"

Shortly after that, having crossed the coast, our course took us into the Ruhr Valley area of Germany, one of the most heavily defended areas of the Third Reich. Soon the sky was filled with bursting 88-meter shells. Instantly the singing stopped and was replaced with heavy, heavy breathing with a gasp or two interjected.

Bradley had a good comeback, – "Sing now you son of a bitch!"

When the mission was completed and with no enemy fighter reaction – we headed home – group in tact.

Bradley had another order. "When we are on the ground, I want every pilot to assemble in the Tower area." We dutifully lined up while the irate leader paced back and forth demanding to know who!

No confession. End of funny war story!

February 1944 LOSSES:

| | |
|---|---|
| Dick Klein | POW |
| Lloyd Hubbard | MIA |
| James M. Lane | POW |
| Jack Turk | KIA |
| Tony Radojits | MIA |
| Joe Krebs | POW |
| J. Don Munger | KIA |
| Al Barris | POW |
| Col. Ken Martin | POW |
| Richard McDonald | MIA |
| J. Don Mattie | POW |
| Billy Bronston | KIA |
| WauKau Kong | KIA |

354th AIR CLAIMS TO DATE
 121½ destroyed
 23 probably destroyed
 100 damaged

CHAPTER 20

# MISSIONS AND LIFE

**W**E DID HAVE LIFE between missions. In late February, we had a dance at our 'O' Club (and combination mess hall). All went well with our newly formed group dance band actually playing quite danceable American jazz music. People seemed to be having a good time, although some of the young ladies recruited from Colchester didn't quite dig the jitter bugging style of dancing. Then again, some lonely Americans were holding the young ladies in nearly imperceptibly moving embraces that led one to think their minds were on something besides music. Still, it was a fine party until about 2130. First, there was the wail of sirens. A young lady or two screamed. The music stopped and somebody dimmed the lights, which suited a few couples just fine. A number of us went outside to see the show. A half dozen searchlights lit up the skies. One finally picked up a lone raider; about 10,000 feet up and immediately a few big anti-aircraft guns added their explosions to the show.

Just outside the club building, an air raid shelter had been constructed and, with the ack

ack fire, several wandered into the security of those thick walls. An immediate shout from them indicated an even more interesting show...a pair of dancers had evidently sought privacy for more serious togetherness and the first ones to enter after the air raid, found them frantically trying to don and position their wardrobes. Of course, the shouts drew a few more to watch this display, quickly out-drawing the miniature air raid.

The lone raider eventually disappeared and the guns fell silent. The searchlights went off and the sirens signaled, 'all clear'. The show was over except for the crude group of guys needling the erstwhile lovers until the lady was obviously in tears.

All went back in and the music and party resumed.

I've flown a half dozen missions and I'm sure I have what it takes. The flying part is no problem.

The graduation book in primary flight school quotes me, "I can do chandelles better than my instructor." I could! I can do that up, down, sideways, every way. I have very good peripheral vision and excellent eyesight. I discovered a secret. Don't focus your eyes on anything in particular. It is easier to detect motion. Then concentrate on the mover.

The old saying, "beware of the Hun out of the sun" is indelibly etched on my mind. I raise a hand to block the sun and search around the perimeter. Usually using just a thumb to do that will work. This game of aerial combat is a deadly one. Many times the loser dies.

Don't give the bad guy an even break. You may find yourself in a fair fight but that's not what you want. See him first and go for the kill. My God, this is exciting!

When will I get one of the enemy to my credit?

"LIVE BAIT" may sound like a strange name for a weapon of war like my P-51B, and all later models, but the evolution of that name came about in logical fashion.

I had started naming planes in the states when I was assigned a nearly private P-39 as "C" Flight Leader. The name painted on the nose was one I secretly used for my blushing bride, "Lil' Pigeon". I was so 'bleeping' proud of it that I would stand beside the nose of the plane and beam at it for minutes every day. Unfortunately, for the first "Lil' Pigeon", however, it made a 'wheels up' landing with another pilot at the controls, and was wiped out. I got a replacement plane within a week, but it was another week before the squadron artist was able to fancy the nose with the name again. Two weeks after that, again with somebody else flying it, the second "Lil' Pigeon" cart-wheeled across the desert on a misjudged practice ground strafing run, and both plane and pilot were no more. I tried once more and while the third plane lasted longer than one and two, it also met an untimely end. I decided it was NOT a very lucky name! We went overseas before I could come up with a change.

About that time we were assigned our own P-51B and Smitty inquired as to what I wished to name it. I toyed with "Lil' Pigeon", but I wanted no unlucky names and so GQ-I was just that with no name for several weeks.

On a later mission, I came back with Bob Stephens, two alone, after being separated on an escort mission from the rest of the group. We were flying a spread mutual support formation when Stevens, obviously feeling feisty, suggested, "Why don't I drop back and get above you, maybe you'll get bounced and we'll get some action." Now, I wasn't against that, but I didn't relish being the bait in such a trap and said so.

"Hey! What the hell do you think I am? Live bait?" He said yes and positioned himself above and behind me on a direct line to the sun. The trap didn't work, but I guarantee you I kept my head and eyes moving to make sure I wasn't drawing an attack.

We laughed about it when we landed at Boxted and a day later I told Smitty to have the name painted on the nose.

I liked it. Big box letters in orange paint with white trim. It proved very lucky. The first "LIVE BAIT" lasted until it was retired as 'war weary' with over a hundred patches covering flak or bullet holes in the skin and yet it never failed to bring me back. Near the end we were painting red circles around the patches instead of trying to hide them. The same name went on the "C" model, later the "D", "K" and "L". Me and "LIVE BAIT" and my ground crew were a team and we stayed together through the war. I should say 'almost always brought me home', because of one bail out in October 1944.

Finally I found a mission to put a dent in the enemy's fleet of aircraft. It was spring and a rare good day to fly.

Sleep is not a guaranteed thing around here. We had a wake-up call a little after 0500 for a big go to the Mannheim area – escorting the big boys. Long before we finished breakfast and briefing and headed for the flight line, the crew chiefs, armorers and others were working in the darkness to ready our birds. Not to complain – they could have their jobs! I always approached briefings by peeking around the corner to see how far the ribbons went for that day. Today they were all the way into Southwest Germany. My ass would be numb by return time. I could feel it already. Our new Deputy Group Commander, Lt. Col. Teschner would lead the three squadrons for the first time. Brueland would lead the 355th.

We trucked to the line at 0620, got strapped in and started engines. It takes awhile to marshal 3 squadrons for take off. Today we had 53 Mustangs, 48 for the mission, three spares and two for radio relay. We needed those on these extra-long missions, to do exactly what it sounds like; fly out to the middle of the Channel and position themselves at altitude. From there, they listened to our calls from the mission and relayed them to our base. I flew that job once and hated it. Three or 4 hours of circling, with one of two feelings; you were either bored silly or, if you could hear talk of good action, jealous as hell.

Teschner was off the ground at 0651 and the rest in pairs a few seconds apart. Once in the air, the leader had to fly giant circles until all had joined up, then set course. An hour later, we made rendezvous as scheduled and spread out to cover all the B-17's who were pretty strung out themselves. The escort was nothing. No enemy fighters although a few miles down the line, the 356th squadron found two JU-88's. They shot one out of the air and hit the other a few times, but he headed for cloud cover. Jack Carr, a new pilot tried to chase him and paid with his life when the '88 tail-gunner hit him with a 20 mm and he broke up.

When a group of P-47's relieved us to take the bombers home, Brueland rallied the 355th and we headed home at lower altitude, looking for anything to shoot at. Boy, we found it! A German airfield crowded with lots of birds. The squadron made a great circle left, descending as we did so we came out at very low level heading directly across the field. The Bosche don't like losing airplanes on the ground and this field was very heavily fortified, as always, to avoid that. There is a tendency to scrunch down a little to make yourself a smaller target every time you find yourself on the way through a wall of fire.

I always did that. Because we were hedgehopping our way in at high speed, the anti-aircraft gunners didn't have a lot of time to aim. Thank God.

I found myself going down a line of ME-109's parked in front of a hangar. I could hardly miss. The first two burst into flames. I hit others – no time to see what happened to them. After I passed the hangar, I found a DO-217 parked by itself and had time to riddle it before roaring over it, again no time to see if it burned. Now we were over the field and starting to climb when what did I find in front of me but a barrage balloon. Few rounds started it down in flames. Danny Richards on my right wing had fired at it when I did. Elation! We created havoc and made sure a lot of enemy aircraft would not be flying again soon, if ever. More elation followed. We joined up and all 16 of us were there. No losses! As we started for home, that ended. Bill Simmons' in Green flight was trailing smoke. He had time to say goodbye and climb a little before bailing out. We were seeing a pattern and it wasn't a good one. The 355th had never crossed an enemy field without losing at least one plane. That would continue throughout the war.

We went home exactly 5 hours after the 0651 take off. And, my butt *was* numb – but, we painted two victory marks on "LIVE BAIT"! And there were four more, at least damaged and a barrage balloon down. I wonder if those count?

CHAPTER 21

# EMOTIONS

ON APRIL 13TH, I experienced a variety of emotions from lucky and to mad. I got robbed. We flew an escort for heavies on a mission to Schweinfort. It would be a long one to an area generally bringing enemy opposition. That happened.

We had a late mission – take off at 1151 and making rendezvous more than two hours later for our job of taking the big friends into, over and back out of the target area. I led White or the second flight of 355.

Within minutes of rendezvous, all hell broke loose. I don't know how many enemy fighters were involved, but they were everywhere. I had Kallas, Hawley and Richards in my flight, but none were with me as I locked onto the tail of a single 109. Whether he saw me or not I am not sure. We were in a shallow left turn down. Before I fired, I checked my own tail. Good! I had been joined by two red-nosed P-47's coming in. I had 'help', I thought.

With my attention on the 109, I closed to less than 100 yards and opened fire. I saw multiple hits on the fuselage and left wing.

Then the world exploded! I felt a blow to the back of my neck as if belted with a baseball bat. A good part of my canopy had disappeared and I found myself in an involuntary snap roll, which became an out of control spin. I was stunned – not sure I was still alive.

After dropping several thousand feet, I reasoned that I must still be alive because I know I am spinning earthward. I went through the motions of a spin recovery and leveled out. Without the plastic canopy, I felt the bitter cold air – maybe it helped revive me. As I leveled out, I put a gloved hand to the back of my neck. When I examined it, it was dripping red. Blood? Must be.

Now I looked back and found the two P-47's coming in again. Frantically I rocked my wings. They didn't shoot this time and pulled alongside of me. Red-nosed P-47's of the 56th fighter group. Two-foot high identification letters on the side – HV – Gabby Gabreski's squadron! In a rather stunned condition, I did not remember the individual code letters. Then they compounded the crime – they peeled off and left me.

All alone, I took note of my condition. No canopy and dozens of holes in my wings. I decided the red fluid dripping from my glove was hydraulic fluid. There was a line of puncture holes in the fuselage and turning back, I found the armored silhouette behind me was distended four inches in the neck area, but not penetrated. God bless the people who put it there! I also knew what had caused the blow to my neck. Well, my engine worked and I found the radio still worked. Now alone and badly shot up, I had to take stock of my situation. Nobody around me but a stream of B-17's still headed east far above me. At least they are friends, or are they? After the P-47 attack, I wasn't sure about anything.

I started a climb toward them at the same time switching to the fighter-bomber channel and seeking recognition. I finally got a response from the leader of one box who said he had me in sight – to come on up. After assurance that his group would not fire on me, I was invited to join up. I slid under the left wing of the leader.

I felt more secure but I had not solved my problem because we were still headed into the target area. I didn't have fuel to go at their speed and make a round trip, even if the target flak barrage didn't get me. I alternated between fighter-bomber channel and our own calling for help. Old friend Lowell Brueland finally answered and he was alone and said he would fly along the bomber stream to find me. I felt better.

That lasted for maybe two minutes when I heard a series of fighter reports from the bomber crews. The box I was with came under attack by probably 25 to 30 ME-109's in an overhead pass. They were quickly through and gone. I'm sure some of the B-17's were hit, but I saw none go down. I wondered if taking this battered P-51 in chase of a bunch of enemy would be a good idea. It didn't seem as if it would be. Besides, I was cold and getting colder at 22,000 feet.

Brueland found me and I thanked the bomber boys and headed home. We went down a few thousand feet to warm me up. P-51's always look good, but never had I enjoyed seeing one more than seeing Brue's come by.

Next problem – no hydraulics. That meant manually pumping the wheels down – a task that takes time and a lot of energy. It also meant a 'hot' landing with no flaps. Then I wondered if I had brakes! If I get it on the ground I will do a ground loop. With the wings already shot full of holes, who cares what happens to them next!

I was experiencing all of those emotions as I pumped the wheels down. I was angry! What the hell were those guys thinking of? They weren't! They were strictly head up and locked! God! I could easily have been killed by friendly fire. And to compound the situation, they left me alone instead of escorting me home.

And I was lucky. I didn't know how lucky until I climbed out of the cockpit once safely on the ground and saw the extent of damage. I had flown Bob Stephens' plane, so He needed a new one. Good! My own was not involved.

Then the anger including the fact that I was robbed of a

1927 Clayton and Orien Jr. "The Gross Pilots"

Clayton Kelly Gross

Orien Wilford Gross, Jr.

Impressive line of BT-14 trainers at Randolph Field, "West Point of the Air"

"If you're an aviator, you should look like one." Air Cadet Gross with aviator glasses and pipe. Glamorous – No?

Wedding Picture 9-6-42 of four room mates at Randolph Field Chapel. Newly-Commissioned pilots and officers back row, left to right: Lt. & Mrs. John Hamilton, Lt. & Mrs. Gean Hale (Judy Hale was Gwen's Maid of Honor), Lt. & Mrs. Ed Gunter. Front row: Lt. & Mrs. Clayton Gross (Gwen)

Glamour Boy Gross and P-39 at Oakland Army Air Base

First landing ever at Aurora Airport after forced landing & spinning 180 degrees – 1943

Picture at 355th Squadron Officers' party at Portland Air Base in 1943. Gwen and CKG are seated second and third from left.

P-39 in shop in 1943, Portland, Oregon. Pilots left to right: Al Johnson, Vern Rhing, Tony Radojits, Earl Wulff

355th 'C' Flight at Portland Army Air Base 1943 Ryan standing top, Radojits, Emerson, Gross, Center, with Brueland, Hoehn, Turner standing

Three 'buddies', Gross, 'Lanny' Lanowski, Gus Allen at Boxted 1944

My un-named P-51B being readied for long range escort – 1944 Boxted

CKG ready for mission in P-51B at Boxted

P-51B from 'A' Flight belonging to Maury Long. Publicity photo of 355th pilots from the Northwest. Kenyon of Walla Walla, Talbot of Portland, and Gross of Spokane.

Dick Kenyon's *Bad Penny* went down on March 22, 1944

Radio Silence?

CKG and *Live Bait* P51B at Boxted

Rare sunny day at Lashenden just prior to D-Day. Note no dispersal.

"Uncle George", George R. Bickell, squadron commander and later group commander. His P-51B *Peg O'My Heart* at Boxted 1944

Excited and happy pilots. Jim Edwards on left, CKG on right, Major Burris (I.O.) on left interviews Col. George Bickell who led two D-Day escort missions, June 5/6, 1944

Surviving 354th F.G. D-Day aces. At 6 o'clock and clockwise: Brueland, Franz, Hunt, Turner, Stephens, Eagleston, Bradley, Beerbower, Emmer, Goodnight, O'Conner.

355th pilots in front of "OPS" office at Lashenden, June 1944. Identified from left: "Cuz" Lasko, Lynn Cocker, Bill Davis kneeling center, two on right are Gus Allen and Earl Knier.

Living Area and pre-fab buildings for officers and "O" Club area is between Marne River and Marne Canal. Before flood.

After the flood.

Two Spokane aces in publicity photo on day I bailed out. I'm wearing borrowed "Chute" that proved too small! Harry Fisk and Clayton Gross.

Whenever we carried bombs, they were "safe" until take off. The crew chief would pull the pins and hand them to me. I tucked them in my jacket pocket. Fifty years later, I found these still in the pocket. (Courtesy of *The Columbian*, Vacouver, WA)

Picture by Major Art Mellor at ALG1 on June 14, 1944
just prior to takeoff after emergency landing.

LIVE BAIT ready to take off from emergency landing on A-1 shortly after D-Day.

CKG on a rather desolate air base in France in early 1945.

Grave of Billie D 'Bucky' Harris in Omaha Beach area of france. I have visited this and other American cemeteries several times since the war.

The other side of GQ-I (*Live Bait*). "Smitty" wanted his wife's name there and I was happy to ok that.

"Smitty" (S/Sgt. C.E. Smith) who "crewed" *Live Bait* for me all my combat and training. P-51-D late in the war.

Spokane flyer again honored: at a 19th tactical air command pioneer fighter base in France, Capt. Clayton K. Gross, W137 Twentieth, where his wife, Gwen, and his parents, Mr. and Mrs. O. W. Gross, reside, is decorated with the silver star by Brig. Gen. O. P. Wayland. Gross holds, at last report, eight air combat decorations. (S-R A. A. F. photo.)

CKG directs pilot delivery on way to mission. "Tex" drives "carry-all", with Lynn Cocker on fender and Chuck Hawley on hood.

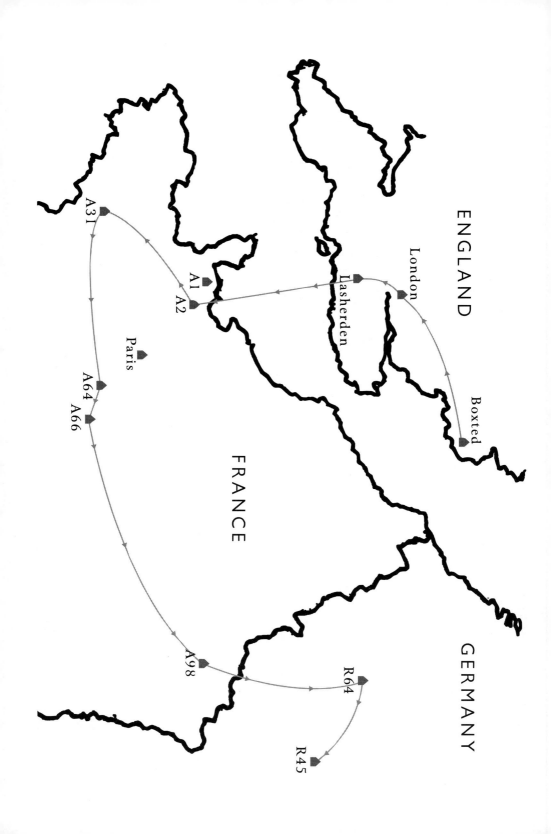

CKG and Smitty reunite 25 years post war, Portland, OR 1970.

Kurt Lobgesong and wife with CKG 1995 at meeting of "Gemeinschaft der Jagdflieger" (Association of Fighter Pilots) Germany. The pilot of the ME-262 I destroyed.

At the dedication of the Monument to the 354th Figher Group on the site of A-2, our first base on the continent.

victory hit me. Nobody knew what happened to the 109 I was hitting. I was locked on his tail and had multiple hits. Did he go down? I could only claim a damaged!

Thirty minutes after landing, I climbed into another plane and headed to Boxted, our old base now occupied by the 56th Fighter Group, I landed and headed for Group Headquarters. They ushered me to the office of the famous Ace, 'Gabby' Gabreski, although out-ranked by several grades, I was mad enough to lay my case on the line in no uncertain terms.'Gabby' stated that I was wrong with my identification, "We weren't even in that area today!" "Not so!" said I. Those Jugs were not 20 feet away from me and those ID code letters are indelibly marked on my brain, not to mention the distinctive nose and tail markings. It was your planes!" Then 'Gabby' allowed as to maybe they ranged that far and had one pilot who actually admitted firing at a Mustang, but did not hit it. "Hey" I said. "This guy may be the the best shot you have! Please come down to Headcorn and take a look at his handy-work."

At that time 'Gabby' sent for a pilot. When he got to the office, I had calmed somewhat and the young man, for that he was, was quite shaken. The three of us had a heart-to-heart talk for several minutes and then I shook hands and forgave him. I thanked 'Gabby'; truthfully saying it was nice to meet him and feeling much better. I left closing the door behind me. About ten steps down the hall, a thought struck me. What a souvenir it would be...the gun camera film of me being blasted! I ran back to 'Gabby's' office and opened the door without knocking. 'Gabby' was in the middle of an intense conversation with the pilot, thumping a forefinger on his chest as I entered.

I broke in by saying immediately, "Hey how about the gun camera film?" Like a mother hen protecting a chick, the Colonel stepped in front of the young pilot and spread his arms. "It was accidentally destroyed. When he removed it, the Crew Chief accidentally dropped the can and it popped open exposing the film. I'm sorry."

All I could do was leave saying to myself, "I'll bet!"

During the 354th stay at Boxted from November 1943 until April 1944, a Polish pilot had been assigned to our squadron. His name was Vitold Lanowski and we became friends. He had flown with the Poles against the German invasion – not really a fair fight. He managed to escape and make his way to England.

We would not allow him to fly combat missions, but he checked out in P-51's and flew training missions with us. And he harbored hatred of not only the Germans but our Russian allies as well. I recall one night at a movie showing propaganda film depicting our wonderful Russian friends was included. 'Lanny"' as we called him, jumped to his feet and shouted "No! No! Is not so!" Gus Allen and I sitting with him told him to sit down – "You're just mad because they stole your country." In retrospect, that was rather cruel.

After our move from Boxted to Lashenden in April, the 56th Fighter Group had moved in and Lanowski stayed, joining them. I visited Lanny occasionally and on one of those trips, I asked where he might be. "He is probably sacked out". And they told me which Quonset hut he would be in. When I got there and entered, I saw one lone body on the very last bunk and went back to see if it was Lanowski. It wasn't but it was the young pilot who 'Gabby' said 'might have shot me up'. He was asleep on his back and I had leaned over him slightly to identify him. When he awoke and jumped a foot off the bed, crossing his arms defensively, I laughed and assured him it was not an attack.

---

FOOTNOTE: Years later, 'Gabby' and I became friends. At American Fighter Aces Reunions, we would go to Mass together on Sunday. I would ask if he had confessed the lie about the gun camera film and he still wouldn't admit it!!!

on Sunday. I would ask if he had confessed the lie about the gun camera film and he still wouldn't admit it!!!

March 1944 LOSSES:

| | |
|---|---|
| Horace White | POW |
| Bob Silva | MIA |
| Edward Fox | KIA |
| Ridley Donnell, Jr. | POW |
| T/Sgt. Don Dempsey | POW |
| Al Ricci | MIA |
| Dick Kenyon | POW |
| Ernest Ditewig | MIA |
| Bill Aney | POW |

| 354th AIR CLAIMS TO DATE | GROUND CLAIMS |
|---|---|
| 159½ destroyed | 2/0/6 |
| 24 probably destroyed | |
| 110 damaged | |

CHAPTER 22
# MORE ACTION?

IT SEEMS FROM A little change in our missions that the war must be changing gears. We were flying more armed reconnaissance or dive bombing missions interspersing our usual bomber escort. It's not for us to question. This one was of the old order – an escort of the Big Friends.

Nowadays I know that smoking can be dangerous for your health, but in 1944 nobody told me that. From the time Lenore, my first steady girlfriend teased me into learning to use cigarettes until I quit cold 25 years later, a smoke was my favorite recreation. In fact, nearly everybody I flew with was the same.

On one particular long-range escort mission into Germany, I found an acute hazard associated with the habit. Our segment of the escort ended when we were relieved by another group half way home, on the withdrawal leg. The flight up until that time had been uneventful. As we set course for England cruising at 15,000 feet, we had been airborne for over three hours and my butt was numb! Step one to relax involved unlatching my seat belt and rising just one inch off of my seat pad. Oh that felt good! It's amazing how such a simple thing can bring such pleasure in some circumstances. Next, since conversation was not needed and oxygen was optional, I peeled my oxygen mask/mike away from my face and wiped the perspiration from the mouth area. Then I removed my gloves and dropped them into my lap.

The chest strap on my parachute was next so that I could zip my jacket down slightly and retrieve a package of Luckies from a shirt pocket. Then I rose off the seat again to find my Zippo in a side pocket. Finally, I was lit up and deeply inhaled the first drag. Ah h h! Pure pleasure! And, just then, all hell broke loose. A voice screamed in my ears, "Break left. Break. Bandits!" I reacted instantly spitting the lighted cigarette onto the floor and feeling a chill pass through my body as the dangers of my situation sank in. The centrifugal force of my violent turn was holding me tightly to the seat without a seat belt, but what would happen should I need to reverse suddenly in a dog fight. Would I go through the canopy? And that damn burning cigarette somewhere on the floor. What if there had been or would be a fuel leak? And what about oxygen? What if we had to grab a few thousand more feet? I had one hand on the throttle, one on the stick and I couldn't let either foot off the rudder pedals.

"Oh my God, what if I had to bail out?" Still in about a 5G turn, I was swiveling my head frantically trying to locate the bandits. More conversation and I heard, "Focke-Wulfs," but gathered it was not my tail they were on so I rolled out and reversed directions to try to spot them. Though I did it carefully, I raised slightly off the seat and found another hazard. Though I didn't find the cigarette, I did find a few ashes…in my face and eyes.

In about five minutes, all was calm. My flight never had visual contact with the enemy. We leveled out and continued home. First I fastened my seat belt. The I looked for the cigarette but couldn't find it. It had burned out on the cold metal floor in that low oxygen atmosphere I found later. I re-buckled my parachute, managed to find my gloves, put them on and replaced my oxygen mask. I also made a few resolutions about relaxing prematurely over enemy territory!

I told the whole story to 'Smitty' after landing and the next morning he had a surprise for me. Installed on the instrument panel was a neatly constructed aluminum ashtray with a flip lid. On the lid were clips that held two cigarettes and several wooden matches. I could retrieve them, strike a match on a panel on the front of the box and light up without undoing anything. I tapped the ashes into the box and the lid snapped closed, was airtight so a lighted cigarette would go out and no ashes could fall in my face. I didn't use it a lot, but it stayed there and was moved from model to model when we got new birds. Now smoking was not quite as hazardous to my health, thanks to 'Smitty'.

A large detachment Lt. Bruce Plath and several dozen EM's left Boxted as the advance party for a move to the southern coast of England. Things are happening, but at our level, who knows what! Anyway, on this particular night, we used it as another excuse to party. The beer flowed freely in the 'O' club until the witching hour approached and six remaining stalwarts decided to head home. We might even have to fly tomorrow if this damn weather should ever clear.

The Officers' Club, a Quonset hut sat on a rise and so did our living quarters, but not the same rise. From the exit of the club, a paved walk several feet wide meandered a winding path to the lowest level where 'Cocker's Creek', as it had been dubbed earlier, flowed. Then up a small hill 50 yards to our quarters.

When we stepped into the inky blackout, we found it further complicated by a fog so thick you literally could not see your hand in front of your face. Bob Stephens, our new Squadron Commander, was confident and he said to prove his leadership qualities, would get us home. "I know every step of this trail! I could do it blindfolded. Follow me."

Bill Davis put his hands on Steve's shoulder followed by Brueland and me next. Red Emerson followed me as Jim Dalglish brought up the rear of this chain gang but he soon aborted.

I had just retrieved several articles of my finest uniforms from Bowers Espy Dry Cleaning Service, so I carried them over my right arm and held onto Brueland's shoulder with my left. In lock step, we started down the path, "Hup, two, three, four, hup, – etc." as he stayed on path for the first 20 feet. Steve's confidence swelled. We went a little faster.

Now there is a wooden bridge across the creek and on each side, a railing, no more than four inches high guarding what, I don't know. As we reached the bridge, our pace had increased to a normal walk. The first indication of trouble was interruption of the cadence, "hup", SCREAM. Splash and another scream, splash! Brueland started over and I desperately held his shoulder while doing all in my power to keep from losing my cleaning in the mud. I must admit that, when it came to a decision, I had had to drop Brue, my dear buddy.

He joined Steve and Bill who were struggling in knee-deep water and mud to gain footing and with his superior weight and strength, the CO managed to nearly drown Davis. After Brueland was retrieved, the rest of us howled with laughter, all the way home, each feeling his own way into the darkness at much reduced pace.

Oh yeah! It was called "Cocker's Creek" because Steve and Bill were not the first to spin in. Lynn Cocker did it first on a trip home from the club...alone and in daylight. God only knows why, but I have my suspicions!

On April 5, 1944 the morning rain and low clouds lifted enough to get mission off by early afternoon. Forty-eight Mustangs plus two radio relays were directed to the Orleans, Chartres, Conches area on an armed reconnaissance mission, another one of those bomb and shoot everything you see jobs. After three aborts left, the rest of us did just that. The 355th Squadron dive-bombed a large railroad marshalling yard and then split looking for other targets. We could hear the chatter of the 353rd who ran into some aerial opposition. No such luck for us!

A few minutes later we found an airfield with some grounded Luftwaffe birds in view. We made a sweeping left turn into position and fanned out to start our strafing run from about a thousand feet. We weren't very far into the dive when the sky lit up around us. The field was very heavily defended. Between flinching from the heavy ground fire, I found a truck and small staff car parked in front of my line of flight and opened fire scoring heavy hits on both before I had to level off. A little to my right two Mustangs were firing at some 109's and the hangar they were parked in front of. The plane shooting at the aircraft set two of them on fire and pulled up. The guy firing at the hangar didn't. I was shocked as I watched him fly straight into the side of the hangar that exploded into a huge fireball. It was Edward Rody Ryan, the last of the three great 'R' pilots who joined us in Portland, Oregon.

Ed was the 37th pilot lost from the group; nearly half the number we had brought to England and just four months and four days from the date of our first combat mission. It was a very sobering thought. So also was the fact that Ed's loss kept alive the record that of never crossing an enemy airfield with all surviving the strafing runs. It was impossible to start one of those runs without thinking about it.

I got back to London a few weeks later. It is an experience; a huge city blacked out in wartime, still with thousands of people on the streets visible in the moonlight and mostly in uniform. The air-raid wardens were quite visible with white belts and shoulder/chest straps and the only ones with torches as they called them. There was a fair number of our troops, many British, but most of them females, akin to our WACs. Australians were in evidence as well and oddly enough, when soldiers overdid the Mild and Bitters and a street brawl occurred, the American and the Aussies sided together against the British. I found that many English, who described us as, "over paid, over-sexed and over here," really didn't appreciate us. Can't say that I blamed them.

When it began to rain that night, three of us signaled for a taxi. Fifty feet before us a very proper looking British gentleman was doing the same. A cab started to pull over for him, but saw us and quickly went by him to get us. He was irate! Before we were loaded, he was at the cab, banging his 'stick' on the window and telling us and the driver what he thought, and what he thought was not at all proper! He said, "You Americans have ruined our country. A taxi will not stop for us if there is an American in sight because of the way you throw your money around." Then the cabby, "you should be ashamed. You care nothing for your own countrymen!" Then he drew himself up to full stature and began shouting for another taxi. We were quiet but nobody offered to get out and give him the cab. After all, he had an umbrella.

I thought about this for a bit, actually only until we were delivered to another pub or bar. I thought we would be welcomed here, but evidently not everybody feels that way.

Anyway, I did like his 'stick'. The next morning I visited a department store and purchased what is called a 'swagger stick'. Officers and gentlemen carried them, usually in folded gloves. They were great for getting attention when needed. Of course, the person tapped on might not think so. While I was at it, I bought a Sterling cigarette case, post card size, but very thin. It still held a pack of twenty of the weeds. To be even more proper I had it engraved 'CKG'.

Now properly outfitted, I learned to say 'bloody'. "Call us a bloody cab. Give me another bloody pint." And when the sirens blew and the searchlights lit up the sky, it was, "the bloody Huns are at it again!"

★ ☆ ★ ☆ ★

April 1944 losses

| | |
|---|---|
| Edward R. Ryan | KIA |
| Jas. B. Campbell | KIA |
| Young M. Davis Jr. | MIA |
| John M. Cartright, Jr. | MIA |
| Dennis L. Johns | POW |
| Edw. V. Parnell, Jr. | POW |
| Ralph A. Brown | POW |
| Geo. W. Hall | POW |
| Robt. L. Plank | POW |
| Robt. R. Kegebein | POW |
| Edw. E. Phillips | KIA |
| Billy J. Lamb | KIA |
| Jack H. Carr | KIA |
| Wm. J. Simmons | MIA |
| Franklyn E. Hendrickson | MIA |
| Joseph A. Lilly | MIA |
| Edw. R. Regis | POW |
| Jas. Cannon | POW |
| Richard N. Hudson | POW |
| Paul W. Kallas | KIA |

354th AIR CLAIMS TO DATE — GROUND CLAIMS
250½ destroyed — 22/6/37
39 probably destroyed
191 damaged

CHAPTER 23

# PICADILLY CIRCUS, THE BEST SHOW IN LONDON

IN THE EARLY SPRING, I decided I needed a break and some entertainment. Bonotto and I boarded the local out of Colchester and chugged our way into the huge station in Central London. We grabbed a cab from there to the Park Lane Hotel, a fine and famous accommodation, now in wartime used as an Officers billet. After a scrub up and a change into our finest Class A uniforms, we lit out for a night on the town.

First stop was in the hotel bar where Bradley, Stevens and I had our introduction to London at night soon after arrival in England. It held nothing for us that we could see, and the bar offering was limited to Gin and Orange and those get old fast! We headed out to walk to the famous Picadilly Circus. The night was mild with enough moonlight for people visibility, despite the blackout. It was a ten or fifteen block walk to the center of "action" and action there was! Hundreds of men, and some women in uniform, with no shortage of the opposite sex.

A news vendor on the corner waved his wares hollering, "Times," get your "Times," and then in a slightly subdued voice, "condoms, condoms." Even in the moonlight, we decided those wouldn't be a bad idea, given the caliber of some of the women.

This really happened! As we passed an alley, an American GI bolted out pulling up his trousers as he ran. Closely following was a female shouting in a full Cockney accent, "Stop him. He screwed me – now he won't pay! Stop him!" I guess the gentlemanly thing to do would be to collar the delinquent 'screwer' and tell him to pay his bills. But Carl and I were bent over laughing so hard we could not react so I guess he got a 'freebie' unless an M.P. grabbed him later down the block.

There were plenty of M.P.'s, both British and American, but their purpose was to guard against real trouble – not to interfere with the seamy life on exhibit. I could not tell the professional ladies from the just lonely type and was not interested in either.

As we sauntered around the Circle – it is a circular intersection with a statue of a famous English Admiral as the centerpiece, or is that Eros? A young blonde girl joined us by coming up behind us and linking her arms in ours. "Do you know what I like about you Yanks?"

"I can't imagine," I answered smartly. She unlinked arms and slapped each of us on the butt. "It's your silk underwear. We can't get it over here now, 'ya know."

"I would give you mine, Maam, but I don't happen to have an extra with me."

She walked a little further with us. Then gave up.

After an hour of this floorshow of life, we mutually decided it was not for us and headed back toward the hotel. The traffic of people thinned to zero as we left the vicinity of the Circus. About three blocks from the hotel, we detected two ladies near a corner. There was enough light to see they were a class or two above what we had just left. Both wore fur coats and high heels and what looked like silk stockings. They were both attractive and smiling. In an accent we found to be French, the brunette spoke to me.

"Good evening, gentlemen. Could you use some companionship?"

My mind was racing and my conscience in turmoil. The darker-haired girl who had posed the question to me was really attractive! I had a brilliant answer. "How much?"

"Two pounds, or ten for all night."

Each English pound was frozen at $4.12 American. That made it expensive, but they looked like real class and I had about 150 pounds in my pocket. My conscience lost. "Okay," I said, and she took my arm.

"I have to stop at my hotel for a moment."

"Why?"

I pulled out a two-inch thick roll of bills. "I need to leave this in the hotel safe." I counted off ten and one extra for tip or emergency. The lady was hurt, but it was a sale made and she walked to the hotel where I asked the desk to put the roll in the safe. Then we went to her flat not too far from the corner we had found the ladies waiting. I had no idea where Carl had gone, nor did I care.

For the balance of the evening and in the morning, I was educated and entertained. I awoke to find Mimi beside me, and a maid delivering a delightful breakfast on a tray – in bed. And the eggs were real! "All included?"

"All included," she smiled. I was smitten!

Before I left, I was given a phone number should I get back to London. I also got a life story that made sense. She had married young to a Brit who now had been gone fighting in Africa or wherever for two years. When France fell, she was trapped in England. "What's a girl to do?"

While I went back to Boxted to continue to argue with my conscience, I found it difficult to forget M. Morton. That was the name on the door of her flat.

By mid-April the 354th was on the move. The pilots flew to our new base of operations, Lashenden near Maidstone in the Duchy of Kent. Gone were some of the "good" perks of Boxted. We flew from a dirt field instead of asphalt runways. We lived in tents rather than Quonset huts. England was still cold and we had to rely on a pot-bellied stove to heat our 'quarters'. Brueland, Emerson and newly commissioned Flight Officer Danny Richards and I shared one tent.

We were cold and we usually were hungry. Danny had a turn at keeping the stove functioning and one cold evening he developed a plan to do it easily – he thought. When it had descended to embers only, he added more coal and took an open can with a little gasoline that he started to pour in. Of course, the embers ignited the gas that quickly ran up the poured stream to the can. He instinctively threw the can skyward which managed to start numerous fires in the canvas of the tent. The can landed on his own cot which served him right. I had a rack of uniforms by my bed that survived, or I might have killed him myself. We got a new tent.

And hunger! We were all young and relatively virile, usually hungry. We weren't the only ones. There had been so much theft from the kitchen that the Mess Sergeant had booby-trapped the slightly subterranean storage area. He neglected to tell one early morning cook or the cook had forgotten. He stepped on one of the steps and it blew up – not too big a charge, so the cook survived but did get a few days in the hospital – probably for his nerves more than injuries. Our tent was very close to the area and we definitely arose early that day.

We had the easternmost tent on the line of 355th pilots. It was the closest to the cook tent, which made it even easier to think about food that didn't seem like there was ever enough. On a spring night in 1944, we discussed the situation until it was decided there was only one option! Somebody had to go steal some food. But stealing was not a nice thing for officers to do. Your military career could very quickly go down the drain if found out. On the other hand, young men do not starve to death as long as they could breathe and move.

We suggested to Danny who, as a newly commissioned Flight Officer and as the lowest ranking of the four, it was his job. "Bleep you," was his answer. He suggested we draw straws from the stub of a broom. It was robbed of four straws of varying lengths. Danny might as well have taken our original suggestion. He got the short one and soon disappeared into the darkness. I tortured myself dreaming of something to chew on.

The storage area was out of the question, but with the mess hall close by, it could be entered by crawling under the flap. With great anticipation, we waited for Danny to return. Ten minutes – fifteen. Maybe we should go search for him! Then he pushed in the flap, a bit breathless, but holding food in both hands. In one he had a partial loaf of cheese about the size of half a pound of butter, in the other, a fairly large dry onion. "That's it?"

"Listen, I'm lucky to find anything. That place is bare."

We carefully quartered both prizes – everybody worried they wouldn't get their fair share. I had never eaten an onion in my life so I tried to barter.

"My onion for half your cheese." No way and they all turned me down. Then they tried to talk me out of it.

"If you aren't going to eat that, can I have it?"

"Bleep you, buddy!"

I ate my cheese and then stared at the onion. Finally, I took a nibble – wasn't bad! I ate the whole thing.

In early May, we interrupted our armed reconnaissance-type missions with another long-range escort. We could hear the heavy's overhead before we got to breakfast…an unending roar of how many thousand Pratt and Whitney engines in a stream miles long on their way to dump another lethal load on the Third Reich. I wondered how they must sound to the German people. Not very pleasant I wager.

The briefing had said, "Maximum Effort, to and out of Berlin". Penetration and withdrawal. I was one small part of that Max, one of probably a thousand fighters to protect more than a thousand bombers. We relieved a P-47 group a half-hour before the target. I was on the right side and above a box of 25 B-17's, weaving to maintain position. Then they flew into an ungodly amount of anti-aircraft fire – thousands of those black clouds appear suddenly and hung there to let you know they've been there. My God! They are taking a toll! I see one guy lose a wing and spiral down out of formation. I watch and watch for chutes. There aren't any! Another in a steep descent and on fire, two more slowing and dropping from formation with less than four engines still working.

I know there are ten guys in each of those wounded birds. How many will live out the day? Only our Creator knows now. I feel tears in my eyes because I can't do a damn thing to help. Have I cried since childhood?

I can't do it now – eyes must be clear – maybe they'll send in fighters next and I must be ready.

The stream of bombers flies on with more falling – and more – and more! I fly on. After five or six hours in the air, I should be home in a cold dreary English countryside. I'll go to the bar and drink to get rid of the vision of the hundreds of bomber crewmen who can't do that. War is truly hell!

As I grew up, I had a mop of curly blonde hair and I did cry when some mean kid made fun of it in 1928. My mother soothed things when she told me Lindbergh had curly hair. Well, okay! If he did, I didn't mind being like him.

I'm sure I cried a few more times in those days with skinned knees or elbows, but tears in those days were not like the ones that showed up after that Berlin trip. Ten men in each one and they didn't have a chance. Oh well! It can't happen to me.

CHAPTER 24

# CONTEMPLATION

I T'S HARD TO FIGURE these guys out. These are the only men you've known for some time now. These are men you live with, eat with, work with, fly and fight with. These are storybook characters in the flesh and you are one of them. They don't look it and you don't feel it. In all this time, you're not sure you know them at all and hours of trying to figure yourself out make you realize that you may be crazy!

That one is tall and good-looking. He's young and he shows it at rare times when he's in a good mood. I guess he's got what it takes. He's a leader and he's a killer. You've heard him tell his story after a mission. He'll have a grin from one ear to the other, but his voice doesn't jive with the smile. "Jeezus," he'll say, "I blew those bastards to kingdom come! Pieces'll be coming down for the duration." That voice is a mixture of hate, joy, nervousness and well – you don't know. He's a good Joe. You know he loves to fight. He can take care of himself, too, and raise a lot of hell with those he's fighting. You've seen him scared, too. He didn't try to hide it and you or nobody else said anything about it. Hell, brother, you've been more than excited yourself!

He was laughing an hour ago. Now he's sitting in a chair quietly. He thumbs through a book of secret and confidential 'poop'. Maybe reading about the latest secret weapon those bastards have started to use. Then he closes the book and just sits there or looks out of a window. He actually doesn't know just what he wants or what he's doing. Maybe he and the rest of them do know and you're different.

And then there is Ralph Hasbrouck. He wrote a poem about his best girl. It opened him up for us to see and know a little better. His aircraft was named "Miss Finnigan".

'CO-PILOT, MISS FINNIGAN'

*I wonder if you know about*
*The flights you make with me*
*I hope you keep on making them*
*I love your company.*

*I don't know how you get there*
*You're not there when I start*
*Do you hide behind the dashboard?*
*Or deep down in my heart.*

*Do you sit upon a cloudbank?*
*And wait till I go by*
*Then climb into the cockpit*
*I know not how or why.*

*Will you answer one small question?*
*Do you just go for the ride?*
*Please let me know the reason why*
*You're always at my side.*

*Perhaps you're there to guard me*
*To see that I'm not harmed.*
*Your gentle voice to soothe me*
*When I get quite alarmed.*

*When flak is bursting 'round me*
*My very life at stake*
*You're always there to tell me*
*The safest course to take.*

*When things are nice and peaceful*
*We just sit there and chat*
*Of what we're going to have some day*
*Our home and things like that.*

*Then when we're getting near the field*
*You say for now…Goodbye*
*But I'll be seeing you again*
*Tomorrow, in the sky.*

*You steal a kiss and then you're gone*
*You vanish in the blue*
*Then once again, I'm left alone*
*With just my thoughts of you.*

*If I don't fly for several days*
*It drives me nearly mad*
*Not seeing you up in the blue*
*Makes my whole day quite sad.*

*Right now it's time to go to sleep*
*I'll say…Goodnight, my love*
*And pray, tomorrow I've the chance*
*To meet you up above!*

*Ralph C. Hasbrouck,*
*1st Lt., Air Corps*

He was a good pilot. Now we knew he had help!

I started flying before the war and it was all very dramatic. The small flivver planes were about the heighth of my imagination, but they were enough. Then this "flying cadet" business interested me and I decided to try that. The war started. The thought of me in a fighting machine was still too much for my limited imagination so I was content to get myself through training, maybe dreaming sometimes of the "story book" characters who were actually fighting.

The training phase of my career was the first contact with the men I live with now. Then they were like me, a bunch of guys full of glamorous dreams, but more intent on the realistic present. Probably they couldn't see themselves really in it either. At least I couldn't. The day I graduated, I really began to wonder. I was going to get a job now.

The Major behind the desk at your first station asked if you thought you would like the P-39. He said it with a smile. I still couldn't believe I was a fighter pilot! The Major's smile broadened because he had seen lots of new men like the others and myself with me. He might even have understood me then. Would he now?

For awhile, I let myself dream of being really in it, but just for awhile. Flying a fighter settled down on the routine training. I could fly it all right and I read the headlines in the paper about the guys flying and fighting 'over there'. I couldn't believe I would really be a part of it!

I was married and for a period of a year, the war went on without me. I lived at home. I drove to the field in the morning and back at the end of the day's work. It wasn't much different than it had been before you started all this. At least I felt normal. I never sat down alone and questioned my nerve, or maybe my sanity.

Maybe we've all changed but that fellow by the window looks no different. He hasn't moved or said anything for a few minutes, but if somebody brings him out of his trance, he could laugh and joke with the best of them. I think it beats me really.

I didn't fly today, but others did. While I lingered over a cup of coffee after lunch, somebody came in and said the guys were back and they had seen something. On the way to the interrogation room, I thought it over with mixed emotions. If I had missed a good show, I would kick myself around for a week. Still, I hoped they got a million of the bastards. Hell, why does this damn war go on anyway? The French say it simply 'cest la guerre' and let it go at that, but at times it doesn't make much sense to me.

The interrogation room is a hubbub of excitement. At the center of each crowd is a man. He stands out from the others like a sore thumb. You can't push through the circle around him, so you stand and watch and catch a few words of what he says. Over his nose and around under his eyes are lines cut where his oxygen mask wore deep and sweat and dirt collected. His hair is disheveled by the recently removed helmet. His face is a grim mask and there is nothing funny about it. He shot down an enemy aircraft and the corners of his mouth turn up in a simulated smile when a newcomer congratulates him, but it is only so deep. He fought for his life to do it and two others didn't come back because they lost their fight.

The other pilots watch him with eager faces and he tells his story a dozen times because a dozen of them wanted to hear it for themselves. It is told with short, sometimes unfinished sentences together with motioning hands. Another pilot over here got one too. It was his second mission and he still doesn't know how it happened. He says it pulled up in front of him and he hit it. It went into the ground and blew up and it took him a minute to realize what he had done. Then he was too busy to congratulate himself 'til he got back' and now he's still too nervous to be happy about it. He also saw a midair collision. Who were they? It's a lot of war to see in the first few hours you fight it.

Tonight I stopped by the club for a short one or two. On the way home somebody made a sharp quip about the war and I laughed like hell for a minute. The two men who didn't quite make it today had been two of the men I worked with. Two good friends of mine, too, and I had hardly thought about them since they went down.

It sounds kind of funny, but damn it, I couldn't think about them. I had to forget and go on. I started laughing at something else.

CHAPTER 25

# SCORES IN THE AIR AND THEN D-DAY!

**W**E WERE DEFINITELY GETTING busier as the weather sometimes improved. I flew eight combat missions in the first ten days of May, evenly divided, four dive-bombing and four escorting bombers. Three of those were to Berlin. On the eleventh, in another escort of B-17's, this time to Saarbrucken, I finally scored in the air!

The group put 52 P-51B's in the air in an afternoon mission. I led Green flight of the 355th. Chuck Hawley was on my wing, but had to abort and Billy D. "Bucky" Harris filled in. We had rendezvous without any problems, but were responsible for a huge part of the armada and so spread out over several boxes of the Forts. Bucky and I were alone on the right of one group.

For ten uneventful minutes we used a slow weave at bomber level. Then I saw a large number of bogeys coming in about 1000 feet above us and to our right. I called them as bandits and Bucky and I turned toward them. I decided that coming up underneath them would allow us to attack without being observed. They were ME-109's and I estimated at least thirty or more in number. I again reported them as bandits and heard no response except Harris. As we continued our climb, I checked our own tails and discovered a second gaggle of like size. I leveled out watching both groups carefully. There was no apparent notice of our element as we allowed the second bunch to pass over us and then resumed our climb.

I could not believe what I was seeing! A huge number of enemy fighters so close we could actually read numbers. When the last plane cleared us, we spread out and climbed the last few feet to their level – no more than 50 yards behind the trailing 109's. I selected a target and opened fire. Bucky did the same. My first one exploded in a ball of flame and smoke and slowly winged over in a steep twisting dive. I had no time to watch. I slid over to another target and started firing. I had multiple hits, but about that time, all hell broke loose and I could not follow him.

Why they had not yet attacked the bombers, I don't know. They were in great position. Our shooting had sent eight trails of tracers through the formation and planes were breaking in several directions. There easily might have been mid-air collisions; we didn't have time to witness. It is one thing for two of us to attack 70 enemy from the rear, but quite another to stay and fight the survivors, out-numbered as we were. We rolled over and headed down.

I leveled out around 5000 and found no one chasing us. We headed West in mutual support. Five minutes later I found another target. A lone ME-109 below us was on a reciprocal heading. I did quick 180 and settled on his tail and opened fire. I doubt that I had fired 100 rounds in a short burst when his canopy came off. He had continued to fly straight and level. Since the canopy ejection signaled surrender, I quit firing and slid off to his left – now no more than fifty feet away. He stuck his head out that side, saw me and quickly went to the other side and jumped. I was on cloud nine! Two definitely down, maybe more. A big formation broke up before they could attack. Harris had flamed a third!

I checked to make sure we were not targets ourselves and then made a pass by the parachute to wave to the pilot and let him see the name "LIVE BAIT". Maybe he will warn the rest of the Luftwaffe to beware of me. He didn't wave back. We headed home.

I could not resist the temptation when we got home. I went down the runway at ground level and pulled up into two perfect slow rolls to signal my victories. Harris did one behind me and we landed in true fighter tradition.

George Bickell was waiting at my hardspot when I rolled in. First, he listened to my story – then he shook my hand – then he fined me $10, $5 for each roll. Later he recommended me for the Silver Star and Bucky for the Distinguished Flying Cross.

He did not recommend me for promotion. No matter, I was still on cloud nine.

Two days later on my next mission, I had another claim of a damaged 109 that I lost before seeing what happened to him. Maybe my luck is changing

The aerial activity continued without let up through the rest of May. I flew 19 missions in that month. We had more escorts – some the ass tiring kind to Berlin and Magdeburg. The Luftwaffe put up little opposition – at least in our areas. That is until the 28$^{th}$ on an escort of heavies to Magdeburg when they made up for lost time! German fighters struck en masse and for a few minutes we had a king-size dogfight. In short order, I lost sight of white flight which I had led. I tagged onto an FW-190 but lost him and almost myself in a near mid-air collision with something crossing my path.

Group claims that day would eventually total 17½ destroyed and five damaged, but I had not fired as yet when the enemy disappeared as fast as they had arrived.

I picked up a wingman as we started home. Shortly I saw a

B-17 several thousand feet below us with one engine feathered and obviously in trouble. Further examination showed he has more problems than one bad engine. Boring in from his rear was a ME-109 closing rapidly. I had altitude and a good angle to intercept. I did a rapid wingover and poured on the coal. When I saw the 109 start firing, I could not wait to close as far as I would like. From 200 yards I opened fire with about a thirty-degree deflection. It worked. My first burst hit at his wing root and cockpit area. Like the sparrow to my slingshot, he dropped. That is he rolled over and began a straight down dive, which I followed to the ground.

My new wingman caught up and we lent air escort for the bomber as far as we could go with fuel diminishing. There was a lot of waving between us and the bomber crew as we told them we must depart. All I could do now was pray they made it the rest of the way.

Now what? We are confined to our base – no leaves. This may be it. I flew one more escort mission on the 31$^{st}$ and for the next few days nothing – no missions. There really was no question of the reason for our base confinement. The big one we knew – and the enemy had to know as well – was close to happening. We put up with confinement.

On the evening of June 5, we ate dinner and as usual headed for the club for a nightcap – or two. Half way through the first beer, Espy, the Group Adjutant, burst through the door.

"Close the bar!"

"What the hell do you mean – close the bar?"

"Exactly what I said. Briefing in thirty minutes." And he left.

There was a hell of a buzz of conversation – mainly to do with the hour. This had to be the big show. "---but for Chrisake, it will be dark before the briefing is over. And the weather doesn't look all that good anyway. What the hell are they thinking of?" almost in unison from one or more anonymous sources.

Dutifully, we left unfinished beers and tromped to the briefing building. It *was* the big show! We were to rendezvous with C-47s towing troop gliders and escort them to the Cherbourg area of France. Those troops were the airborne units to drop beyond the coastline and disrupt enemy wherever they could before the beach landings at dawn! Wow! We were part of the most important part of the war since America entered it.

Initially pumped by this thing – all we had to do was walk out the door into the darkness and 'less than ideal' weather and a few reservations popped into mind. In the blackout someone said, "Hold your hand up. Can you see it? How the hell can we see to escort?" When we finally fired up, we could see each other by exhaust stack flames. That's something.

Uncle George himself would lead the group from 355$^{th}$ squadron. I led Blue Flight. We were off the ground, 48 in number, a few minutes before 2100. The cloud cover was down to 2,000 feet but in time we were able to form and set course for rendezvous. It didn't take long and we spotted our charges visible only by their exhaust stacks. Six planes aborted for various reasons and I could understand how a guy might hear or feel a hundred things wrong with his aircraft, but we stayed on the job.

To myself I thought, if a German fighter were to find us in the dark and fire a string of tracers through the formation, we might all spin in. It didn't happen and a half-hour later, the real excitement started.

As the formation neared the coast of France, an absolute *wall* of fire erupted from the ground. Those poor bastards! They have to fly through that and they have little or no armor protection. With no enemy aircraft to oppose – some of us did the only thing we could do to help – dive at the obvious points of fire and squirt a few rounds of return fire. I don't know if it helped, but it couldn't hurt.

Now with the job done, we headed for home, but new problems. The weather had closed in over Lashenden and we couldn't get there. After a few abortive attempts, we were directed to an alternate airfield some miles west of our own and got safely down thirty minutes after midnight. For the first hour we were full of fire and wide-awake. Then Colonel Bickell who had been on the phone called us together with a bombshell announcement. "There would be a second mission, but the replacement pilots are there and the planes are here. The same bunch will fly again -- same type mission. Take off to start at 0530. Try to get some rest and you will have to pre-flight your own planes. Any questions? Good."

I found a wooden bench, maybe a foot wide and short enough that my feet hung over the end. I used my helmet and gloves for a small headrest and tried my best to rest. My thoughts were with those airborne troops. I wondered how they were doing – how many had already died. By 0300 I was up and basically sleepless. There was some coffee from I don't know where. It helped.

We gathered for a briefing about 0430 – more of a pep talk than an information session. We wrote new times on the back of our hands – press tits – TO, rendezvous.

I did a pre-flight on LIVE BAIT, mostly kicking tires and making sure the pitot tube was uncovered. I climbed in and the first thought was I should have slept here. It was more comfortable than that bench!

Bickell was off by 0530 and 40 plus of us remaining followed. It was dawn and we saw our escort charges plainly this time but this wasn't the main point of interest. Below us in the cold light of the new day was a sight I could not believe or will ever forget. It was more ships than I knew existed. They ranged from battleships pounding the coast to the LST's closer to the shore.

We followed our charges in watching the gliders release and head down. Again I cringed as I watched some come apart upon touching down.

When our escort ended, we patrolled the beach area for awhile, then headed home. This time we were able to get into Lashenden and were greeted by our own people. The pilots who didn't get to fly were upset but their time came quickly. More missions to the coast were scheduled.

There was a microphone set up and members of the press there to hear our stories. A royal visitor also joined us. King Peter of Yugoslavia, resplendent in an RAF uniform with a lot of paraphernalia. He was exuberant because the invasion meant he would someday get his kingdom back freed of the Nazi's.

Although I had already been up for almost 30 hours, it was several more before I went to my bunk. I felt those two missions were the most memorable of my war to date. I will never forget what I saw!

★ ☆ ★ ☆ ★

May, 1944 LOSSES:

| | |
|---|---|
| David W. Henley | POW |
| Frank E. Weber | KIA |
| Wm. B. Dehon, Jr. | MIA |
| Robert L. Shoup | POW |
| Thomas S. Varney | POW |
| Eldon E. Posey | MIA |
| Wm. T. Elrod | KIA |
| Don McDowell | MIA |
| Glen H. Pipes | POW |

| 354th AIR CLAIMS TO DATE | GROUND CLAIMS |
|---|---|
| 325 destroyed | 43/6/46 |
| 39 probably destroyed | |
| 213 damaged | |

★ ☆ ★ ☆ ★

CHAPTER 26

# ANOTHER VICTORY – WAR IS HELL!

On the 14th of June, we flew escort for B-26 Marauders to the Alecon/Ste. Hilaire-Aur area in France. Escorting these mediums is much different than the heavies. They fly lower – about 12,000 vs. the 25,000 feet the 17's and 24's flew. In addition, their speed was such that it was not necessary to continually weave to match speeds.

Shortly after rendezvous, the Luftwaffe put up some opposition and for a few minutes, we had a royal donnybrook ranging from 15,000 feet to the deck. I found an ME -109 in a climbing turn left and was able to cut him off closing to 75 to 100 yards before firing. My first burst hit home solidly and his turn became a very slow wing over as he trailed smoke and fire. I followed long enough to see him go in. No ejection by the pilot.

We claimed 6 destroyed that day with a probable and a damaged – no losses. More importantly, I had air victory number four.

Shortly after the D-Day invasion of France, June 16th, Hitler unleashed a new weapon, the V-1 that had little effect on us but raised hell in London where they were targeted. We were sound asleep on our Lashendon airfield at about 0200 when the first one of these pilot-less drones putt-putted across our field at 200 to 300 feet and within a few moments all hell broke loose from the anti-aircraft positions bordering the field. Everyone was awake and outside the squad tents, clad, of course, in night wear which was generally the same skivvies we had worn that day. The AA, of course, missed everything and the "buzz bomb" continued on its way to the big city. We were about to go back to bed when a second one came over and a few thousand more rounds of ammunition were wasted. One gun position in particular irritated the pilots who watched the brace of four 20mm cannons start firing at the intruder, and hold the trigger down until it had disappeared over the horizon, and burned out all four gun barrels. They were replaced and when the next V-1 appeared, the same thing happened again. The helmeted crew in heavy flak jackets did not appreciate a few fighter pilots in their shorts appearing on the sandbagged revetment to tell them how to fire their guns. So when we felt that a few more hints on how to do the job might get the guns trained on us, we headed back to bed.

In a foxhole, dug according to instructions, along side our tent, we found Alfred Joseph Disiere, Jr., the youngest pilot in our squadron at 19 years. Not only was Alfred tucked down in his foxhole in fetal position, but also his steel helmet was in position with chinstrap fastened. To us, he looked funny although he was doing exactly what we were instructed to do in the event of attack. Some guys were rather cruel in their comments and his reaction and words have been indelibly etched in my memory forever since. Still from the foxhole, blinking back what appeared to be tears, he shouted with forefinger pointing. "You wait. I'll be alive when all of you are dead!" I gathered he almost was wishing we were.

The comments stopped and we went to bed leaving him in the foxhole. We were to find out that Lashendon was in a direct line from the German launching sites to London and almost hourly for the rest of the night, the strange craft wended their way across our field and the roar of anti-aircraft made sleep very difficult. No one, however, got up again except Alfred.

At 0710 the following morning after an even earlier briefing and precious little sleep, the group lifted off on an armed reconnaissance mission to the Bricquebec area of Northern France. We were loaded with 500 pound bombs with eleven second delayed action fuses, ideal for the job the 355th squadron was given which was to cut a rail line and thus a supply route to German troops. Since the krauts were so good at rebuilding track and even engines after our attacks, we were going to block a tunnel and knock down the hillside site of the rail line to see how fast they were able to re-do it. The delayed action fuses allowed you to deliver the bomb precisely and give you 11 seconds to get out of the way before they blew up. From a couple thousand feet we went in pairs. I led the third or blue flight with 'Cousin' Lasko leading White in front of us. Disiere led his second element. Circling above the target, watching results and deciding on my own run, I saw Lasko and his wingman plant their bombs in the bank directly under the track. Good job!

I was thinking I might put mine above the track and possibly bury the line with a slide when I suddenly realized Disiere and Gray, his wingman were already on their run and the bombs of Laskos element had not yet exploded. I tried to shout a warning and maybe Gray heard or realized their mistake for he pulled up and right just before the explosion. While he was rocked to a 'fare thee well' his plane held together. Not so for Alfred! The blast ripped his wing off and he immediately rolled in that direction and struck the ground in a flaming ball of fire. It was 0830. Alfred was dead less than six hours after his prediction to outlive us all.

I missed the dear little guy and it was another lesson to file away in your memory to keep yourself alive. He was the 70th of the 80-some pilots we took to England to be lost and on that June 17th, we had been in combat for just six and one-half months.

Not a one of us lacked confidence, however, because we had 294 of the enemy planes confirmed destroyed and another 202 probably destroyed or at least damaged by that date.

June 17th would be a very long day for me. We landed at 1105 from the sad morning dive-bombing mission. After debriefing and chowing down, I headed for the sack to make up for the sleep I lost watching the Buzz bombs cruise across Lashenden. It didn't last long. In the late afternoon I was rousted out for another briefing and after supper, the 355th put three flights in the air with another load of bombs to dump on anything we could find in front of our troops. Time off the ground – 2000 hours in the still daylight summer evening. I led Blue flight. For a target, I followed a single rail line to a junction with a second track, not a very big area, but the best I could locate. About 20 yards south of the junction was a neat white cottage. I made my run from about 3000 feet, releasing my two 500-pounders at about 500 feet, then pulled out, climbed steeply and rolled left to look back at the target. The white cottage had disappeared! I sincerely hoped that it was peopled by German rail controllers and not a French family! I had been aiming for the Junction.

Back to the war – we climbed to a few thousand feet and cruised the French countryside looking for movement. I found a truck barreling down a two-lane road and made sure he didn't go anyplace, anymore. At 2145, with shadows lengthening, we started home.

I had noted several sputters in usual purring performance of my Merlin engine, but as we crossed out over the French coast, I felt a quite severe hesitation, in fact, it cut out, then caught again. I looked at the expanse of channel ahead of me to be traversed before I could reach the southern part of merry England and my base. I hadn't realized that it was quite that far, like completely out of sight and more. I didn't feel I should try it. Thank the Lord that our forces held the Omaha Beach area below me.

We had been briefed on the emergency landing strip, which had been given priority shortly after the area had been secured. Because my power plant sputtered again, I decided to give it a try. I found it easily only a thousand yards or so from the beach area, George Hoehn, my wingman, volunteered to stay with me and I surely appreciated the company. We circled the strip only once at about 800 feet so that we could be identified and not used for target practice by nervous ground gunners. The strip appeared to be at least 1500 feet long and had been bulldozed quite flat covered with metal planking. Each of the four corners was marked with a burning bucket of flammable something to easily outline its limits. As George and I flew the pattern, I could not help but count thirteen wrecked gliders of the type we had escorted on the two 'D' Day missions. The field was obviously one of their target landing areas and from the condition of those wrecks, I felt sorry for the people who had landed in them.

We set down without incident and taxied the two Mustangs back to the area of the half-buried 'control tower' truck. A few uniformed people gathered around as we parked. I found out quickly they had no aircraft mechanics or parts or anything else for my ailing engine, but they did radio our base for help that was promised for the next day. Hoehn and I would spend the night with the infantry. We were Jeeped to the area of a bivouacked company of that branch of service where they would try to find us some chow, and a place to lay our heads for the night. The Major himself came over to meet us and I got a shock in the 'in this a small world department'. It was Art Mellor, a family friend from Spokane, Washington, half a world away. I hadn't seen him for two or three years and didn't even know he was in the service. He had lost track of me also and we were together on Omaha Beach in the middle of the war.

The Infantry didn't have much, but Art saw to it that we got a fair share of what they did have. We soon had mess kits and went through a passable chow line. Art also got us space in a squad tent for the night. No cot, but a plastic sheet under us with several blankets. We slept in our flight gear, what sleep we were able to get when the temperature dropped to 30 or 40 degrees. Slightly the worse for the wear, we were up at dawn and back to the chow line, then back to the emergency strip to wait for help on my plane.

About 1000 it got there. Talbot flew the mechanic in the back seat of an AT-6. An hour later we were able to lift off and back to England.

I thought Hoehn and I were the first of our group to spend the night on the continent, but maybe we weren't. The advance echelon of our group, some crews, ground support and other non-flying personnel had sailed from England to prepare our home to be Advanced Landing Strip 2 on the 17th. We didn't know that as we spent the night with the Infantry. A-2 was near Cricqueville, France about 4 kilometers inland from A-1 in the Omaha Beach area.

This is the most haunting and maybe the only memory of the war that has continually returned through the years. I am sure that in dropping hundreds of bombs and firing thousands and thousands of rounds of ammunition at the enemy and their targets, I killed people. In two or three of my aerial victories, it was pretty certain the pilot did not get out, but if you must fight a war, the beauty of doing it from the air is that you don't have to look at the results. It was always possible you had done your job without anyone dying.

On this particular day, however, I could see it. We were on an armed reconnaissance with bombs and during and after our drop, we were attacked by German fighters. The engagements lasted only seconds and I never found a target, but the net result of the confusion left me alone. That is a bad situation for any fighter pilot – knowing the enemy is in the air, but rather than waste time looking for others, I decided to barrel all out for A-2 at low level. It should be no more than ten to twelve minutes away.

I skimmed across the French countryside ten to twenty feet in the air and with my head on a swivel. Moments later, as I crossed a road, I spotted a German military truck speeding toward me from the right. Although concerned about my own safety, I could not resist the chance to play for real, a dirty game I learned in Tonapah during training period.

While flying in Nevada desert country it was a simple matter to spot the movement of those rare automobiles who found the reason and fuel to motor along endless miles of road. What great sport it was, on spotting one, to circle a few miles ahead and start down the road toward them at automobile level. I could visualize the feelings of a driver who suddenly found an airplane about to hit him head-on. On pulling up and looking back, you would invariably find the car off the road and driving across the desert. Although I had done this several times, I was not really bothered by my conscience because the countryside was flat enough not to cause a rollover and traffic was zero. At the time, I didn't even know what a coronary was and didn't think about it.

The memory of those fun runs returned as I spotted the truck. I continued to hold at low level straight ahead for about a mile to a low hill on my left. The road the truck was on had turned north to go around that rise. Perfect! I banked over and began my run. When the driver spotted a Mustang ahead of it, it was too late. I must have opened fire exactly at the spot my machine guns were bore-sighted to converge because it appeared that every tracer entered the windshield at once in the one-second squirt I fired. The driver undoubtedly saw me just before I opened fire because at high speed he began to waver – then when hit, the vehicle burst immediately into flames and went off the road. I pulled up and looked back to see it burning furiously, upside down in the ditch. I had a very funny feeling as I resumed my low-level dash for home. It was not the first time, but surely one of the most vivid! I had caused the death of some mother's son and probably several.

It did not take a hit by a freight train to make me realize my military career, as a career, ended with Bickell's attitude after the train crossing incident. It did not affect my love of the flying and of the 354th to any degree. I took what I got and didn't feel bad or even consider it a downer. I eventually was relieved as 'C' Flight Commander and appointed assistant operations officer. That wasn't a demotion. It could be considered a promotion. The excitement of preparations held my interest totally. When we reached England where we could see and hear the war, I was one of the three group pilots selected to check out the new fighter, the P-51 Mustang and check out the rest of the crew. I felt as if nothing had changed really, except George no longer acted like a buddy. He had promoted me to 1st Lt. just a few months after I graduated as a pilot and new 2nd Lt. He was a Captain and Squadron Commander at the time. I watched him go to Major, Lt. Colonel and full bird Colonel and I was still a 1st Lt. It had not affected me mentally until I began to realize that I was apparently frozen in grade. I think when Glen Buer got Captaincy a week after D-Day; it hit me hard for the first time. He joined the squadron six months after me. I held job that rated promotion a year before he did. I had four victories in combat and he had zero. For the first time, I did sink into a funk. It just wasn't fair! I asked Bickell for a transfer.

A few days later I had forgotten I ever asked. It was love of the guys I trusted with my life every time we went into combat. I was still enjoying my job. Maybe another week later, I got an official note. "Transfer denied." I was happy it had been. The war went on...

There are no Atheists in foxholes – I'd heard that long before combat and it didn't take the war to make me a believer. My mother, daughter of John B. Kelly, an Irish policeman and Mary, his mostly French bride was raised a staunch Catholic and raised her three sons the same way. Her faith was such that my father, who was reared in a Christian Fundamentalist home, eventually adopted the Catholic faith as well. I spent my primary school years under the Holy Names Sisters and again my freshman year of high school. When we moved back to Spokane in 1935 I entered a public school for the first time in my life. Not to worry, Mother, I know all the prayers by heart and I never miss Mass on Sunday. Still, until I started flying, religion was rather mechanical for me. I think, on my first ride in the Porterfield when I started flight instruction, the 'Hail Mary' occurred to me. I said it under my breath, but with more fervor than ever before as my Instructor pushed the throttle forward and we rolled down the dirt field of Felts Field airport. Especially the "---pray for us sinners – -now and at the hour of our death – Amen!"

That became a part of my flying routine and even today in the passenger section of a Commercial airliner, I help out on take-off with the same prayer.

Once we reached England and became combat ready, my belief in the Almighty was stronger than ever. But war is a seven-day a week job. It was difficult to tell Sunday from the rest of the days unless Father Ryan, the Chaplain who serviced our group and several others stopped by my office to remind the 'Mackerel Snappers' and me that the Mass was about to begin. I appreciated that.

June 1944 Losses:

| | |
|---|---|
| John H. Arnold | POW |
| Albert Charles Huffman | MIA |
| William R. Perkins | KIA |
| John Rody | MIA |
| Alfred J. Disiere, Jr. | KIA |
| Thomas L. Donohoo | POW |
| Robert K. Porter, Jr. | KIA |
| Clarence H. Stewart, Jr. | KIA |
| Patrick E. Moran | MIA |
| Wm. J. Walbracker | MIA |
| John D. Carpenter | KIA |
| Earl W. Knier | MIA |
| Daniel L. Richards | KIA |

354th AIR CLAIMS TO DATE
   370 destroyed
   41 probably destroyed
   222 damaged

GROUND CLAIMS
61/6/48

★ ☆ ★ ☆ ★

CHAPTER 27

# POST D-DAY – ORDERS HOME!

AS IF MY EGO needed another blow – Brownie, our PR guy came up with an idea. He gathered the eleven surviving pilots who had scored five or more confirmed air victories and attained Ace status for a publicity photo. They were arranged in a football-type huddle with the photographer on his back in the center.

I, with four confirmed, stood on the outside clenching my teeth in envy. I considered jumping in my trusty P-51 and searching enemy territory until I got one more, but that was not reasonable. It would have to wait!

On June 19th we moved our base of operations to the Continent – the first fighter group to do so. The field was designated A-2 and situated very near the coast and Omaha Beach. It was a leveled grass field with a mat of iron webbing for the runway surface. That was adequate for our purposes. A truck with a plastic dome was half buried at mid field and served as our 'control tower'. I liked to lift off and turn as I reached that point – to kind of spice up the controllers' lives a little. They probably didn't like it. It was close sometimes.

We were quartered in tents but the weather had warmed, but that, too, was okay. The missions were usually dive bombing, fighter sweeps or area patrols. The Luftwaffe generally stayed home.

The group flew multiple missions each day – sometimes a half a dozen. The danger of these low-level missions was quite apparent. From our move until the end of June, we lost thirteen pilots to ground fire. In that same time, we scored only eighteen aerial victories – far below our won/loss average.

On June 25, I was on an eight-plane mission to patrol the Cherborg Peninsula and we spent two uneventful hours doing that. Takeoff had been at 0600 and we were back on the ground just a few minutes past 0800 in the morning. Brueland had led the mission and since the day was warm and sunny, he and I decided to satisfy our curiosity about the battlefront we had been observing from the air. Although the peninsula had been cut off for some time, the Germans were still holding Cherborg and there were conflicting reports as to the severity of fighting. We had seen practically nothing on our patrol. We soon had a Jeep and a map and with tin helmets and side arms like real soldiers, left Cricqueville for the great adventure.

From the A-2 area, we drove a small country road southwest until we found a main road west and a sign pointing that as the route to Isigay and St. Mere Eglise, names we had heard of, and could find on our map. I drove and Brue navigated. Since it was truly a nice day, we put the top and windshield down to take advantage of a cooling breeze. Before we reached Ste. Mere Eglise, Brue felt the need to stop and in the small village of St. Laurent, I stopped while he went into what looked like a public house. I decided to rest and tossing the uncomfortable helmet into the back seat stretched myself out by placing my feet up on the folded windshield, closing my eyes and folding hands on my chest. I had nearly dozed off in the sunshine when I became conscious of the sound of a Jeep passing us at fairly high speed. That did not make me open my eyes, but then I heard the sound of brakes hit and tires sliding on the road. When I next heard gears changing and a Jeep backing up, I did peek to see what the commotion was all about.

A Sergeant driving the vehicle had stopped exactly opposite my position and in the passenger seat next to him was the very familiar face of Omar Bradley scowling at me from under a three-star helmet. He did not say a word, but I surely understood the look. My feet were down, I twisted and in one motion retrieved my helmet and replaced my crush cap with that bulky thing, then saluted. General Bradley's eyes twinkled; he nodded and returned the salute while motioning his driver onward. I could not imagine an Army Commander headed for the front in time of battle with time to stop to see that a Junior Officer followed his directives!

I told Brue the story when he came back and we continued in the same direction Bradley had gone. I think Brue did not completely believe my story. Still some distance from Cherborg we were stopped by an M.P. who couldn't believe he had sightseers in the area. We were told there had been German activity in this area within the past four hours. We decided we had gone far enough and turned around.

Before we had gone a hundred yards, we spotted a field just east of the road with literally hundreds of German prisoners. We stopped for curiosity, but soon were drafted to help. There were not more than a dozen of our troops handling the prisoners on a hundred-to-one basis. An officer gave us the routine. Line them up, tell them by signs to empty their pockets in front of them and pat them down. I couldn't believe it, but for the next couple hours, that's what two fighter pilots did.

The Germans had been holed up mainly in several huge pillbox types of fortifications. There were two French whores, complete with high heels and fur coats in June, who had been with them. The girls had huge stacks of money when they exited, but it was quickly appropriated by some GI's, to screams of anguish from the girls. I patrolled a line of prisoners, talking to some that spoke a little English, picking up and looking with curiosity at some of the things they had placed in front of their feet. I saw several GI's with their blouses stuffed with money stolen from their prisoners, but I didn't take a thing. I suppose it was lost to the GI's later. I felt out of place and when we got some relief, Brue and I went back to being fighter pilots.

Just after the invasion, I was involved in a low level-strafing mission in the heart of France. We had made a run at and destroyed two German trucks and in the doing found a 'flak tower' returning our fire. Those things are a real enemy of strafing fighters, so we made another run to try to knock it out. As I passed the tower after my run, I was no more than 15 to 20 feet off the ground. Straight ahead of me, standing on a road with no attempt to hide from the two-way exchange of machine gun and cannon fire and apparently without fear, was a lad no more than six or seven years old. He had removed his cap and was waiving it to me.

I rocked my wings to let him know I got the message. On the way home I could not help but think of him. Obviously he was happy to see the hated Boche punished for invading his homeland, but if he continued to stand around in the middle of a battle zone, I doubted if he would make it until the time we liberated the area.

On June 28, I flew an area patrol mission over the American and British beaches where huge amounts of material was being delivered to the Continent. It was uneventful. At this time I was so indoctrinated by my job that doing anything else had not entered my mind. In the next few days, I found a bit of sunshine that lifted me to 'Cloud Nine' without my plane! I had finished 200 hours of combat missions. I would be one of the first pilots rotated home. That group consisted of Bradley and Eagleston of the 353rd, Fisk and Depner of the 356th and Talbot and I from the 355th

It took a while for orders to be cut and transportation to be secured but within a week, after many emotional moments with those staying, we were on a C-47 which delivered us to the U.K. More problems which in the Army, came under the heading of SNAFU – situation normal all fouled up, but eventually we arrived in Liverpool and were told we would soon be on a ship home!

We had no way to tell us how long before ship transportation would be available. Assigned quarters, we were confined to base because the call could come on very short notice. That got old in a hurry with nothing being the total of things to do for entertainment.

On the third night, we corrected that. Immediately after dark, in very non-officer-like manner, we went over the fence. To do that, we donned Class-A uniforms, climbed a barbed-wire fence and tiptoed through a cow pasture to the nearest road where we were able to flag down a truck and get to town. The tiptoeing was necessary because of numerous cow droppings. Coming back after a few hours in town, I managed to step (stagger?) into a fresh one.

The first night over the fence, we managed to find, purchase and bring back, two bottles of Scotch. The next night, the four of us gathered in one of the cubicles that passed for rooms. Except for two, double-decker bunks and two freestanding wall closets, there was no furniture. Talbot was on one upper bunk and

'Eagle' on the other. I had climbed from one bunk to the top of a closet where I sat in cross-legged relative comfort. Bradley, alternately sat on a lower bunk, or paced the floor. Half way through the second bottle, Jack walked over to his buddy, the reclining 'Eagle'. He cradled the 'Eagle's' head in one arm, then suddenly put a hammerlock on the unsuspecting one and flung him the five feet, four inches from the top bunk onto the concrete floor.

From my vantagepoint, I knew the 'Eagle' was dead. He hit the deck with a sickening thud. Bradley calmly surveyed his handiwork. Talbot and I scrambled to the 'Eagle's' side. He emitted a weak moan and stirred slightly. Determining that there were no spinal fractures, Gil and I gingerly returned the 'Eagle' to his upper bunk. Bradley had not said a word in all this time and stood aside while we tended the wounded one. Then as we returned to our previous positions, he walked to the 'Eagle's' side. "I'm sorry buddy," he said sounding quite sincere. He patted the moaning 'Eagle' on the head and then suddenly, with another damned hammerlock, re-deposited Glenn onto the concrete floor!

If I didn't know these two guys thought the world of each other, I would have decided this was a feud to the death. I decided it was the whiskey and I thought about quitting forever. Instead, while Talbot and Bradley were looking at the 'Eagle', I stole the rest of the bottle and wandered out into the woods to think about life.

Orders finally came. The ship was okay – it was headed home. There was no huge convoy. We were alone. There were no big poker games, but Talbot and I faced Harry Fisk and Earl Depner in a continual Bridge game – ten days across the Atlantic. By the halfway mark, Harry had threatened to throw Earl overboard at least ten times. You can understand that we were winning.

The ship docked in New York Harbor. What a thrill to see the Statue of Liberty with up-raised torch. Until transportation could be authorized, we were billeted at Fort Hamilton. It didn't take long to dump luggage and head to the big city – Gil and I on our own.

The subway ran directly by the Fort and two small-town hicks, resplendent in Class A uniforms sporting ribbons to impress the natives, boarded for an adventure. We had no idea of our destination except to 'go downtown'. After a dozen or so stops, we asked another passenger when we would get there and were told, "we've been there for the last ten stations". We disembarked at the next stop and climbed to street level. I am a firm believer in fate and this cemented the feeling. Directly in front of us at this busy intersection, was 'LONGCHAMPS' bar. We went in.

After ten months in the war zone where the standard question to a bartender was, "What have you got?" We said that here in America.

"What do ya' mean – what have we got? What do you want?"

We ordered a couple of 'Old Granddads' and water. A toast sounded in order, so we clicked glasses and proposed "To the $354^{th}$" and drank them down. Also, unlike England, the bar never ran out. We began toasting individuals. Neither of us remembered how far down the list we got before lights out. Now another 'never to be solved' phenomena – we both woke up on a subway with sunshine beaming through the windows, obviously no longer underground.

We were clothed in a way, but both of us had been stripped of all accessories. Our pockets were empty – not even a handkerchief. Our belts and shoes, all insignia and decorations were missing. Fort Hamilton was the next stop. Fate again? We got off.

At the gate we were denied entry for lack of identification. A call in to our other $354^{th}$ members finally arranged for them to vouch for us. It was a night to remember – if we could!

★ ☆ ★ ☆ ★

A couple days later we were on our way again, this time by train and a week later, I was home – a thirty day leave, plus travel time. My beautiful wife was prettier than ever and I made it home in time for our second anniversary. Life was wonderful! A second honeymoon it was, but all good things end. The parting was even tougher this time because we knew what I could expect – the first time I was heading into the unknown.

★ ☆ ★ ☆ ★

July 1944 LOSSES:
    Thomas W. Cannon, Jr.    MIA
    James D. Masen    MIA
    Billie D. Harris    KIA
    Lt. Miller    MIA
    Theodore Dickter    MIA
    Villas D. Balk    MIA
    Joseph J. Roberts, Jr    MIA

354th AIR CLAIMS TO DATE    GROUND CLAIMS
    410 destroyed    64/6/48
    47 probably destroyed
    242 damaged

★ ☆ ★ ☆ ★

CHAPTER 28

# BACK TO THE WAR

THE 30 DAYS WERE gone and I took leave of wife and family sorrowfully. I would not go empty handed, however. I had learned in my first combat tour that except for Doc's ration of one ounce after each mission with a second thrown in for each enemy aircraft claimed, there wasn't a drink of bourbon to be had in all of Europe, and it was my favorite alcoholic beverage. I planned to change that during my second tour.

In early 1941 a small Coeur d'Alene, Idaho liquor store folded and my father, in either the world's greatest demonstration of foresight or the greatest stroke of luck, had purchased the entire stock of spirits at a bid auction. It was originally intended for the lake lodge he was planning for the future, but when liquor rationing became a way of life during the war, the liquor remained stored in our basement.

Dad was so proud of me that I think he would have given me the whole batch if I had asked and he did not hesitate when I told him I wanted a case to take back with me. Not selfishly for just me, I intended to split it half and half with Crew Chief, C. E. 'Smitty' Smith who I was convinced was as responsible as my mothers prayers for my living through the first 11 months of combat.

We picked out a case of 'Old Granddad' and reinforced the box in every way possible, then secured it with double wrapped rope that also was designed to give me a carrying handle. I tried it and it worked although before I left home, I noticed that after lugging it more than fifty feet, my fingers felt like they were coming off. Just thinking about opening the first bottle in the land of no bourbon gave me the resolve to try it.

My orders were to Atlantic City on the East Coast – by train again. Here I was reunited with Gil Talbot and eventually with the other four members of the 354th Group. Otherwise, the trip was uneventful. Who knew what to expect in Atlantic City? Certainly not our gang who was numb enough at this stage of the war to do what we were told when we were told.

Day one of our arrival we were installed in a plush hotel on the famous boardwalk. Gil Talbot and I shared a room on the twelfth floor. It was huge and richly furnished. Man, we decided our wives would love this. That led immediately to an investigation – just what is our schedule?

We found that to begin with, we would have two weeks "R & R" in these surroundings. Then after a physical, and mental as it turned out, we would be assigned, maybe back to our outfit, maybe elsewhere. "Look forward to a few weeks right here!" That was all Gil and I needed. We busted tails to the nearest phones and called Gwennie and Peggy. We didn't care how they got to us, but be here! The quicker the better!

Peggy from Portland, Oregon and Gwen from Spokane, Washington to Atlantic City, New Jersey in the middle of a war proved to be no easy task. The best was the same way we had crossed the country – by train. It took some string pulling to even arrange that, but it was done. Estimated time was about a week. That seemed an eternity, but even if it took that, we would still have the second week of "R & R", then probably a week more for exams and who knows, maybe more. I was elated at the thought of more time with the beautiful Gwendolyn. That night I made another booze bet with the "Deacon". A fifth of the finest whiskey available, "we have a child before you do". Both of us had been married two years with no heirs.

The week that followed went slow for both of us, but not for lack of things to do. The boardwalk and beaches were still there, war or no war and with so many males in the service. There was no shortage of available females to look at. All we did was look, but we did do that. Beside the bathing suited amateurs on the beach, the 1944 Miss America Contest was in full swing with opportunity to watch America's most gorgeous in their competition. Poor lovesick me was certain Gwen would beat any of them.

The rumor also started that one enterprising fighter pilot had managed to stash Miss 'Something' from the contest in his room at our "R & R" hotel. We tried, but never verified it.

We walked. We drank our share of real American whiskey and we counted the days until our brides would arrive. Finally, we got a telephone contact from them enroute. They were traveling together and due in Atlantic City on Saturday morning. We made arrangements for another room starting that day.

Friday a hurricane hit Atlantic City. Born and raised in the Northwest, I wasn't used to this type of thing. I had been through the big blow at Kelly Field just before graduation and here it was again, even worse.

Nobody had to tell us twice to stay off the streets. It became almost impossible to stand up with the winds and large debris was flying in all directions. Our room gave us a ringside seat to watch. Somebody a door or so down the hall made an entertaining discovery. He opened the window and discovered that anything tossed to the window was sucked out and up! He tried paper, and then pillows, then somebody tried a chair. It also went out the window and straight up out of sight. If cooler heads had not prevailed, everything in the room would have been ejected – 'in the interest of scientific experiment'. It was pointed out that everything the wind sucked up into the sky had to fall back to earth somewhere and somebody could be hurt by a chair hurled by 100-MPH winds. We lost interest and went looking for another bottle.

Room telephones started ringing everywhere about that time and I picked one up. The switchboard operator informed me that the hotel had to be evacuated. "Do *not* bring your luggage. Lock your room and come immediately to the lobby. Do *not* use the elevators. Come down by stairway! This is an emergency!" I passed the message on to the Deacon, grabbed my hat and coat and as an after-thought, my Contax II which I did not trust alone in the room. We closed and locked the room and joined a bunch in the hallways headed for the stairwell. I could still hear telephones ringing in some rooms as we followed a gang already on their way out. Twelve floors down are easier than twelve up. We were in the lobby, or close to it, in a few minutes despite the crowd. I say close to the lobby because we held up for a few minutes about three steps from the lobby level because from there down looked like a swimming pool. Water was two feet deep. It caused a bottleneck as we sat to take off our shoes and socks and rolled pants up as high as possible.

The MP's were directing traffic out of that mess and about three blocks north to the Civic Auditorium where we had been earlier in the week to try to get a peek at the Miss America show. We had to go away from the ocean first to get there. No sign of the boardwalk. The ocean had swallowed it, I guess. The gale was still howling but we leaned into it to get there. I couldn't help but look up occasionally to see if the chairs thrown out of our hotel window were headed down yet.

The floor of the auditorium was a mass of humanity. I didn't like it but it was dry and more fun than the howling winds outside.

We found a corner and holed up for the night. Before dawn the next morning I had had all the 'rest' I cared for on a carpeted stair step and Gil and I left our sanctuary for the great outdoors. The storm was gone but so was the power in most areas and what remained was devastation. Great sections of the famous boardwalk were curled up and leaning on shattered storefronts. Some merchants were assessing the damage and cleaning up by candlelight and probably had been since the winds quit and the sea went back to its hole.

An MP informed us that an emergency military kitchen had been set up in one of the larger hotels fronting the ocean so we headed that way. That location also lost power, but a few twinkling candles and lanterns gave off enough light for us to find our way. As is usual, there was a chow line. While Gil held our place in line, I located the form of a large grand piano in the darkness and, lifting the lid placed my valuable Contax II on the wire strings and put our hats over it. It felt good to rid my neck of the camera after it had dangled there for 18 straight hours.

We had a lousy breakfast in semi-darkness but it beat not eating. Thirty minutes later we retrieved our caps and the camera was gone! Some dirty rotten no good son of a bitch! I guess I had not been covered by the darkness as much as I thought! If I had left it in the locked room, I would probably still have it.

A few hours after the sun came up we located the emergency housing office and badgered and bribed them until they came up with alternate housing. While we were allowed to enter our original plush hotel to retrieve baggage, it remained closed for fear of weakened foundation. Gil and I had separate rooms and a quick investigation showed mine was no prize, but clean and adequate. I was on the second floor of a wooden three-story structure with no elevator. We moved into the rooms and headed for the depot. There we were informed that the train had arrived hours earlier. Somewhere the gals were out there looking for us! With that startling bit of information came another blow to further sink me into deep depression. The "R & R" leave was cancelled because of the storm damage. We were scheduled for the physical the next morning and we were to leave Monday for New York to ship out to Europe. I counted 47 hours with Gwendolyn, provided I found her! Another hour later they found us and I was in temporary heaven.

Late in the afternoon Gil and Peggy rang our room and suggested we find a place to eat. We decided to celebrate the fact that we were together for however short the time.

Power had been re-established in most areas and we got dinner reservations in one of the nicer hotels. Not a great deal is clear about the rest of the evening, but I surely remember the start. If this was to be one of our last evenings together for some time, hang the cost and enjoy it. We started with Champagne cocktails at dinner. Champagne was new to all of us and the nose tickling bubbly seemed to fit the occasion. We kept them coming through the entire meal. When that was finished, we found a club with a floorshow and ordered more Champagne. A few hours later the four of us literally staggered back to our temporary quarters.

Our room was immediately at the top of a wide carpeted stairway. I had to prop Gwennie against the wall to search for the key. Damn! I had forgotten to get it. I steadied Gwen, whose eyes had not been open for some time, and went down to the desk. Ten steps from the top on the way up, I saw Gwennie slowly sliding down the wall. At two steps at a time, I got there just before she hit the floor. I don't remember any more that night.

Sunday morning I awakened with the worst headache in my memory. I had no time for breakfast before my physical. All the way to the scheduled auditorium location I sucked in as much air as was possible and repeated over and over again. Oh! My God! Oh! My God! Never again! It would have to suffice for my Sunday worship that day.

The physical was a farce, I thought, in my tender condition. There were about ten lines with a bored physician at the end of each, who either put a cold stethoscope against your chest or banged your knee and instep with a small rubber hammer. Nobody found any flaws and so I moved along in agony until the last one, which stirred my interest, somewhat. It was a psychiatric evaluation that was something new to me. I tried to straighten up a little. That's the first time I noticed that I had forgotten to shave. By the time my turn came, I was fairly sober. The Psychiatrist had a canvas wall secluded area for a degree of privacy and he was seated at a bare desk. I sat in a wooden chair beside it. For a few seconds he said nothing, but stared into my reddened eyes, which stare I gave him back as much as I wanted to close them and go to sleep.

Finally he spoke. "Do you want to go back to combat?"

I wondered if it was a chance to stay home with Gwennie. Without one second hesitation I answered, "Hell no!"

Just as quickly he answered me. "You're normal. Send the next guy in when you leave, please?"

Sheez!

Parting with Gwen was even tougher than the one two weeks earlier. I had promised myself a few weeks with my beauty that had tragically become two nights. With real tears, I bid her adieu and headed back to the war zone. We put the girls on one train and ourselves scheduled for another – back to New York Harbor and another ocean voyage.

I didn't like my second voyage to England as well as the first. I found a few poker games, but no "arrangements" like the Athlon Castle, all-nighters with super food and other amenities. No private rooms, for four, either. I had a bunk in a room of fifty of the same and this was Officers Quarters! The days were boring. Not enough to read and little else to do besides BS sessions where those of us who had already experienced combat proceeded to thrill and scare those who hadn't, with stories of our talents and courage.

One incident spiced the trip for a while. I was lounging on the top bunk of four listening half-heartedly to a loud mouth "kiss and tell" pilot sitting on the bottom bunk directly below me telling everyone who would listen of his easy conquest of a 'broad' he met in Cleveland. As he proceeded in great detail, to sully the poor girl's reputation, a guy directly across from me began to stir from his prone position with increasing interest. A moment later, the ass bragging of his amorous affair was stupid enough to mention the girl's name, "in case any of you are stuck in Cleveland". There was a blur as the man across from me literally projected himself downward on the talker. It happened by a miraculous chance that the young lady in questions was his sister. I recall his screaming over and over as he pummeled the surprised lover that he would *kill* him. By the time the other dozen of us were able to pull him off, he had a pretty good start on doing that with his bare hands. It actually took most of us to restrain him. He was dragged away and I understand had to be locked up for some time where he continued to shout his intentions toward the sad sack whose story had started this. I am sure that guy learned something about buttoning his lip in the future. I know that I did and I was just an observer.

Ten days later we docked in Liverpool.

August, 1944 LOSSES
| | |
|---|---|
| Edward H. Pinkerton | MIA |
| Lloyd J. Overfield | MIA |
| Thomas F. Miller | POW |
| Charles H. Simonson | MIA |
| James D. Harbers | KIA |
| Don M. Beerbower | KIA |
| Wallace N. Emmer (Died as a prisoner) | POW |
| Robert M. Parkins | KIA |
| Garland N. Page, Jr. | POW |

| | |
|---|---|
| Thomas H Whelan | MIA |
| Arthur V. Mares | MIA |
| Charles E. Brown | MIA |
| Kenneth H. Dahlberg | MIA |
| Tadeusz Skowronek | MIA |
| Harry P. McClure | MIA |
| Norman B. Mayse | MIA |
| Geo. J. Hoehn, Jr. | MIA |
| Harold L. Gray | MIA |
| Caryl P. Bonotto | MIA |

| | |
|---|---|
| 354th AIR CLAIMS TO DATE | GROUND CLAIMS |
| 524 destroyed | 100/6/51 |
| 48 probably destroyed | |
| 259 damaged | |

★ ☆ ★ ☆ ★

CHAPTER 29

# PARIS!

THE DIFFERENCE OF OUR second arrival in England versus the first was like night and day. On our first time into Liverpool we had traveled as a unit, marched off the ship in line, knowing little of the future, in line to board a frigid train and on an all-night ride to Greenham Commons.

This time Gil and I were two veterans and alone with orders back to the 354th. "Where the hell are they?" we asked an I.O. "Somewhere in France". "Oh, great! How do we get there?" "We do have shuttle planes to Paris. Then you're on your own."

That sounded good! Paris–wow! I think I started singing the song my father taught me, 'Mademoiselle from Armentieres, Parlez vous'.

A few hours later we were on a C-47 in bucket seats with barracks bags at our feet and of course, the case of 'Old Grandad' I had lugged all the way from Spokane. It wasn't comfortable, but it was exciting and an hour or so later, we touched down at Le Bourget. I'm not exactly sure how the next part worked, but we were two officers wearing wings and a row or two of ribbons and carrying official orders to return to our group. We were given a bus ride from the airport to downtown and a hotel taken over by the Americans.

The ride was exciting seeing Paris and its life-style for the first time. I hollered at Gil who was looking out the right side while I watched the left. "Look at this! Look! Look!"

The bus had stopped at an intersection and I was feet away from a young mother with her little girl, maybe 5 years old. The young one needed a 'potty stop' and the mother lowered her panties, put her feet against the curb and held both hands while lowering her out over the street. A stream of 'piss' soon went into the gutter. I had never seen anything like that but I was told it's nothing. The French think nothing of relieving themselves publicly. I found that true a few blocks further when I saw my first sidewalk public urinal only chest high so users could easily be seen.

Later when our bus stopped on a main street we exited and were directed down a small side street to the hotel entrance. Just in front of us a taxi made a quick right turn into the street and in doing so, pinned a pedestrian to the wall. He screamed and the cab stopped and backed off a little to free him. While he didn't seem badly hurt, he screamed what sounded like the French equivalent of, "You rotten, no good SOB!" What amazed me even more was the cab driver shouting back as if he had been the wronged one. Then he drove off with the pedestrian shaking his fist in that direction but then continuing his walk as if nothing had happened.

"Gil," I said, "these people are truly different".

We went into the hotel.

The hotel was nice. I could imagine that it had been one of the better ones in its 'hey day'. We had separate rooms and while not large, mine was something else, especially the bed. I would nearly sink out of sight into the softest mattress I had ever seen or felt. The pillow, too, was huge and soft. After the tents and cots of A-2 and the stacked bunks on the ship, this was heaven.

The lobby had a wide marble staircase leading to a mezzanine level and there was a large public restroom at the head of the stairs. It had a prominent sign on the door stating in French and English "Men Only". The French mingled in such areas as I had already discovered on the bus ride from the airport. American WACS and nurses, however, objected to such familiarity during their ablutions and so the American hotel divided and labeled them.

Before we had been there very long, I had to use the head at the head of the stairs. A line of a dozen urinals lined the wall and a huge mirror in front of them so a user could see who opened the door behind them. I did that. It was a female carrying a pail and some rags. She went to the first urinal and began scrubbing it, and I did my best to turn away and still hit the bowl. I guess to her, it was no big deal. After I finished, she was only feet away and I nodded as I buttoned up. "Bon jour Monsieur". I nodded again and scrubbed and left. I'm with the nurses and WACS – I'm not ready for this kind of togetherness.

I met Gil and we ate an adequate, if not great meal in the dining room. In doing that, we luckily met another officer, a Second Lieutenant, wearing Silver Wings. Remember we still had no idea where our group was stationed. "Hi, what do you fly?" "Mustangs". "Great. What group?" He proudly answered, "The 354th!" Now we knew we could find it. "That's our group, 355th squadron", we said. "Hey, you must be Captains Gross and Talbot."

It was plain for him and everyone else to see that I still wore the Silver bars of a First Lieutenant and mention of rank rankled me whenever it came up. I pointed to my bars. "No, you've been promoted! I joined the 355th squadron in July and just got my first leave. Everybody in the squadron is waiting for you guys."

I couldn't believe it. Uncle George must have run out of people to promote, if he finally got to me. Gil went to his room and got a spare pair of railroad tracks and I proudly pinned them on. "Let's celebrate". F. Duncan McCleod, our new friend, volunteered to show us Paris and we freshened up to get ready for a night out.

I had no idea what 'peace time' Paris had been like, but I can report that newly liberated Paris, still at war, wasn't bad. Even with blackouts, the streets were bathed in moonlight on this October evening. McCleod showed for our night out with a date, not too bad looking. "Met her a couple days ago" he said, "doesn't understand a word of English, but who needs to talk". Watch this. "Isn't she a pig?" he said smiling and putting an arm around her shoulder. She demurely lowered her eyes and smiled.

I didn't think it was all that funny, but it was his date. He led us straight to a darkened door and inside the double black out security, we found a beehive of nightclub activity. It was crowded, but we eventually found a table and found that the French didn't share England's shortage of alcoholic beverages. After the first two drinks, McCleod and his mam'selle who had been playing footsy under the table, excused themselves for who knows what. Gil and I ordered another drink.

The club was jammed with both civilian and military. Over a few more drinks we had enjoyed people watching! Now, I had need of relief and went to the bartender. "Hey, buddy. Where is the men's room?" I got a quizzical look and a two handed gesture which I took to mean, "I don't know what you're talking about."

I used pantomime demonstrating washing my face and hands. His eyes lit up in understanding and in rapid fire French with gestures, I guessed it to be around the corner of the bar and down the stairs where I immediately went. There was only one door at the foot of the stairs and I entered. In front of me was one only enclosed toilet and in the open foot of space I could see high heels and panties around the ankles. I tiptoed out and ran back up the stairs.

To the bartender – "Men – not women!" I got a shrug. Since time was of the essence, I looked elsewhere for help and found a Sergeant making eyes at a pretty French girl.

"Hey, Sarge, where is the men's room?" He gave me the same directions I got from the bartender.

"No, there's a lady in there!"

"Oh. They use the same one here."

I again went down the stairs and carefully opened the door. This time there were size ten men's shoes visible. I patiently waited – hoping he would hurry. Then the door opened behind me and I found a very attractive lady entering.

The man exited nodding to us and I turned to the lady, "After you."

"No, Mo'sieur – apres vous."

I panicked and ran out the door. Fortunately I didn't have an accident before she came out. These French!

The following day we requisitioned a Jeep and got directions from McCleod and headed for the current 354th base – designated A-66.

★ ☆ ★ ☆ ★

September, 1944 LOSSES
    John D. Wigglesworth    MIA
    John S. Miller    POW
    Robert Reynolds    MIA
    Frank John Pavelick    KIA

354th AIR CLAIMS TO DATE    GROUND CLAIMS
    579 destroyed    117/6/55
    48 probably destroyed
    265 damaged

CHAPTER 30

# PARTIES, MUD AND FIVE DOWN

THE RETURN TRIP, PARIS to A-66, was uneventful. We did stop at a French country home to ask for directions and a glass of water. Water was not good enough for us they proclaimed so broke out a bottle of Champagne that was handed to me to open. I struggled for minutes, unsuccessfully, before a young man with no right arm (with the FFI we were told) took over and deftly tucked the bottle under his left arm. With probably two or three pushes with his thumb, popped the cork out to cheers from the rest of us.

Since thirst was satisfied, we moved on. It was mid-October 1944.

On the two-week voyage across the Atlantic, I had again felt strong temptation to salve the boredom of convoying with one little old container of 'Old Grandpappy', but I didn't! When I finished the last hundred feet down the boardwalk to my first tent home of this tour, I still had the whole case intact. I opened it and took my half out with verbal threats to Talbot who I was sharing space with, then re-roped the box and stalked out to the enlisted area where I found Smitty. I made him the most popular Sergeant in the Air Corps with half a case of good whisky of his very own. He deserved it! I looked at my reddened, swollen fingers that would rest now and decided I would do it again. The next morning Smitty was reassigned as my Crew Chief and whoever he crewed for in my absence could find a new one.

We never needed an excuse to celebrate what with a bit of pressure from daily combat missions; the officers club bar did a brisk business every night of the week without an excuse. Whenever something special did happen, and our return from stateside leave did qualify, maybe a little more enthusiasm went into the evening festivities.

The 355th had done themselves proud at the new station A-66. The 'O' Club was housed in a wooden pre-fabricated building liberated from the Germans and it contained a reasonable facsimile of a real bar with the addition of a fine upright piano for entertainment. The bad part was that our recent efforts to scrounge something to drink had brought only Champagne and I still remembered the hangover from our last night in Atlantic City. Nevertheless, it seemed appropriate for toasting our return. The other problem was a shortage of glasses, but then it would have been a bother to keep going back to the bar for refills if we had them. The system was simply for each guy to buy a bottle at a time and drink from that. It worked very well except that people began to feel the effects rather rapidly. The guys who had not had a leave as yet wanted a first-hand report on what it was like on the home front and we wanted to be brought up to date on the war.

I shed a real tear when I was told my friend and one of my favorite wingmen, Billie D. Harris, had been lost, clobbered in a frantic dog-fight shortly after I had headed home.

We had had losses, but not as crucial as the 353rd Squadron. Don Beerbower had taken command from Bradley the morning we left on leave. He was killed two hours later while strafing an enemy airdrome. Wally Emmer succeeded him and was lost on a flight that afternoon. By the end of the day, the 353$^{rd}$ had four different C.O.s!

After the stories were traded back and forth, the party gradually centered on the piano where, with Champagne jugs dangerously waiving back and forth to the music, we took turns volunteering some of the 1,000 verses to "That was a pretty good song. Sing me another one just like the other one. Sing me another one. Yo!"

If there had been a sober person present to evaluate the real caliber of the singing, it would have been interesting to hear what they had to say. But no matter, they all sounded great to us. After about an hour of such good sport, someone in the crowd, no doubt carried away by the camaraderie and wishing to demonstrate his good feelings, drew his '45' automatic and fired a shot through the roof for punctuation. It worked so well that within a few moments several others had imitated the act and it seemed like so much fun that another dozen of us had side arms drawn and aimed when Uncle George intervened.

I guess that's why some people are commanders and others aren't. The Colonel had had as much to drink as the rest of us, but had the presence of mind to shout, "Hold it!" With both hands in the air, he got the quiet he wanted and then with very measured speech said, "THERE WILL BE NO SHOOTING IN THE OFFICERS' CLUB!"

I was standing next to my dear friend, Maurice Long. Both of us had '45's drawn but had not fired when Uncle George ended the fun. We stood there for a moment and then I nudged Maurie. "He didn't say we couldn't shoot outdoors!" Maurie grinned and nodded and we quietly tiptoed to the door.

Outside it was raining steadily with a ceiling of about 100 feet. That meant that with the blackout, you could hold your hand a foot in front of your face and couldn't see it. Directly out the door of the club building was a small wooded area with trees whose trunks were no more than four inches thick, about three or four feet apart. There was a wooded boardwalk straight out the door for seven or eight feet that turned left and right to the living areas. Maurie made a suggestion, "You go right and I'll go over here and we'll have a little duel."

It sounded like fun! I was giggling as I stepped off the boardwalk and through the muck into the trees. I had advanced about 20 feet, still giggling when I heard the roar of a '45' and *heard* a slug pass close by. My laughter ceased as I went to a low crouch position and fired in the general direction of the flash of his shot, then quickly changed position so as not to advertise my location. Good thing! I saw another flash and heard the whine of another projectile. I fired back and this time got to my knees in the mud in another location. We traded shots until I heard Maurie, after the 7th round of his clip say, "Hey, I'm out of ammunition!"

"That's too bad. I have one left." I let fly toward the general vicinity of his voice. There was silence and I was almost afraid to ask, "Are you all right?" "Yeah!"

We both started laughing as I tried to find my way back to the club, arms outstretched to feel my way through the trees. The sound of the piano and a dozen officers was my beacon. We met at the door. I started to open the outer door when Maurie laid his arm across me to hold us up. "We can't go back in there with this evidence," referring to the guns. We both threw our empty, uncleaned '45's up on the roof and covered with mud, arms around each other, went back in.

Nobody had even missed us.

Can you imagine the condition of the guns when in the cold light of a new day we climbed to the roof to fetch them? It was still raining.

Besides catching up on all the happenings since our departure, a little partying to celebrate whatever, and seven shot duels with friends, there was the business of flying. I had not been in the air since June 28th and so October 15th strapped myself in a P-51B. After a few minutes of laying hands on all the familiar dials and handles, took it up for an hour. The weather was not to brag about, but gave me enough room to wring it out a little and find that it fit me just fine. I felt as if I had never left.

Our major mission at this time was supporting General Patton's Third Army. Our base had moved twice during my leave; first into Brittany and then to our present field designated A-66, and located on the banks of the Marne River. We lived in Squad Tents, both the officers and the enlisted. I got my job back as Assistant Operations Officer and moved in with Gil Talbot who was the OP's officer, Doc Shirley, our group Dentist and Doc Start, our Squadron Flight Surgeon.

We selected a nice area at the end of the row of pilots' tents and not too far from the French farmhouse which was the only permanent building in the area. It sat on a rise 200 yards east of our living area. The farmer still had a smallish flock of sheep that the Germans hadn't confiscated or eaten during their occupation. He and his dogs jealously guarded the flock now to keep us from doing the same. He grazed them in the field between the Marne River and the Marne Canal directly in front of our tent area. Several of us tried to engage him in conversation, but he spoke no English and our French was generally confined to 'Voulez – vous' and a few other phrases that didn't help. All we got from him was a little pointing at our tents, a little negative head shaking and a lot of gibberish that we decided meant he didn't like us being there. Doesn't he understand we are on his side? Forget it old man, we're here anyway. In a few weeks we would learn what he was really trying to tell us.

The weather stayed bad. Rain everyday making for terrible flying conditions and deteriorating living conditions. I got a new airplane, a P-51C that wasn't much different in most ways, but great with one important addition. It had a "Malcolm Hood" bulging out of the cockpit to allow much, much improved visibility, especially in that one most important area, your tail. Smitty and my armourer spent hours in the mud boresighting it to my particular wishes and otherwise preparing it. In the ten days since my first checkout, the squadron was able to fly only one mission. On the 25th it cleared a little and I took the new LIVE BAIT up for a two-hour slow time and orientation ride. Three days later, I started my second combat tour with a three hour dive-bombing mission to the Mossela River Bridge area, uneventful after laying the bombs. The next day wasn't.

I led Blue flight as top cover for two flights dive bombing in the Bookingen area. Jerry was evidently upset by our activity because he resisted, in force, for the first time in weeks.

Walt Meyler, a new jockey in our squadron, was hit on his dive-bombing run and bailed out. Shortly after that, a wave of 109's hit the group and a weird dogfight ensued. It was strange because of a partly broken layer of clouds at about 2000 feet, with the top a few hundred feet above that. Everybody I chased disappeared into it, up or down, including my own flight. I soon found myself alone in the world and climbed up on top. Being alone in a fighter when you know there are enemy fighters in the area is a very uncomfortable feeling. Survival depends on your head being on a swivel, something I tried to do. Very soon I spotted two P-51 silhouettes traveling directly away from me on top of the cloud deck and I poured a little more power on to catch them. I was probably 500 yards away, identifying myself by radio when between me and the haven of my two little friends, an ME-109 popped out of the clouds, saw them, but not me. For some unknown reason, maybe to lose speed, he dropped his landing gear and rolled a few degrees right to the tail of one of the Mustangs. I hardly had to adjust direction to close in on his butt. All four of my 50's concentrated on his tail, cockpit area and wing roots. He began to trail smoke and slowly rolled over, landing gear crazily pointing upward, then headed straight down through the low overcast. From the lack of violent evasive action I gathered that the pilot was done, but that victory, if it was one, was the most important of my life because it would be number 'five' and make me an *Ace!* All the pain and jealousy I felt when the group Aces were photographed a few months earlier would go away. I would be one of them!

In a not very smart maneuver because I didn't know what was below us, maybe a mountain, maybe a dozen of his 109 buddies, I had to know what happened to him so I rolled into a tight spiral and went straight down where I had seen him disappear. On the ground 1000 feet under me as I pulled out was a flaming crater, no parachute in sight. I felt sorry for the pilot, but my spirits were dancing on the clouds. I climbed up on top again and found the two Mustangs waiting for me. I told them of the victory so it would be reported in case I didn't get home and that's where we headed.

The group score on that day was 24 destroyed, 2 probably destroyed and 8 damaged. In doing it, we lost four of our own including Earl Depner of the 356th Squadron. He and I had been on our 30-leave trip and had played a few thousand hands of bridge from A-2 in the Omaha Beach area all the way across the ocean by ship and across the U. S. and then all the way back to our outfit again. Fortunately, he made his way back through the lines and rejoined us a few days later. The other three weren't that lucky.

I was. I was finally an *Ace!*

By the first of November we began to understand the French farmer's concern over the location of our living area. The ground grew soggy and then worse. We constructed boardwalks from area to area to stay out of the mud, but the water level continued to rise so that the walks had to be staked down to prevent their floating away. On the night of November 9th, both the Marne River and Marne Canal went over their banks and flooded the entire area. I found out about it when I heard Doc Start cursing the war, France, the River and anything else that came to mind. I woke up with the noise of his discourse and asked what the hell his problem was. He answered by suggesting I check my shoes that were carefully placed under my cot. I put my hand down to find water within inches of the bottom of the cot and my shoes long since floated away.

The rest of the night was spent piling everything from ground level onto the cots. No more sleep. At dawn we were able to see the total mess of our living site. The next thought was our planes. The field was also covered with a few inches of water quickly deepening and soon likely to do something Jerry hadn't been able to do, put us out of action. Those that could be moved were immediately flown to a landing strip on the other side of St. Disiere. A-64 which was perched high and dry. Some had to be towed, pushed and literally lifted out of the mud of A-66 to reach areas where they were able to taxi to the runway. By the time we got all the birds to A-64 that field was jammed with combat aircraft since ours was not the only field to be flooded out. What a place for the Luftwaffe to strike if the weather had been clear enough to see.

It was an eight-mile truck ride back to our living area where we waded in knee-deep water and mud to move to an area high enough to keep us dry. Even then it was necessary to lay the boardwalk through water six or so inches deep to get to certain facilities, one of those being the Officers' Club. Pilots and crew personnel trucked back and forth to be able to fly missions and we never missed a day if the weather was good enough to get off the ground.

As if we hadn't had enough trouble, Gil developed a new problem of his own. He and Doc Start woke me about midnight a week or so after the flood. The right side of Gil's lower jaw was swollen double normal and he was miserable with the pain. The flashlight showed Doc Shirley's bed was empty and had not been slept in. Start was telling Gil what had to be done. Although I had known him for over two years, I found out for the first time that he was a Christian Scientist who didn't believe in treatment. Through the pain, Doc convinced him he didn't have time to heal it by faith, that it would have to be lanced immediately. We left Gil sitting on his cot and Doc and I dressed to go look for our dentist friend. On the way, we roused a corpsman to aid in whatever would be done.

Doc Shirley was sitting in the 'O' Club talking to one of our young pilots and he was absolutely stinko. When we told him the problem, he bravely stood up and promptly fell down. We had the corpsman make a pot of coffee and we poured several cups into Doc. He still couldn't walk without help. After more coffee, we started for the dental tent area with Shirley claiming, as do most drunks, "I'm fine. I'll be just fine." He wasn't.

Start and I came up with a plan. I was walking on his right side and Doc Start on his left. At a signal, I let go and stepped back. Start gave him a gentle nudge and Shirley stumbled off the walk and face first into six inches of cold water. We immediately retrieved him with apologies, and then on another signal, sent him headfirst off the other side. After about four dives on the way to his 'office', he began to demonstrate a somewhat remarkable recovery. I ran to get Gil while they poured one more cup of black coffee in him and readied him for the operation.

I was glad it wasn't me and Gil kept his eyes closed so he didn't know what was happening. Doc Shirley selected a very sharp looking scalpel and with a flourish and only a little weave, approached the swollen area and plunged in. I watched until I saw what comes out. Then because I didn't care to be sick myself, turned away. By 0300 we were all back in bed.

On the 17th of November we were officially moved to A-64 near St. Disiere, France. Patton is a hard man to keep up with!

October, 1944 LOSSES:
- Sheftall Coleman, Jr. — MIA
- Thomas H. Whelan — POW
- R. L. Dowell, Jr. — POW
- Fred D. Buckner — KIA
- Robert B. Harrison — KIA
- Ira J. Bunting — POW
- Kenneth J. Herman — KIA
- Earl G. Depner — MIA
- John R. Bowers — POW
- Walter P. Meyler — POW
- Richard J. Boes — KIA

354th AIR CLAIMS TO DATE
- 606 destroyed
- 50 probably destroyed
- 274 damaged

GROUND CLAIMS
122/6/55

## CHAPTER 31
# I GET SHOT DOWN

THE MORNING OF NOVEMBER 18th, PR guy Brownie called Squadron from Group and said my hometown paper –"The Spokesman Review" – has asked for a photo of Harry Fisk from the 356th Squadron and me, the two remaining Spokane pilots with the group. It was fine with me, but I was leading a mission with takeoff scheduled at 1500. It would have to be taken before that. Brown said he would round up Harry and get back to me. I didn't hear for a while, in fact, forgot it until he called back around 1400 and wanted me on the 356th flight line.

"Hey man, I don't know if I can make it". He assured me it wouldn't take more than a few minutes so I went for it. I was nearly ready so hurried to finish in order to go directly from photo to my plane. I zipped up my flight jacket, pulled helmet on and grabbed my gloves, then headed for the parachute storage. The bin that normally held my chute was empty.

"Oakley!" The corporal in charge of such things came a running.

"Where the hell is my parachute?"

"It's being re-packed, Captain. You'll have to borrow somebody elses."

A quick look at my watch showed 1430 I grabbed a chute from another bin and slung it over my back. Sgt. Cahill took me to the 356th area while the rest of my flight headed for our flight line. The pictures taken in front of Harry's Jug took five minutes, then back in the Jeep and all out to our flight line. Before Cahill drove away, I stooped to fasten the leg straps on my borrowed parachute. They didn't come within five inches of being long enough to fasten! It was 1445 and I was supposed to start my engine in five minutes. I stopped to think seriously, hell; you really never need these things except for a backrest! Should I or shouldn't I? Then I decided you really never know and I jumped back into the Jeep and had Cahill highball back to the parachute area. I grabbed another chute and fastened it right there. It fit. Back in the Jeep and to the flight line. I arrived just at 1450. My engine was started two minutes later and with no real warm up, I taxied out, leading the flight to the runway.

We were off the ground exactly on time. A little over an hour later I would be hanging in that borrowed chute for the first and only time in my life. Later I felt chills down my back when I thought back to the decision of going with the chute that wouldn't fasten. If I had, the force on opening could have shot me out like a greased pig from the swine chute and left an empty parachute to drift to earth.

Who says a mother's prayers don't work?

I think it is true that the Almighty really does give those in combat situations, the feeling that the terrible things that happen around you could never happen to you. I suspect that's why infantry troops can crawl out of trenches and charge. I know for sure – that's why after a year of aerial combat watching friend and foe fall from the skies in flames, I was sure it could never happen to me.

On this day we had a very routine armed RECCE mission. Instructions – find any enemy movement and destroy it! Forty minutes after take off I had a beauty – six German lories crawling on a narrow road east to west. The decision required no time at all. The execution was only a gentle turn into our dive attack position. Kinmon was on my wing, his second combat mission, never had he fired his guns; and this was a great place to start with no return fire that we could see.

All the trucks stopped on the first pass, and one in line of my fire burst into flames before I passed over their position. I pulled up in a casual turn left and observed three of the six burning and destroyed. With no opposition, I decided to make another pass so none of them would move again. On the second pass, spread nearly in line abreast, we went after the remaining. Kinmon on my wing was overly excited with the success of this strike against the enemy and had pulled a few feet in front of me. No sweat – I had no indication that our efforts were answered by return fire. I waved him back and held our position ten feet off the ground waiting for him to drop back. If I had made my turn left at that altitude, my element would drag in the ground. In the next few seconds, I was surprised to find great numbers of German uniformed troops in those fields, on their knees firing rifles at the formation. "Those dirty bastards," I mentioned to my flight. After he dropped back into proper position, I began my right turn and climb. Never would the threat of rifle fire threaten my armor-plated Mustang! I was wrong!

As we climbed away from our victorious attack on the convoy, I counted and reported the visible holes in "LIVE BAIT" that I could see; four through the right wing, two in the left and one that rather concerned me. Metal erupted outward on the cowling about two feet in front of the windshield. That SOB had to go through the engine to come out there. I thought no more about it as I continued to climb.

At 8000 feet it concerned me! We spread into a mutual support formation headed for home. A mental bell rang when I found my engine coolant temperature gauge banging on the post – well past the 'no go' mark. No coolant, no engine! Before I even throttled back, I felt the power loss. Those dirty bastards. They got me. And, with rifles!

I had to say it once on the radio before it sank in. "I have to get out of this SOB." What am I saying? This time it's me! No power. My beautiful Mustang began to glide like a rock! Even with power off, the engine idling soon froze up and began to smoke and burn. I had the presence of mind to call Ragbone for a homing. "Setting 275 – forty miles to go to our lines. Can you make it?" It pained me to say it, but I had to be honest. With the present rate of decent, more like 40 yards, no way forty miles. I made preliminary moves to get out. The red handle for the canopy release that I had looked at and noted a hundred times. This time I pulled it and the canopy simply disappeared as promised. My air speed was about 115 MPH. It seemed so easy to look over the side and visualize easy exit that I was not concerned, as I should have been. The different ways to get out crossed my mind only briefly. Roll over and drop out. No way! It looked too easy to dive out!

At this point I started the strained messages of bravado I had had a part in when friends had been forced down before. "Hey you guys, take care. George, you owe me 40 damn dollars. Don't forget it, cause I won't." I used probably two minutes of radio time in my ever-increasing glide angle time to pass and receive these dumb comments. I pulled my seat belt release and it fell free. With a silent prayer on my lips, I lunged toward the left wing. I was probably three to four inches off the seat before I hit the shoulder straps, not fastened, but laying across my shoulders enough to drop me back in the seat. That effort had taken all the guts I could summon. And, in failure, I decided to relax for a moment. I picked up the microphone and said another fond farewell to the flight.

That done I eliminated the cause of the failure by throwing the shoulder straps back and off. No seat belt. No shoulder straps. I could see no reason why a dive out would not be 'duck soup'. Deep breath...Look at the place on the left wing I would dive for. Short prayer, then leap!

No seat belts or shoulder straps held me back. I made it inches off the seat before I hit the end of the radio cord, plugged into my helmet. It snapped my head around and I dropped back in the seat. "This is ridiculous!" As long as I was back and the radio was plugged in, I picked up the 'mike' and said another goodbye to the guys. Unplug the radio. Do the same preliminary steps, especially the prayer, then leap!

The leap couldn't have been too powerful. Since nothing else restrained me, I got my head out into the 100-mile an hour plus slipstream. My goggles from the top of my helmet were stretched six inches away from my head. That startled me enough that I pulled my head back. The goggles slammed back against my head and I dropped back in the seat. "I can't believe this!"

As long as I was back, I plugged the cord back in and said goodbye once again, then threw the helmet on the floor and jumped. IT WORKED!

While I dove for the wing, I never hit a thing. I found myself barrel-rolling lazily through the air and I pulled the ripcord instantly. Wham! I stopped as if I had caught up on a giant hook. A look up and I reassuringly found that beautiful white canopy spread over my head. I was about 2000 feet when I left my bird. Before I reached 1999, I started a prayer out loud. The sound of my voice scared the hell out of me. I could not believe the quiet I found myself hanging in! In the distance, 1900 feet straight down, I could hear gunfire, both big stuff and small arms. But in my area, deathly still. Because the parachute drifts with the wind, no sound of breeze, or anything else, in my prayer, I got as far as "...who art in heaven..." before the sound caused me to stop. I finished it silently, to myself.

I had almost forgotten my beautiful P-51C until the sight

and sound of the explosion grabbed my attention. Man alive! Was I glad I was not sitting in it at that moment! Now I took stock of the situation. There was obviously fighting below me but I couldn't do anything about that. Speaking of below me. The ground didn't seem to be getting any closer. I looked up to see if I was caught on anything. I did notice I was drifting backwards. From the distant past, I remembered that one should not land that way. People have been dragged to death, unable to get to their feet, turn and land with the wind. The big problem was I couldn't remember how that was done. I wound up my arms and swung in circles several times with varying velocities and each time, I found I returned to exactly the same direction. I was still trying when I hit the ground.

I certainly had always been in favor of regulations in the military, but on this particular day, I was hard-pressed to find one I hadn't broken, at least regarding uniform. Suntan uniforms were 'verboten' in the European Theatre, but RHIP or at least for second tour veteran pilots. I was wearing khaki shirt and pants with absolutely *no* insignia of any kind, hadn't had time to change from another shirt before take off. I usually wore my "dog tags" but they irritated my neck. This morning I left them on the apple box nightstand by my cot. We didn't wear oxfords when flying, always high top boots because, heaven forbid, if you had to bail out, the shock of chute opening could pop them off. We were expected to escape if we dropped behind enemy lines and that would be hard to do in stocking feet. Yes, I was wearing oxfords. Fortunately they stayed on.

The government had developed new jackets for our wonderful guys in mechanized tank monsters. They were padded olive green body with a warm, comfortable fur collar – really neat. Someone, I swear I don't know who, had liberated a few on their way to the front. I was given one and had it on. The tank men hadn't even seen them yet. On top of that, inherited from my father's side of the family (and my blonde mother) I had the Aryan look, blonde hair and blue eyes.

As I experimented twirling on the way down, I discovered a small village in the direction I was headed and fairly close. Another warning came to mind. If you are captured let it be by military, not civilian. Many civilians had lost loved ones and they weren't concerned with rules of the Geneva Convention. You might find yourself impaled on a pitchfork or such implement. I made a mental note to head away from the village when down.

I hit in fairly soft ground about 20 feet from a narrow two-lane road, surprised that it didn't seem to hurt at all. I went over backward but my chute collapsed and I bounced up quickly gathering the parachute and diving for a large bush bordering the road. The ground fire was still audible but not right around me. I got out of my harness and stuffed the chute under the bush to hide it.

Within two minutes while still deciding my plan of action, I heard a heavy vehicle rumble into the open field. I peered around my bush at what I saw to be a German half-track (truck front and tank track rear). Two helmeted soldiers were standing up with raised rifles looking for me. It's hard to hide in a descending parachute so they know I'm here. I might as well give up now. I raised my arms and stepped out into the open. The soldiers spotted me and with rifles at ready beckoned me toward their vehicle. With heavy heart, I started the fifty yards separating us. After maybe ten paces, I noticed a crude white star, hand-painted over the German cross. Also, those were our helmets on the soldiers. They're GI's! I'm not going to sit out the war in a POW camp!

I put my arms down and started running toward them. Both raised their rifles aiming directly at me. I shouted, "Don't shoot. I'm American." They didn't, fortunately. I continued toward the half-track, arms raised and constantly chattering to keep them assured. While my English sounded genuine, the aforementioned uniform and physical appearances didn't look that way. They didn't believe me! These guys were both from New York I found out. I could guess from their accents. I was told to keep my arms up while we talked.

"Where are you from?"

"Spokane, Washington" I responded.

"Uh, what's the capitol of Washington? One asked.

"Olympia!"

He turned to his buddy, "Is that right?" "How the hell would I know!" the guy answered. They tried something new. "Who da' Brooklyn Dodgers?" Thank God I was a baseball fan. I told them including a run down of the entire National League and started on the current roster of my favorite team, the St. Louis Cardinals before they were convinced. "Okay, okay. Get in. We got to get outa' here!"

I put one foot on the track wheels before I remembered my parachute. "Can I get it?" "Alright. Hurry!" I ran back to the brush while they wheeled the transportation after me. I balled up the chute and climbed in. My ride was about 50 feet out onto the road and east toward the village I had decided to avoid when we met a Jeep coming in the opposite direction. The driver was a black PFC and his passenger standing like a ship Captain at the 'bridge' was a bird Colonel. The Jeep was completely armored, including the windshield with only slits for the driver and passenger to see through when seated.

My GI friends explained who I had said I was and hopefully proved and the Colonel ordered me into the Jeep for a ride to his headquarters. When I was seated in the back with my parachute he turned and offered me a cigarette. I needed one! From bailout to this moment was probably twenty minutes. It seemed longer and not until I reached for the cigarette did I realize that the "D" ring with it's three-foot cable dangling, was still clutched in my white knuckled right fist! Nothing nervous about me!

I was in the Jeep for half an hour and only one thing about it sticks in mind. The Colonel, who never sat down, cursed and shouted at his driver from minute one, until we stopped at a two-story farmhouse that would be temporary headquarters for the Armored Group for the night. Never have I heard one human treat another like that. The driver never uttered a sound in the entire trip but from my rear seat position, I could watch the muscles of his jaw tense and flex. Outranked by a few grades and beholden for what I hoped would be return to my outfit, I couldn't say anything. I've wished ever since that I had anyway.

We did detour slightly to the crater where "LIVE BAIT" had hit the ground, maybe to verify my story that it was an American plane. An awesome sight! Again, I gave thanks that I hadn't been in it.

The farmhouse had been a German headquarters only hours before we arrived. This was the way Patton moved his army across the countryside. Our people were still moving in and I was pretty well ignored. This would be our resting-place tonight as dusk was upon us. Within five minutes, we heard a muffled explosion upstairs. The krauts had booby-trapped the building. They told me not to move around too much until they checked it out. I wondered if I looked so dumb, that I had to be told! If I hadn't been standing in a passageway, I wouldn't have moved either foot until dawn. I didn't move very far, only to a corner where furnished with a box of K Rations and a very coarse German blanket, I curled up with my parachute for a little rest and sustenance.

Maybe dozed fitfully for a bit. Can't remember much, until I heard the Colonel and another officer talking earnestly with a tall, black-clad and beret-capped stranger. Nobody objected when I moved closer out of curiosity. It was a Frenchman. His accented English, if not his appearance, told me that. He was huge, at least six inches taller than my 5'11" and with broad muscular shoulders tapering to a wasp waist. A broad leather belt around his waist held numerous and a strange array of weaponry from grenades to an automatic pistol, one of the largest 'hunting knives' I had ever seen and several wire loops with wooden handles at each end. I listened but stayed out of the conversation that centered on what they knew of the enemy troops ahead of the Third Army. The Frenchman's face was as blackened as his pants, boots and turtleneck sweater, and a truly awesome character. After a while, they ended the conversation and with firm handshakes all around, Pierre (that was what they said his name was) left, into the darkness.

"Who the hell was that?" I asked.

"He's FFI. We drop him behind German lines at night and he raises all the hell he can with their already confused, retreating troops."

My God! I shivered with the thought of an unsuspecting enemy sentry who suddenly found one of those wire garrotes around his neck! Well, they deserve what they get!

At dawn I opened my eyes still shivering, but not for the German sentries, but because those damn scratchy blankets were next to worthless for warming tired bones.

We were southeast of Metz and the Third Army was driving north to surround that city. When I could locate an officer who seemed to have a moment, I asked what they planned to do with me. I had no desire to fight the war from this level. I was told to sit tight. They would soon have transportation back for me. A selfish thought occurred to me. I wondered if Gwen had already been notified that I was missing in action. Maybe it wouldn't hurt to have her concerned for a short time and get me a little sympathy, and they could tell her I was back today before she grieved too much. Just maybe the letter flow would be better after a shock like that.

I stayed near the house until about 1100 when somebody brought in a grinning staff sergeant who informed me he was a pilot who would fly me back to A-64. We Jeeped to a hillside field (?) where an L-2 Cub was parked on the edge of a cleared hillside which sloped gently down to at least a 20% grade. I couldn't believe it! "We're going to fly off this?" I asked. "Sure!"

I reluctantly got into the back seat and the Sergeant handed in my wadded up parachute and harness filling my lap to my chin. He spun the prop to life and jumped into the front seat.

I think at that moment, I felt like an old tired gunslinger faced with the neophyte in the next town. He wanted to test me to show me how good he was and I didn't want to learn. I just wanted to go home…safely.

After latching the door, with no warm up, no MAG check (God I hope he just came in this thing and knows it's ready), he poured on the coal and started laterally across the hillside. It was probably no more than a ten-degree grade, but it seemed like 45 to me as we rolled across the hillside, right wing down. When he reached about 40 MPH, he kicked right rudder and we started downhill. I'll be damned if we didn't get airborne before we got to the bottom. Sarge grinned back at me. I would rather he watched where we were going. Nevertheless, within 40 minutes we touched down on A-64. We rolled the cub into the 355 area and I was waiving to pilots and crew of my gang. I held center stage when I got out. Nothing would do but I slip into the harness and show off the chute. This time the wind was blowing and if I had been backwards, I might have been dragged. That was enough of that. As soon as I determined that the chute had already been written off, we cut it up for hot pilot scarves for the pilots in the 355.

I was back and they hadn't even told my family I had been gone!

November, 1944 LOSSES:
| | |
|---|---|
| Horace P. Stanley | MIA |
| Allen B. Prosise | POW |
| Frank Q. O'Connor | POW |
| Richard A. Stayton | KIA |
| Edward E. Hunt | KIA |
| Max A. Steiner | KIA |
| Clayton K. Gross | MIA |
| Richard F. Poole | POW |

| | |
|---|---|
| Russell W. Erb, Jr. | KIFA |
| Frank P. Davey | POW |
| William F. Koerner | MIA |
| Ivan R. Henry | MIA |
| Haydon H. Halton | MIA |

354th AIR CLAIMS TO DATE
   661 destroyed
   52 probably destroyed
   293 damaged

GROUND CLAIMS
172/7/73

★ ☆ ★ ☆ ★

CHAPTER 32

# BACK TO FIGHTING WITH BIG CHANGES – P-47'S

From my horseback-riding days, I remembered the advice, "If you get bucked off. Get back on before you lose your nerve." That seemed a logical bit of advice for a pilot who had bailed out and so I climbed in a P-51 a couple days later and went for a ride. I was at home again. On the 26th, I flew a three-hour dive-bombing mission to a railroad yard in the Frankfurt/Darmstadt area. One bomb hung up which skewered my dive slightly but no problem. I shook it off.

The next day the Squadron made a major change from our beautiful Mustangs to the monstrous P-47 Thunderbolt or 'Jug' as they were called. The 356th Squadron had converted two weeks earlier.

All of us had to go through the usual cockpit time and check to make sure we were familiar with instrument and control positions. Because of my day and a half absence, I was a little behind and didn't feel a great urgency to catch up. It didn't help any when we had an accident the first day of flying.

The pilot was not airborne before reaching

the line of trees at the end of the runway and took one out with his P-47. At the Commander's conference two days and an another very similar accident later, the matter came up.

In the question session after a briefing someone spoke up, "Colonel, about those trees at the end of the runway…"

The Colonel interrupted, "Yeah. I know. They're coming down."

The originator's answer brought the house down. "Yeah, one tree at a time."

A couple days after that, I was ready to try it. Our squadron line chief had one plane that had just arrived and needed a test hop. I thought it would be as good a time as any to take my first ride, so I volunteered. The Jug looked bigger than ever when I strapped myself in it and waved the crew chief off to put all those 2700 horses to work. I took my time in engine warm-up and taxi time to the end of the strip. At the far end I could see the line of remaining trees and I gulped and pushed the throttle to the firewall. The great radial engine roared and I started my roll. I knew of the water injection system, but had never used one, and in the middle of the roll, I was a little reluctant to experiment. When I went by the tower truck, I had enough speed to get the tail up but that was all. I could see the tree-line fast approaching and very well felt a cold sweat on my forehead and the back of my neck. A few seconds later I made the judgement that I had to get off the ground now or not at all. With both hands on the stick, I pulled back with all the strength I could muster. I actually felt as if I lifted it off myself, all 25,000 pounds of it.

Now we come to the bitter bit. There was no way of holding it. I managed with brute strength to climb just above the treetops and could not get it any higher. With both hands holding the stick, the throttle remained wide open as it had been for take-off and I was rapidly gaining speed, but no altitude. Any experienced pilot knows the answer, even on his first ride. The question was, could I hold it with one hand long enough to hit the trim tab? I had to, and did, and immediately the nose went down, not up. I had an increased pressure to fight. In a cold sweat, I thought over my situation. I knew I had rolled the trim tab back. Could they have forgotten to tell me they work backwards in the P-47, or could the crew have installed it backwards? Since I was fast running out of strength, I had to find out. To hold it above the treetops, I was now skimming by two to three feet and freed my left hand; I slid my arm around the stick to hold it in the crook of my right arm. Then, whispering a prayer, I slowly rolled the trim tab wheel forward and the pressure eased! I spun it more and the jug finally began to climb. I was probably ten miles from the strip but I was flying and alive!

For the next 40 minutes, I experimented. It seemed to me that the monster cruised at about 190 MPH with normal throttle setting. It did the same in a power climb and when I simulated a dive bomb attack, I found myself at the fantastic speed of 190, or possibly a mile or two faster. I brought it back convinced we were ruined by the loss of our Mustangs. It happened that the crew, not my own, had installed the trim tab backwards and they apologized profusely. "Hey, no problem. I made it," I said. But I did develop an intense dislike for the P-47 on that first ride. I would find some positives in the next few weeks of using them in combat.

I developed great respect for the firepower of those eight 50-caliber machine guns in the P-47 over the next few missions. I already knew they hit like a hundred sledgehammers from the time one of Gabreski's lads had mistaken my Mustang for an ME-109 and clobbered me in the Berlin area. Still I wasn't ready for the demonstration I got while strafing a train headed toward the battle lines early in December. I made a strafing run at a boxcar from a 90-degree angle. It didn't blow up as some had done under those circumstances. It simply tipped over on its side, off the tracks and partially taking the cars on each side with it! I couldn't believe the power of my guns!

I would fly a dozen missions in the next few weeks using my gun power to destroy a dozen trains and road vehicles and dropping a few dozen bombs. We were truly destroying Germany's ability to move in daylight and Patton's troops were taking advantage of it. Dare I dream this war could end! No, we move forward again to A-98 and it goes on.

I went to Paris for a short R & R with the intention of using the 354th 'Apartment'. After the liberation of Paris it had somehow become a Mecca for most of the Group officers.

How it came about, I don't know, but knowing Bowers Espy, it did not surprise me. I don't know if it was in existence when Talbot and I passed through on our return, or was developed later. Of course, it was unofficial and word of mouth was the only advertisement. I decided to try it. I never got there.

I had been given the address but Paris streets were not easy to find or follow. My search went by a bar and I paused there for directions and a drink that led to conversation with another pilot and another drink or two. He intended (horrors) to try a local house of ill repute about which he painted an exciting picture. I tagged along.

I am not that well acquainted with 'whore houses' but this one surely was different from what I had heard. Entry was by a long narrow stairwell. A single door at the top opened into what appeared to be a small 'Bistro'. There was a bar and several small tables. There was some cushy over-stuffed furniture and probably a dozen people – half female and only one other uniformed man when we arrived. The women were clothed but not overly so. One wore a nearly 'see-through' outfit.

We sat at the bar to survey the group. I ordered a drink and discovered that the attractive lady bartender spoke very good English. A Frenchman sitting in a lounge chair soon began singing what I assumed was a love song, very good considering no musical accompaniment. Everyone stopped talking and listened, applauding when he finished. Me too, although I had no idea what the words were.

Occasionally a couple would leave the room, but most simply enjoyed the entertainment. One of the girls broke into song and it was good as well. I was enjoying conversation with the pretty bar girl, ordering an occasional drink.

I sat there the entire night enjoying what I thought was becoming a relationship.

Hours later, at dawn, the young lady asked me to go downstairs and wait for her. "We will go to my apartment." I was excited. I waited outside in anticipation, smoking a cigarette, when the door opened and my lady wheeling a bicycle exited. She mounted it and pedaled away, leaving me to holler, "Wait. Wait."

She was gone and I was alone and tired. Nevertheless, I had thoroughly enjoyed the evening in a whorehouse – and never even held hands with a female!

In the moves from one advanced landing ground to the next, we often found the 'field' facilities not quite ready. That is, the strip might be operational if you didn't mind a few bumps or a little slope right or left in the middle of the take-off or landing run, but definitely needing work.

They didn't leave them that way for long. Lacking major equipment to do the job, the French made up for it with manpower. I have seen a fall morning dawn with 500 Frenchmen arriving on bicycles, each with a knapsack and each knapsack with a loaf of French bread projecting from one corner and the neck of a wine bottle from the opposite side.

A dump truck would arrive to deposit a load of rock near the mat and the manpower would render a head-size boulder to gravel size with muscle and sledge hammers. When the gravel was ready, it would be placed in the low areas in need and foot tamped to level by dozens and dozens of the workers. It was primitive, but it worked.

Two things about the workers were unforgettable. When lunchtime arrived, the entire crew seated themselves on the ground with their backpacks. The routine from then on was so similar with all those hundreds it seemed choreographed. Everybody had a loaf of bread, a hunk of cheese, a bottle of wine and a knife. The bread was tucked under the left arm, the cheese held in the left hand. The wine bottle, once opened, was held between the crossed legs and the knife was in the right hand. Each would deftly slice a piece of bread, then ditto a slice of cheese, eat it and immediately wash it down with a gulp of wine. Then repeat again and again. I suppose in that mass of men, there were left handers who did it oppositely, but they all looked the same to me. It was fascinating to watch!

The other unforgettable habit was a deadly one. When it was time for a mission take off, or return, the French had to be cleared from the strip. They lined both sides of the runway for it's entire length. It was a weird feeling to face that gang on take off, a corridor of faces reminding me of the thousands who lined a fairway to watch Ben Hogan tee off in a tournament. They wouldn't have dared offer me that narrow opening to hit a golf ball through, but Ben seemed always to keep it down the middle to give the crowd more confidence. The same with the workers!

With each takeoff run, they crowded in a little more despite desperate hand signals to move back. On day two of this procedure, Jack Bradley blew a tire on take off and careened into the crowd. The whirling propeller threw body parts of the ten or eleven Frenchmen who died a hundred feet in the air. Believe me, they moved back for the rest of the mission, but with each day, they closed back in until a week later, someone landing lost control and ground-looped into the mob again with similar results.

Would you believe they crowded back in day by day again? At least we had to stay alert on take off and landings!

War ending or not. I felt need of and was granted a two-week leave. The Air Corps had taken over a large resort hotel on the French Riviera. Max Lamb from the 356th Squadron and I took advantage of the offer.

A half-hour after his scheduled arrival time, the C-47 that was to fly us down, finally arrived. I never met a Fighter Pilot who didn't like being one and probably the number one reason was –you were the boss! You had the best seat; the only one and you alone controlled what you did in the air. The worst thing you could do to a fighter pilot was to put him in the back of a big bird where he not only had no control but also couldn't *see* what was going on. For that reason *and* his tardy arrival, Max and I immediately decided the '47 pilot was an untalented imbecile. A little later he proved we were right. He took off from our field and was supposed to fly 15 lumbering minutes to another base to pick up more R & R guys. Believe it or not, he set a reciprocal heading 180 degrees from the course needed, to go to the next stop.

After a 15-minute trip and no base below where it should have been, he discovered his error and turned about. That meant a 30-minute ride to get where we should have been much earlier. We were livid until we landed to discover a number of ME-109's had strafed the field 40 minutes earlier. If our pilot had not made a stupid error, we would have been an unarmed sitting duck over that base at the time of the hit. I guessed the good Lord had guided us the wrong way to start the trip. Max and I decided to drink to that as soon as we landed, and we did.

Our hotel, the Martinez was great! A real luxury spot in better times. It had great, very large rooms. The bath alone was as big as many hotel rooms I had experienced. It had something new to both of us, a bidet. Max decided it was some fancy kind of urinal and tried it, but the flushing water went straight up so we decided to, henceforth, use the toilet we understood.

The room cost us the equivalent of $3.75 a day, each, and that included breakfast and dinner. Lunch was on your own. Having experienced the exceptional period of poker and the crap table in the weeks before, I arrived on the Riviera with $1400 in my pocket. I guessed I would have at least $1200 left over after our two weeks.

Most of the money had gone for alcohol at a small bar we discovered near the hotel. Both the owner and the pretty mademoiselle who tended bar spoke English, so we settled into a routine of an eye opener about 1000 that dragged into a nooner or more. Then casual drinking through the afternoon until time to find a night club with dancing for the evening. I met a cute little girl on about the third day and we enjoyed dancing, a beer or two and even a little smooching in a doorway before she let me know she had to go home now. No serious romance. She didn't speak English and my French wasn't much past the voulez-vous stage, but we did communicate with eyes and gestures and found we could get along. I don't remember her name because I probably never understood it when she told me.

I remember running out of film for my camera but when I found a store that had the proper Eastman film available, the price was something like $25 a roll. I told them to shove it, but before I got to the door, the proprietor had an offer. A roll for one pack of American cigarettes? Deal!

I was broke, but happy, after eight days and we caught the next flight back to A-98 and the war.

On December 4, 1944, the Group diary read, "a rainy – no fun day. A mission got off late with fifteen P-47's to the Pirmasens area of Germany. AJ-I did not return".

The next day we found out why. AJ-I was found a few miles from the base, shot down by our own anti-aircraft. The pilot, M. J. Slavlan, was dead.

Now just a damn minute! On June 26th I had watched a P-38 pilot murdered by the anti-aircraft gunners around the perimeter of A-2. The poor bastard had evidently had a mechanical problem and just as I had done a week or so earlier, decided not to chance the channel. He circled at about 800 to 900 feet and lowered his flaps and gear. There is no mistaking that familiar silhouette. Even in the gathering dusk, the markings were plainly visible. When he turned on final and began his landing flair at slightly over 100-MPH, the anti-aircraft opened up at him and killed him. The Lightning flipped over and into the ground. Those of us who saw it happen, charged the nearest gun emplacement. "What the *hell* are you doing?"

A grim-faced Lieutenant answered, "I have orders to shoot at anything in the air after sunset. That was 1932 tonight and that's what it was when we fired!" I absolutely could not believe what I heard!

"Write to that guy's family and explain that will you?" I added a dirty word and left. Now a few months later, one of our own was dead – probably in the same manner. I hated German ack-ack gunners who made it so rough to attack their fields. Now I felt the same way about our own. I made up my mind that if I thought they fired at me, I would shoot back, remembering their futile efforts at the first buzz bombs. I will guarantee I shoot straighter than they do. I think we have a weak link in our team.

★ ☆ ★ ☆ ★

December, 1944 LOSSES

| | |
|---|---|
| Gordon T. McEachron | MIA |
| M. J. Shavlan | KIA |
| Eldon E. Posey | MIA |
| William E. Boyden | POW |
| Ralph J. Tyler | MIA |
| John W. Postle | POW |
| Alvin E. Groenbach | MIA |
| Franklin D. Chamberlin | MIA |
| William B. Howell | MIA |

Harold S. Price  MIA
William H. Bush  MIA

354th AIR CLAIMS TO DATE  GROUND CLAIMS
686 destroyed  173/7/73
53 probably destroyed
301 damaged

## CHAPTER 33
# MUSINGS AT THE END OF 1944

**W**INTER IN FRANCE WAS bitter! If the 'pot bellied' stove was not stoked and fed constantly, a triple layer of clothes and bedding was necessary. On one particular morning I woke up, curled under as many blankets and coats as I could pile on me for warmth. The pot-bellied stove had gone out and it was cold enough to see my breath when I poked my head out.

And what did I see? Brueland was stripped to the waist and was taking a sponge bath with cold water.

"Are you nuts?" I asked.

"Haven't had a bath for awhile. Thought I might be getting ripe."

I put my head back under the covers and thought about it. When I stuck my nose out again, decided – no way.

We were living in squad tents with those gorgeous pot-bellied stoves to combat zero degree temperatures outside, *if* you could remember to fire them up and keep them that way. The ground was frozen solid and a thin layer of snow covered the world outdoors. Getting up on a morning like this was not the worst part. Warm clothes were available; especially those fleece lined jackets and boots. I set new speed records from 'sack' to clothes every day of the winter.

Now, being comfortably dressed was not the end of torture. Nature routinely calls, as usual. The officers' latrine was a canvas walled area around a six-foot long trench. Two logs had been peeled to leave a relatively smooth, but icy cold, sitting area. They were spaced just far enough apart to allow the droppings, without the dropper falling through. I think the only time in the entire war I felt resentment for those back home in comfort, was the time sitting on that make-shift 'throne' in winter.

It worked, however, and the excitement of the next mission soon washed away the memory of starting each day.

Our missions were almost totally fighter-bomber type, loaded with bombs or napalm we would put in or on the best targets available. Then we went after whatever was available.

My second consecutive Christmas away from home caused me to reflect on the war and who I was. I was comfortable with myself. I had flown 72 combat missions and was an Ace, still alive and here. 118 group pilots weren't.

The Group had destroyed 514 enemy in the air and probably 46 more. There were just over 300 claims of damaged in the air. 172 more had been destroyed on the ground with seven probably destroyed and many more damaged in those brutal strafing missions.

If there were just two alternatives to aerial combat, that is win or lose, we wouldn't have a lot of first person accounts from the losers. The other side of winning was pretty final in a lot of instances. Actually, a lot of people made it through a tour doing their job and ending fairly even, neither scoring nor being scored upon. Even before the end of the war and ever since, a group of people have researched the winners trying to scientifically determine what it is or was that the top few percent had so the perfect fighter pilot could eventually be structured or at least identified. Some even asked me. If I knew, I would have told them.

I know I had a good sense of coordination, which I demonstrated in sports, although I never lettered in the major sports. It was due more to the fact that I never weighed as much as 115 pounds in high school. Three and a half years later at the start of WWII, I tipped the scales at 142 pounds and was on a frame I wanted to be six feet. Actually 5'11½" was as tall as I ever reached. I was a great bowler; never the world's best because at my peak, there were still three or four in the world who could beat me.

I had good eyesight, an absolute must in aerial combat. Not only could I see quite clearly at a distance however, I found I could unfocus while sweeping terrain and pick up slight movement, which found me many a target, importantly before the aerial kind found me. Then I learned the tricks such as eternal vigilance in the air, head on a swivel, checking everything that moved above you and below. Both sides, in front and in back especially, and also looking at the sun by closing an eye and blocking it with a thumb or a fist so the chance of surprise from that area was minimized.

I *knew* I could fly and maybe that was a part of what I think was the most important part of success – confidence!

Our group had only one combat tested and experienced pilot when we entered the fray in late 1943, Jim Howard who had flown with the Flying Tigers before we joined in the war. Yet we became the highest-scoring group of the war, passing the famed 4th and 56th groups who had several months head start. Why? We had the best aircraft, the P-51 which gave us a good start, raised our confidence level until it became contagious.

It was hard to fly with people like Jim Howard who won the Congressional Medal for a one-man attack on half the Luftwaffe, without some of the hunter/killer instinct rubbing off. I listened on one mission to Glen "the Eagle" Eagleston calmly say on the RT, "Hey you guys, I'm all alone at the back of the bomber box and I've got a dozen of the bastards cornered!"

I had a great feeling about the people who made up the 354th – not just the pilots, but everybody from the leaders to the lowest private. It had been a miracle to call 1000 people from every part of the country and have them meld together to form an efficient and very successful fighting machine. That wasn't true of all the units assembled into the Eighth and Ninth Air Forces.

Just prior to 'D-Day', I led a mission on a day of fearful weather and found nothing to shoot at. To make it worse, we could not get back into Headcorn and finally landed at another fighter base. Thankfully, their Group number does not come to mind. Resplendent in our wrinkled flight suits, we were fed and allowed in the 'O' Club for after dinner libations. There I found the pilot who had led their mission that day and we compared notes. "We saw nothing," I offered. "How did yours go?"

"Same here," he said. "Well, we did see a bunch of ME-109's, but there were over twenty of them and we only had sixteen, so we didn't engage."

I nearly 'urped' on the barroom floor! Harris and I had gone after three or four times that many. Jim Howard earned his Medal of Honor by fighting off a dozen by himself! Eagle had radioed that he was "alone and had a dozen of the bastards cornered."

I thought we ought to get out of that bar before we were infected. Thank God for putting me in the group I was in!

I can't let a discussion of the Group personnel go by without mention of 'Tex'! He was a slow drawling, gangly individual who posed a problem for the C.O. in finding a spot for him. Since 'Tex' was not mechanical by nature, was nearly illiterate and just plain rebelled at permanent KP, he posted a definite problem until we found out he could drive.

The problem was we didn't have a lot of trucks to drive, so he was given the task of ferrying the most precious cargo we did have, the pilots. It was a natural. The pilots liked him and he didn't mind being screamed at by young officers since it rolled off his back with little effect. He mainly drove us to the flight line after briefings, picked us up again after the flight and generally took us wherever we were supposed to go, including to the skeet range on a sunny afternoon at Portland Army Air Base.

One particular day, the pilots were crowded in the rear of a 'carry-all' truck which next stopped at Squadron Headquarters to pick up Adjutant Wentworth Howell, who we affectionately called 'Curley' because of a noticeable lack of hair. The afternoon was unusually warm and when 'Curley' wasn't ready, sitting became quite uncomfortable in the truck. 'Tex' sat in the driver's seat saving the other front seat for 'Curley' who was to conduct this practice session. Finally, one of the pilots bellowed, "Tex', go tell 'Curley' to get his ass out here!" and 'Tex' dutifully climbed down, opened the orderly room door and hollered just that, "Curley' get your ass out here."

While our Adjutant didn't really care for the message, 'Tex' was endeared to the pilots forevermore!

Now please don't get the idea that we overdid the drinking – partying thing. It may be that the stories that come to mind were often related to our efforts to relax between missions. It was important. First in England, and now in war-torn Europe, finding enough to hold these occasional social functions was a problem. The solution was to search for and buy anything and everything alcoholic we could find.

To do that Group C.O. Bickell designated a talented Tech Sergeant as our procurement man. He was furnished a Jeep and trailer and as soon as enough of France had been liberated to give him search room, he was given $2,000 in French money and told not to come back empty handed. He didn't. As soon as he was unloaded and had a day to read his mail, we refinanced him and he left again. I think it was his one and only job in the war theatre. Wouldn't the press have had some fun with that if it had been exposed? Still, Uncle George and the rest of us felt his input was as important, or more so, than any other job he could have done for the war effort. Group morale was very high. The big problem was that at times we did not have enough of any one thing to put on a party.

That's when Purple Passion was invented. Each of the Squadron Flight Surgeons and their group counterpart were issued two quarts of pure grain alcohol each month. The purpose, I think, was external application but it was seldom, if ever used, and so was available for one particular scheduled dance. In addition to those eight bottles, we had scrounged nine bottles of Champagne, about a dozen bottles of beer and two of brandy. All of this was poured into a large galvanized tub and stirred. It looked and tasted terrible. We added 50% water and it improved somewhat.

A Mess Sergeant suggested a couple packages of concentrated Lemon Extract. Purple Passion was the beautiful result. The taste was that of an innocent punch. Unfortunately, we found that it didn't take many to bring the partaker to a quite inebriated state. Purple Passion became the standard bill of fare at all group social affairs.

We had an excuse for such a party on New Years Eve, 1944. Purple Passion was served, as usual. I had had several and was already feeling little pain when Uncle George cut me off by reminding me that I was leading the first flight of the New Year. And so at 0700 on January 1, 1945, I was up quite clear-eyed and ready for the day's work.

We ate, were briefed and at 0945, lifted sixteen P-47D's off the frozen runways of A-98. It was my fifth combat mission and only seventh flight in one of those monstrous P-47's and I truly had learned to hate them. Nevertheless, we got off with the first three flights with bombs and a fourth top cover flight. Our mission was close support for the III Corps in Belgium but hardly had we set course when I received a radio call, "Rover Red Leader, we're picking up a large number of bogeys in your area."

"Roger, large number of bogies." Then scanning 360 degrees around us from above to the deck and all members of the group doing same, we found nothing. Still, everybody was on alert and ready to jettison our bombs, if necessary. We again set course for Belgium.

A few minutes later, the same warning was transmitted and again we could find nothing. "Control. This is Rover Red Leader. Can you give me a vector?" The response confused us more. "Well, we're showing several bunches on both sides of you. Can you see anything?"

"We're at 16,000 feet in clear skies, a broken under-cast about 2,000, have not picked up anything." We again circled with all eyes searching the skies. Not a damn thing! In the next half-hour, we found our target area and were directed to drop bombs on a village that supposedly sheltered some of VonRunstandt's advancing columns. Then we climbed up again and were vectored south of our target to what was again "a quite large force of unidentified aircraft." There was nothing. Then we were sent north with similar results.

By 1300 we were back at our base to find a shaken group of crewmen who had been strafed by a sizeable force of German fighters. Several of our grounded aircraft had been hit and one crew chief fell from the cowling of his P-47 to the frozen ground and broke his arm. No other injuries. Our sixteen planes had been sent all over the skies without ever leading us to a target. It was the last offensive effort the Luftwaffe made against us.

One captured German pilot later said they had been assured that 'all the American pilots will have hangovers and will be out of action on January 1$^{st}$'. If George Bickell had not stopped me, this one might have been. As it was, I think our controllers were out of action!

CHAPTER 34

# PARTY TIME IN FRANCE

P LEASE REMEMBER THAT WE flew five or ten missions for every party we had. The relaxation was important before and after we went out to kill or be killed. In between the 'formal' parties with guests invited, we entertained ourselves in the Group or Squadron bars, depending upon where we were based at the time. There was always a piano and no shortage of people who could at least bang out suitable tunes the rest of us could sing. Some of those songs were not really suitable for mixed company – if there had been any.

One of the more formal parties earned me a few days rest. It had been an easy day and that's good because we had a party that night. Espy found a hall in a village a few miles down the road – intact and with a suitable dance floor. He also spread the word at a nearby field hospital and several dozen nurses signed on. I would imagine they get as lonely as we do although I can't imagine a young lady being as horny as some of our group.

The 'party crew' saved and worked on our 'Purple Passion' and did a good job, as we would find out. It was more potent than ever. They also came up with appropriate decorations. Time to party!

Actually, we nearly didn't make it there. Five of us crowded into a 'liberated' French sedan, a Citroen or something like that. Gil Talbot drove and the rest of us sang ribald songs to get in the mood. We were probably doing 50 on the narrow road when the hood blew open and completely blocked the forward view. Like the great pilot he was Gil held the rig steady on this winding road, evidently from memory of what he had seen before it happened. He got it stopped. The hood was hopelessly bent so it could not be secured. No problem; we ripped the damn thing off and left it in the nearby ditch and went back to singing.

At the dance, I secured my first mug of 'purple passion' and was halfway through it when Col. Uncle George Bickell tapped me on the shoulder. "Take the two-seater to London tomorrow morning and pick up Kestler". "Got you, Colonel. Will do." And then I went back to my drink. I remember the first one and most of the second one I drank while looking over the available nurses. I know I danced a little. Made small talk and had a third one. That's all I remember. Gil must have stayed sober because we made it home.

I woke up reluctantly the next morning when the operations field telephone under my cot jingled me into consciousness. My head was throbbing! "Captain, ain't you supposed to be flying to London?" Oh, my God, I thought. "Ahem, yes, be right there." I dressed in two minutes flat. No shave. Nothing to eat and Jeeped to the flight line.

"I will be okay, I said to myself. A little 100% oxygen and this head will go away." I was surprised my helmet fit.

The two-seater "STARS LOOK DOWN" was ready to go, but the crew chief looked at me and wasn't too sure. "Captain, you sure you should do this?" I was in the cockpit and strapping myself. "Pull the chocks." I started the engine. He didn't pull them and hollered at a few other crew people for help. "Godammdit," I thought. "I'm okay!"

I blasted the engine and finally got over the chocks, but by that time, three guys had hold or my left wingtip and I was going nowhere except in circles. I was still waving them away and rotating when Uncle George skidded his Jeep alongside in a cloud of dust and gave me the hand across the throat 'cut it' sign. I did. Obviously someone had called him.

"Get out," he said. "You've been flying too much. Take a few days off. I'll have somebody else do this." "Yes sir." I was a little pissed because I knew I could have done it. I went back to my billet and plunked down on my cot. Then I remembered I was the squadron club officer and had a full case of Hennessy 3-star brandy under the bed. I got one and opened it. Still no food. Take a few days off he had said, so I will. I had several swigs and began to feel better. I went out and wandered around the area, bottle firmly in hand. I think I offered a few people a jolt, but I'm not sure of that. I might have gone to lunch eventually. Before evening, the bottle was empty, so I found my room and retrieved another one.

"Damn, they make these hard to open!" I said as I fumbled with it and stumbled out again. I could not open it, but there was a convenient stone wall and I simply cracked the neck off. The edges were a little sharp, but I could drink again. That's about all I remember.

I woke up the next morning in a field hospital bed. I couldn't have felt worse. Not only was my head throbbing again, I had the shakes. I mean I couldn't stop shaking. "God, oh God," I muttered. I tried to stand up but couldn't make it. One of the nurses came by and gently pushed me down. "Just take life easy, guy. You aren't going any place." I dozed off again. Once or twice they fed me in bed through straws, which was all right. Most things I would have eaten would have come back up quickly. I slept a lot.

The second day I was feeling better, but still had the shakes. I was started on therapy, which was fine. A nurse gave me gentle massages a couple times. I asked if she had been to our dance, but got a non-committal answer and was too tired to pursue it. On day three, I was well enough to put a robe on and walk through the halls. The shakes had eased mostly.

I remember passing one room where a GI was ranting and raving. Another patient filled me in. "That poor SOB has a real problem. He was forcing a French girl to give him a 'blow job' and she bit the damn thing clear off!" I shuddered thinking about it.

The following morning I ate a real breakfast and they sent me home to my own cot. Well, the Colonel said take a few days off and I did – not what either of us meant.

I put myself on a mission two days later – no problem.

On Wednesday morning, January 8 with weather clearing somewhat and in the midst of the Battle of the Bulge, I was assigned a close support mission in the Bastogne area. Eight of us P-47s, loaded with 500 lb. Bombs headed that way. I made contact with the forward air controller who vectored me about 20 miles Northwest of Bastogne, to a small village where he informed me the Germans had troops and several tiger tanks holed up. For a change, the weather was perfect for such a task. We cruised at about 4000 feet above a 70% under-cast. The clouds gave us good cover, coming and going and the holes gave us the opportunity to spot our objective. When I had positively identified the target, we tallyho'd and screamed down toward the Village. I found myself surrounded by white puffs of anti-aircraft fire as I broke through the cloud cover at about 2000 feet. Involuntarily flinching, but otherwise not concerned, I selected a target building which looked like a likely Tiger tank hiding place and released both bombs at a few hundred feet, then hauled back on the stick to gun for the cloud cover. In a Mustang, I would have been there in seconds. In the Jug, I seemed to hang there, slowly, slowly climbing toward the cover and hardly getting any closer. The anti-aircraft fire continued to burst around us and now, I was concerned. Eventually we did reach it and set course for home.

I landed and turned to taxi to my parking area when several ground crews started running alongside, pointing at the engine area. I stretched my neck to see what got their attention, but could see nothing except a lot of oil on the right side. When I parked and got out, I found that a 20-mm shell had blown two cylinders out of the engine – oil streamed along the side from nose to tail – and I hadn't even known I had been hit! The engine had purred all the way home from the target, maybe a little rough, but not enough to bother me. "Maybe the damned old P-47 isn't so bad after all!"

Then again I thought, "In a Mustang, I probably wouldn't have been hit at all." Still, I thought about the single rifle bullet that put me in a parachute a few weeks earlier.

Shortly after the weather lifted in the Bastogne area and we had been able to deliver air support, the 3rd Army had broken through to free the encircled 101st Airborne Division. Gus Allen and I decided on a day off to go see what all the fuss had been about. We got a Jeep and a map and started up the road. Two hours later we wheeled into the edge of Bastogne. For a few minutes, we did not find a visible living soul, a very weird feeling. Finally, a GI stuck his head out of a cellar door and after recognizing our Jeep and American uniforms, lowered his weapon and disappeared into the cellar. We followed.

The damp, cold, candle-lit basement area contained a dozen grimy American GI's who glanced up with a show of interest when Gus and I entered. They gave no recognition of our rank or uniforms, although it was quite plain that we were officers, both displaying insignia on our A-2 flight jackets and caps. I was wearing soiled but still recognizable 'pinks', an obvious part of officer dress. I think, fortunately for us, neither of us made mention of the lack of courtesy. I got a pack of cigarettes out and passed them around. One of the troops asked what brought us to the area and how did we get there.

"We wanted to get a look at the front; just drove up the road."

"The German's held that road an hour ago," one volunteered.

"You're kidding. We were told it was wide open for a week."

"It has been, now and then. One GI arose and moved to the cellar door.

"You guys want to see the front? I'm going out to an outpost now. Want to come?"

It certainly wouldn't do to back down in front of a group of fighting men so we assented. At the door he stopped to give instructions. "Keep about 30 or 40 yard intervals. When I stop, you stop and get down. Then he took a folded double-panel of parachute silk from his jacket and used it so that he blended nicely with the show-covered ground. We had nothing to do the same for us. I waited until he was a good 30 yards out of the place before I took off after him. Gus did the same behind me. The GI ran in a low crouching position for about 25 yards, then threw himself to the snowy ground, covered by the panels. I stopped feeling silly as hell kneeling in a stooped position. I couldn't see a damn soul anywhere. After a minute or so, he arose and went another 25 or 30 yards, then repeating the process. We were in fairly open territory by now. I was sure Gus and I looked like a couple of sore thumbs to any viewer, but I didn't see any viewers fortunately.

Our guide on about the fifth stop, dived into a foxhole and when I saw that, I skipped the last stop and very shortly dived headfirst in after him. Unfortunately for Gus who came up seconds later, two of us filled up the hole. Our GI told him there was another a few yards to the right and he wasted no time getting there. Two seconds later, Gus bellowed at us. "Hey, there's a dead guy in here!" Our soldier friend told him not to mind, the dead GI wouldn't. It became very quiet in Guses' hole for awhile.

My companion took the binoculars from his neck and rising slightly studied the wooded patch about 200 yards directly in front of us. There was a second group of trees a hundred yards to the right of that and a third visible between the two, another 200 yards removed. After carefully looking at all three areas, he offered me the glasses. I looked at the closest woods for a few moments sweeping from left to right. When a movement caught my eye, I concentrated on one section and was shocked to find at least a dozen men in very obvious German uniform gear. One was staring directly back at me through binoculars. I screamed my discovery to my GI friend. He remained quite calm.

"I know. What do you want to do about it, Captain?"

"What do you mean?"

He showed me a clipboard bearing a crude map. An elongated area in front of an X was marked #1, a second area to the right had a #2 and a third between the two but farther back was so marked.

"The X is us. The woods where you see the krauts is target #1. The mortars behind us are zeroed in. Pick up the phone and say, 'Target one, traverse three. ten rounds.' They will start with a round on the left edge and then fire one every three degrees." He pushed the field phone toward me.

"Do you think we should?" I asked.

"Hell, that's what wars are all about."

"They might shoot back at us!"

"Oh, they will but not us. They'll shoot over us into town."

I thought about it. Gulped! Then picked up the phone and cranked it. When a voice answered, I tried to act casual as possible, repeating the words this GI had given me as if I had done it 100 times. Then I hung up and picked up the field glasses. I was staring at the same troops when I heard the first shell whistle over us and later a "Carump!" I couldn't see any sign of the explosion, but I watched as a second, third and so on went over. More explosions still non-visible. Then the GI pointed at target two where obvious bursts about 15 yards apart was every few seconds.

"Those idiots! They got the wrong target. Call them back and straighten them out."

Before I could do that, a different whine started and every 10 to 15 seconds, we heard the German answers go overhead and into the fringes of Bastogne. "I think I'll wait." I said.

"Fine." He answered and we got out some K rations for lunch. Gus was doing the same and said, "I offered my buddy some of my lunch, but got no answer."

We stayed in the foxholes for another hour or so, then told our guide we had better get back and took off. Neither Gus nor I stopped once in our crouching runs back to our Jeep.

Before heading out, we had an opportunity to see a part of war I would rather forget. There were hundreds of dead soldiers in view. The American bodies were stacked ala cordwood. The frozen ground would not allow burial and they were awaiting removal to proper sites. The German bodies had been left where they fell. Two GI's were desecrating those men to harvest gold. Fingers were cut off to get wedding bands. Mouths were pried open and if gold in teeth was seen, a few blows with rifle buts would break the teeth off so the gold could be retrieved.

We went back to base – happy to have our jobs – not infantry.

★ ☆ ★ ☆ ★

January, 1945 LOSSES:

| | |
|---|---|
| Richard H. Brown | MIA |
| Harry L. Lordi | KIA |
| Harry E. Fisk | POW |
| Alexander B. Durkee | MIA |
| Lt. Brown | MIA |
| Clifford H. Davis | MIA |

George Birkner                    MIA

354th AIR CLAIMS TO DATE          GROUND CLAIMS
   687 destroyed              173/7/73
   53 probably destroyed
   301 damaged

CHAPTER 35

# P-51'S CHEER THE BITTER WINTER

**M**AN! DO WE MISS those beautiful P-51's? In the month of January, the Group flew 64 operational missions. We gave the German war effort hell – fairly well destroying their effort to move in daylight. The Luftwaffe refused to come up and fight. We lost nine planes and pilots although one made his way back five days later. We had zero claims of aircraft destroyed – none! Our E.T.O. leading record of aerial kills was in jeopardy. The only constant was the bitter cold of the 1944-45 winter in France.

February began the same way. Another 51 missions without a claim and with six more losses. That was up until mid-month, February 16th to be exact, when the 356th Squadron got their Mustangs back. That same day, I took a group of 355th pilots to England to pick up our own 51's. Life will be beautiful again! The 356th Squadron made claims of four enemy destroyed on a second mission on the 16th.

A rumor started that General Pete Quesada who had been so proud of our air-to-air record, was responsible for the return of the Mustangs. If so, "Thanks, Pete!"

Party or no party – mission or not – I wrote a letter to my bride nearly every night in the better part of the two years we were separated…

Feb. 15, 1945

"My dearest sweetheart,"

I started every letter, everyday in the same way and they usually had nothing but "mush" – the kind of stuff a lonely guy writes to his ladylove after 15 months apart. My thirty-day leave in the middle of that is now only another memory.

I told her the good and bad news, the good being the trip back to England to bring P-51's back to replace the monstrous 'Jugs'.

The bad was the death of my new puppy while I was gone.

Other good news – "The snow is melted and we hope it won't be back." The winter of '44/'45 was terrible – live through it in tents and you will really understand how bad.

The end of the letter is as usual as well…"Oh Darling, I miss you so much and dream of us being together…I'm yours. I'll be seeing you sweetheart.

Clayt"

The new puppy I lost was a male offspring of Ragbone. We had had a little excitement of a different kind this winter. My dog, Ragbone, certainly with no encouragement from me, had impregnated a French dog called "Pepe" after she adopted the group or visa-versa.

She was really not big enough for what a Springer Spaniel would give her. Anyway, her labor started in early morning and lasted several hours before the seventh and last pup delivered. The delivery room was tent #20. I couldn't watch. Seeing enemy blood was one thing, but the pitiful moans from that little girl and the bloody mess that accompanied each birth, was too much.

We had volunteers to assist her. Sgt. Elste was the mid-wife with Sgt. Widdoes assisting. I checked back every 30 to 40 minutes to get the count. It was mid-afternoon before the exhausted "Pepe" collapsed in a box, padded with grass. The staff did a commendable job of cleaning the little blind rascals. The father showed little interest. I chastised him severely. Man, what will I do when I have real children, and they have children?

I led the Squadron on another half dozen missions in February in the new P-51D LIVE BAIT. One may have definitely dented Hitler's ability to wage war. February 23rd had dawned with the same damn weather – stinking!

They wanted a WEATHER RECON flight to determine the possibility of a full group effort against some of the enemy effort to fight back against Patton's advance. The 10/10-cloud cover was down to 700-800 feet and not exactly room to make dive runs. I'm supposed to find if there are areas someplace where we might do some good. Kinmon flew my wing. "Oh yes, you might as well take bombs in case you find an opening! Great! If we don't – what do we do with a 1000 pounds of high explosives…each?"

"You'll think of something."

We lifted off at 0940, entering the 'soup' in formation. Five hundred feet later, we are in beautiful clear blue sky and peaceful conditions with absolutely no sign of the war raging below. For an hour, we cruise in measured and timed legs with no hint of a break, so we start for home.

This I know for sure...I ain't going to let down with a 500-pounder under each wing. We are still well over enemy territory when I spot a break in the endless carpet of puffy white below us. No, not an opening, but several smokestacks protruding above the clouds – and smoking. That's got to be a factory. We position for a straight and level run from about six thousand feet. Okay, guess at trajectory because we don't have Nordens or any other bombsight. I finish those intricate mental calculations and, at the proper moment hollered "Bombs away" and pulled the handle. Then we rolled over and watched those four deadly missiles enter the clouds, nearly in the midst of the protruding stacks.

No explosives to hear or watch, but I think we surely got a factory or two. "You're beat, Adolph!"

Now we get 'a homing'. Thank God for that ability and let down without incident. On the ground, we go over a map with S-2 and guessed that the target was probably Brunstadt. Ho hum!

I had reported flying conditions passable by radio and ten minutes before we landed, the first of several Group missions was off the ground and on its way to Germany.

Kinman and I chowed down and rested a bit and at 1420 in the afternoon, I was lifting off the field leading 16 Mustangs to Kirn, Germany on another armed foray. We dropped bombs in a large rail transportation center and then scouted the surrounding area for any other moving objects. The 'victim' we found was a 20-plus car train which we stopped on the first pass and then circled to finish off. My second pass target was a boxcar. As I fired at the car, the sides of another boxcar a few feet to my left dropped suddenly exposing an antiaircraft battery and crew. The Mustang on my immediate left took a direct hit and flew into the ground just beyond the train. Total destruction, no chance of a survivor! "Sheez!" A trailing flight wiped out the gun crew but the damage was done. I asked who had gone down – it was Capt. William Hargis. We were back on the ground by 1710 and by 1830, I was as drunk as I could get.

The day Bill Hargis went down was nearly six months into my second tour of duty. I had fourteen months of married life with Gwen and sixteen without her. I lived and died for mail call and a letter from her, yet I found the vision of her growing fainter with each passing week. It was not unusual then that a virile young man of 24, I could be somewhat smitten by a pretty face that was close by instead of a V-mail from thousands of miles away.

We periodically arranged dances to satisfy the social part of our nature and had ever since the first one at Boxted, which I spoiled by the crap game. In Europe, the field hospitals and their American nurses were the source of female companionship. While I went to those affairs and enjoyed them, it never went further than a dance or two or maybe sitting out a dance for a cigarette with a discussion of plans after the war. I never hid the fact that I was married.

Finally, at one of those affairs I met Louise. While I first sought a dance with her because she was the prettiest girl there, I soon found deeper beauty that sent my heart fluttering. She was a 'nice' girl, not one you dreamed only of bedding down, but one that made you think of 'forever' and that sort of thing.

I danced several times with her that evening and then several times before the next dance was scheduled, I Jeeped over to the hospital to talk with her for an hour or so. I continued to write letters to Gwen, honestly professing my love, but in my dreams, Louise's face was increasingly replacing Gwen's. The problem was that Captain Billy Hargis shared the same feelings and he made himself as available to her as I was doing. Poor Louise liked both of us and said so. Hargis had transferred into our Squadron a few months before and so I was naturally not as close with him as with those who had been with us for some time. This rivalry didn't endear him to me either. The situation was stalemated for several weeks before the February 23rd mission that killed him.

My first thought on landing may have fleetingly touched on the fact that I now had no rival, but because I knew she sincerely liked him, I dreaded the fact that I would have to give her the news. Because I hated to think of it, I got a bottle of three-star Hennessy Brandy from the stock kept under my cot and drank a good part of it. By the time I had finished, I had the courage to go tell Louise but others felt I was in no shape to do it. In addition to my inebriated state, the roads were a sheet of ice from the base to the hospital. My Jeep key was neatly removed from my pocket. No matter. I staggered out into the night and had soon stolen a Carryall truck. The Lord was with me and although I had to drive the entire distance with one eye closed, otherwise I saw two icy roads instead of one. I got there in one piece by ten o'clock. I sat outside for ten minutes to collect my thoughts. It's a very good thing that I did not bring more brandy or I would have devoured that also.

I went in finally and announced my presence and intentions to the Officer of the Day and presently Louise came down from the second floor dorm in a robe. I was sitting on a step near the bottom. After she seated herself beside me, I gulped and with real tears in my eyes and voice, told her Billy was gone. She started to cry also. I held her hand and after a minute in a drunken attempt to cheer her, told her she still had me. With that, she jumped to her feet and ran bawling up the stairs. After a moment, I got up and left without looking back and never tried or did see her again, although I am sure I had been in love.

On February 25, 1945, Major Marshall Cloke, 355th C.O. since October, got his orders for rotation home. As he often did, for more than one reason, he headed for the bar. I can't condemn that because I usually did the same thing and most of the rest of us likewise. This night, however, we all, at his suggestion, drank good-bye toasts with him until the good Major could hardly stand up. In fact, couldn't without aid. Gil Talbot who would take over the next day as new Squadron C.O. and I practically carried him to his bunk. When we got there, he should have fallen asleep like a good drunk but instead, wide-awake and argumentative wanted to *talk!*

Cloke was a nice guy, usually, but with a quirk or two that eventually destroyed his career in the military. A West Point graduate, he was very intelligent and good looking. Athletic, on the Army Boxing Team, and with a love of military life, all should have guaranteed him an outstanding future in his chosen field. On top of that, he was posted to the Air Corps after graduation. He proved to be an excellent fighter pilot and fearless in combat. The bad part was a temper with a short fuse. Alcohol didn't dampen that, but rather removed restraints which otherwise might have made for better decisions. When he was transferred to our group and assigned to the 355$^{th}$, he was a Major, frozen in grade for, according to the story, punching an enlisted guard at a base entry gate because he felt he 'was not addressed with the courtesy due his rank'. That's what we were told when he joined us and it made sense even though, for a period of time, he was quite subdued. Later he proved the point when in the officers' bar after the evening movie, one of the pilots was showing pictures he had taken during General Eisenhower's visit to our base a couple of weeks earlier. One picture was snapped, quite accidentally I suppose, just as 'Ike' raised one arm and scratched his armpit. There were chuckles as we passed the pictures around. When Cloke saw it, he immediately decked the picture-taker. Why? For not showing proper respect for a General officer. If the downed pilot had pressed charges, I'm sure Cloke would have been cashiered out of the service, but he chose not to and the incident was covered up.

Since his arrival, he, Talbot and I had shared quarters. On the night before he was to go home, he wanted to talk military. Gil and I had put him in bed but he bounced up to ask us, "You're going to stay in the service after the war, aren't you!"

Like you should do in reasoning with a drunk, I answered, "You bet. I love it. I'll stay in forever. Now, go to bed."

We got him back down and his eyes closed, for about two seconds as we tippy-toed away from the cot. Then he bolted upright again. "Talbot, how about you? Are you gonna' stay in?"

Gil, who had a bad habit of telling the truth at all times said, "When this damn war is over, I'm going to be out of here so fast, your head will swim!"

Cloke staggered out of bed and went for him instantly. Because of his inebriated state, I was able to intercept and restrain him. For the next fifteen minutes, I tried to be a referee, peacemaker and sandman. He finally did fall asleep and the next day, February 26th, he was gone. I doubted that he would remember one thing about the evening, but ten years later on a San Francisco street, I had a chance meeting. The very first thing he said, eyeing my civilian outfit was, "Gross, you said you were going to stay in!" And, I felt terrible. He remembered it all!

I understood that he died a year or so later of a brain tumor that no doubt had everything to do with his, at times, bizarre behavior!

The day after Talbot took over and Cloke left, I grabbed a chance for a leave. A little R & R so I flew back to London.

★ ☆ ★ ☆ ★

February, 1945 LOSSES

| | |
|---|---|
| Phillip J. Holmberg | MIA |
| Alfred C. Cooper | KIA |
| Kenneth E. Gorman | POW |
| George J. New | KIA |
| Edward B. Dickson | POW |
| Kenneth H. Dahlberg | POW |
| Raymond P. Bain | MIA |

| | |
|---|---|
| Robert A. Park | KIA |
| Russell R. Wildon | KIA |
| Melvin E. Thayer | KIA |
| Richard Peterson | KIA |
| Robert B. Warner | KIA |
| William G. Hargis | KIA |

354th AIR CLAIMS TO DATE      GROUND CLAIMS
   696 destroyed                     176/7/77
   53 probably destroyed
   307 damaged

CHAPTER 36

# PATTON MOVING – GERMANY ON THE RUN!

**W**E COULD NOT ALLOW ourselves to think this war was about over. The Wehrmacht was in retreat but fighting bitterly. Our job – keep pounding them in every way at every opportunity. I don't know how many ground vehicles I destroyed, but it was multiple in number. We carried bombs and sometimes another fun weapon – napalm.

On March 9, 1945, a great stroke of luck for the Allies? The bridge at Remagen was taken despite German efforts to destroy it. Explosive charges had been in place and some detonated, but with only minor damage so that some elements of the U. S. Ninth Armored Division were able to cross the mighty Rhine River. Then began the battle to hold it. Our job was to deny Luftwaffe efforts to attack it from the air. To that end we kept constant flights over the area.

One of those missions proved to be one of the most exciting of the war for me. I think I met the re-incarnation of VonRichtofen, if not the Red Baron himself. I led a morning flight of eight to the area to relieve the earlier guardians of the bridge at Remagen. Fifty miles away, I heard the R.T. chatter indicating enemy aircraft were in the area and a grand dog-fight was in progress. We advanced throttles to get there. Still, a couple minutes out I could see the battle in progress. Two dozen aircraft were milling about in a giant ball which extended from 10,000 to 20,000 feet and was just as wide. I was afraid it would be over before I could get there and I pushed it forward a little more. As we neared, it began to break up, just as I had feared. Then I spotted a lone ME-109 dive from battle and head for the deck. I sent the rest of the flight on and hollered for Bill Davis on my wing to follow me. If the Kraut was running, he should be easy, right?

The pilot did not see me or if so, gave no indication. At full throttle, I was closing rapidly in the same shallow dive pattern as the Mersserschmidt. At about 75-yards I fired a burst of six 50-caliber guns, no deflection needed. I saw multiple strikes on his tail assembly and left wing before my catch-up speed caused me to over-run him. As I hit him, he broke hard left. I pulled up to lose speed, then did a wingover to follow my prey. I was shocked to find the 109 flying straight at me. I was suddenly the prey! At the moment I lacked time to imagine what maneuver he used to reverse our situations and in the years since then, I have used the time-honored fighter pilot system of two flattened palms to reconstruct the incident without success. He couldn't have done what he did, but he did!

Now in imminent danger of being hit, I did some rather unconventional and wild maneuvers myself. I slammed stick and rudder pedals violently right, then back left into as tight a turn as I could possibly pull. I looked back at a horrifying sight. My adversary sat directly behind me and the cannon muzzle in the hub of his propeller was spitting shells straight at me in my very vulnerable cockpit. The Plexiglas over my head was no protection. I tried to pull my left turn even tighter and frantically called Bill on the radio. No answer. My only defense was the tight "LUFBERY CIRCLE", a tactic devised by the WWI French Ace, Raoull Lufbery. I was alive because although the kraut pilot was shooting straight at me, he could not draw enough lead to hit me. In order to see him in the vertical turn, I looked back over my head through the top of my canopy and again straight down the cannon barrel. At every flash, I involuntarily flinched which did no good for aircraft control, so I tried to quit looking. I screamed for help from anybody and got dead silence for an answer. Now I knew my radio was out. I dropped five degrees of flaps and it allowed me a slightly tighter turn. I occasionally felt the beginning tremors of a stall, which forced me to ease off the pressure. Now a nervous glance back found the 109 still on my tail but lagging further behind. His cannon was quiet.

For what seemed like an hour, but probably was closer to five minutes we continued the circle. In each turn, I gained maybe one foot on my adversary and if it was possible to relax in such a situation, I did. At least I progressed from pure panic to just scared. Fifty or sixty turns later I had reached a position directly across the circle and it was obvious I would be on his tail eventually if my fuel did not run out. I was alone and over enemy territory. I knew also that whoever broke the circle first would be at great disadvantage. It occurred to me also that while I had no radio to call for help, he probably did. Since we were over Germany, his help was probably not far away. As I continued to close on him, he suddenly rolled over and pulled straight for the deck. Remembering what happened before when I hit him while he was running, I decided to let him get away and with a sigh of relief, headed for home.

Bill Davis and the rest welcomed me. Davis said he had experienced engine problems and he had notified me that he had to leave. With radio out, I hadn't heard it.

I went to bed that night with a great deal more respect for Luftwaffe pilots than I had previously held.

Two days later I led the squadron on a B-26 escort to the

Frankfurt area and up came the Luftwaffe. It was a short battle and they did not get to the bombers. I tagged on a lone ME-109 and was closed rapidly – too much so as it turned out. I had multiple strikes and the 109 began to trail smoke and lazily turned left and down, then I overran him. Ben Kirts had been dutifully tucked on my wing and was able to add more strikes on the unfortunate E.A, which then went into what we both believe was a death dive. We went back to the bombers to search for more activity without following the first victim to the end.

On return, we claimed him destroyed and Smitty added a half victory to my total. Ben did the same.

We stayed busy in March. The Group flew 80 combat missions. I led twelve of them. The claims for air victories were 65 destroyed for the month and another eleven on the ground. Of course, there was the usual cost. We lost another dozen planes and pilots. Two of those losses were in a mid-air collision with both pilots killed.

Another had bailed out, but made his way back without capture – ala Gross a couple of months earlier.

I did add a damaged claim while on another B-26 escort. The rascal got away!

March, 1945 LOSSES:
    Kenneth Coleman                     POW
    Harrison C. Frost                     MIA
    Ernest J. A. Wedlund             MIA
    Lonnie D. Kelly                      POW
    Charles F. Shalen                   KIFA
    Joseph E. Fisher                    KIFA
    Mark Baldwin                         MIA

| | |
|---|---|
| Michael R. Jugan | RMC |
| John P. Ryan, Jr. | MIA |
| Calvin S. Walker | MIA |
| Earnest H. Pearson | MIA |
| Kenneth E. Neidigh | POW |

354th AIR CLAIMS TO DATE     GROUND CLAIMS
   774 destroyed                          188/7/106
   53 probably destroyed
   346 damaged

★ ☆ ★ ☆ ★

CHAPTER 37

# LAST VICTORY – A JET!

I LED THE 355TH SQUADRON on April 14th on what proved to be one of my most memorable missions. It was eight P-51's on an area cover in the Hersfeld, Mulhausen, Weimar area of Germany – take off at 1330. After an hour of unsuccessful hunting, I dispatched one flight of four to the south and I took the rest in a northerly direction.

We were cruising at 12,000 feet, Kline on my left wing and the element positioned to my right in a mutual support formation. My eyes roamed back and forth checking Kinmon and Glover to make sure nothing got on their ass –- then to our left and scanning the terrain below us. You search in this manner without really focusing the eyes at all, like a camera lens at infinity. We were heading north with all eyes, I hoped, doing the same. A few miles ahead I could see the Elbe River, which made a sweeping curve from its north-south direction to an easterly course before again heading south. Just south of the river, I made an interesting discovery highly camouflaged but unmistakably an airfield and even more interesting, movement that made me focus for sure, a plane probably at about 2,000 feet and 10,000 feet below us. What the hell is a multi engine...my heart raced as I recognized the silhouette of an ME-262! A jet and I had 10,000 feet on him and hopefully, he did not see me!

I shouted the discovery to my flight and then, "Follow me!" At this time I had encountered the awesome jets, maybe four or five times, enough to know their capabilities. The first time ever I was escorting B-17's on a deep penetration of the Hitler empire, flying right of the bomber box and slightly higher in a slow weave, when a sudden shout "Bandit's 3 o'clock" caused me to quickly turn that direction. It took me only a second to spot the strange craft at my altitude at about 2 o'clock to me, and bearing straight at the bomber formation. "I got him," I shouted, turning into his attack. Before I completed my turn right, he passed me at unbelievable speed! And while I was wracking LIVE BAIT in snap turn left to follow, he was through the formation and gone. "What the hell was that!" At that moment none of us knew but we were to find out.

A few months later, on a dive bomb mission, one of the now recognized jets attacked me. I had laid my bombs in a marshalling yard and started my pull out when our top cover flight shouted a warning. I had learned to break first and then look and did that. What I saw by twisting my neck most of a 180 degrees, was a lone twinjet 262 skidding past me, as he could not turn with the Mustang. Thank God! In a moment, he was gone, at a speed I could not comprehend.

I knew full well what they were capable of by now, but with surprise and 10,000 feet I felt I had a good chance at the one below me. I rolled over and pulled the stick back to start nearly straight down. To help, I left power on.

My eyes were on my unsuspecting victim, but I stole a glance at the air speed indicator in time to see it at 450 and still winding up. At about that moment, I lost all interest in the jet. The control stick began to feel loose and quickly felt like nothing – as if it had suddenly disconnected. Sheez! I was in a state of compressibility. The phenomenon I had heard described, but never experienced. At extreme speeds the leading edge of the wings would deflect airflow so that it did not follow the wing contour and over the control surfaces, deflected away from it so that controls were actually in a vacuum. I made giant circles with the stick – absolutely nothing – no feel. I really can't remember the indicated air speed if I did look at it, but I had the distinct feeling that one more MPH and my bird would come apart.

From the deep resources of my memory bank I remembered somebody saying to pour more power on, to blow air across the wing surfaces. Already with more speed than I could use, it took courage to hit the throttle, but I tried it for maybe two seconds – nothing. I chopped it off quickly.

I kicked, pushed, pulled everything I had. Nothing. I was sure I was hurtling to sure death and nothing I could do would stop it. I wonder if my flight would tell the world I set a new speed record in doing it.

At that instant, I felt slight resistance on the stick. Oh God! Please be there! I tried easing back slightly, more pressure, easy now. I was gradually pulling out and LIVE BAIT was shuddering as if she would pop every rivet of her being. But they held and I was able to level out in one piece. Now guess what? The original object of my attention was absolutely dead ahead of me and I was closing rapidly. To start shooting I needed no more than a one or two degree correction. My initial burst set his left jet burning and a fairly large section of his left wingtip flew off actually causing me to flinch as it went past me. Now the speed of my dive caused me to overrun him and I pulled off right and up to lose speed, then rolled back to re-position myself.

When you are surprised and hit in combat, you wake up and react before many of those fifty-caliber slugs rip into you. I found that out when the P-47 thought I was a Messerschmidt and tried to do me in over Berlin. That's exactly what the jet driver did. When I rolled back to get on his tail again, I found him standing the 262 on end and climbing straight up! And, accelerating as he did it! I tried to follow with some of my dive speed remaining and full power but Mustangs won't fly that direction for very long. While his left jet was still burning, he was pulling away! My heart sank as I thought I would lose him. Then something happened to his power, he slowed, still going straight up; then stopped and began to slide back down hill, tail first! As it started to fall off, the pilot ejected. I had a jet!

The pilot's chute popped open and I temporarily forgot the airdrome we were over, forgot it, that is, until with the 262 now down, every anti-aircraft gun on the field opened up at me and my flight now catching up. I had started a gentle circle around the chute. Kind of a victory lap to let him know who got him! When the AA started, we busted ass to get out of there. The jet pilot was swinging in his chute, hands on the shroud lines. I instinctively ducked in the cockpit as bursting shells scared the hell out of me, but I couldn't help but think that he needed a little armor plate around him in that parachute but there wasn't any!

A tremendous feeling of elation warmed me. The flight had re-formed and we turned south and west in the general direction of home. I couldn't wait to give everybody the word of my victory. Ten seconds later I forgot it. About ten o'clock to our course and a hundred feet below us I spotted a huge flight of bogeys, radial engines. Were they FW-190's, maybe 40 or 50 of them and cruising 90 degrees toward us? If we were to fight 50 Focke-Wulfs, the four of us, I wanted altitude and we started grabbing it. Maximum climb, with full power. I was so pumped up from the jet victory, I actually believed we could handle all of them. I watched their approach to see if they had seen us. No obvious movement to indicate they had.

What a day this would be if we could surprise and get a bunch of them. Then as they drew closer, I recognized them as P-47's. Damn Jugs! And I wanted them to be the enemy. I often wondered if the Jug group ever did see us. Nobody turned toward us so maybe they recognized us early. Maybe they weren't looking, no sweat! We went home to tell the story!

★ ☆ ★ ☆ ★

Two days later, still with a mindset that I could whip anything and anybody in the air, I spoke to Brueland of a way to increase our 'kill' scores. The war was winding down, but the feeling and spirit of the ultimate hunter was carried and nurtured by most of us. Those who had a few victories prayed for a battle. "Give me a shot at somebody!" Those close to 'making Ace' begged to go on almost every mission.

The evening mission Brueland and I planned and talked Uncle George into, was a sign of that. We were both Aces and confident of ourselves and each other. There was no 'ops order' for the foray. The Germans were hiding – we knew that and reasoned they had to fly back to their operational bases when all allied missions finished for the day. If we were still there, unexpectedly, we might catch a bundle of them. We planned it to the last headlight to eliminate our base for a night return. We took off after dinner, at 1930, to bring us over the Luftwaffe base at dusk.

And it worked like a charm. Flying at 1500 feet over the low broken clouds, we found them just below the overcast, exactly as we had thought they would be, a huge 'gaggle' of maybe fifty to sixty 109's in slow cruise. The cloud opening gave a beautiful undetected attack position. I slid a little right of Brue and selected my first four targets – yeah four! It would be like shooting fish in a barrel. They would have no chance. We started the attack.

Then Brueland pulled up. "Why? What's wrong?" I asked.

"My whole windshield is covered with oil. I can't see a thing. I'll fly on you and you position me to fire and say when," he said.

To change lead position and start a new run took a moment – the target hole closed and I had to estimate their course and time to find them again in a new break. That's when I glanced at Brue and found a pair of 109's closing in on him. The hunt was over. We were now the targets. It took very little evasive action to slip their attack and in the gathering darkness, they and we, too, had little desire for a night dogfight. We went home. The guys at our base were as disappointed as we were, having listened in as we called, "There they are – 50 or 60 of 'em." "I'll lead, you follow." "Break left, Brue. They're on your tail." All of that and the tape on our guns went unbroken.

At the time, my thoughts were, "Damn what a wasted opportunity!"

When the war ended in a few months, and the killing stopped, I had a new thought and it has persisted since then. Did the Almighty God, our Creator, have a hand in the oil leak? Brueland's plane never had the problem before or after and I don't recall that they determined exactly what caused it. Anyway, because of it, a few German boys flying close formation at 1000 feet in gathering dusk might have lived out the war!

Then, just to make sure we didn't get too comfortable, we moved again. This time into Germany itself at Frankfurt AM Mainz. Gil Talbot commanding the Squadron stayed behind to make sure all equipment he was responsible for was properly dispatched to our new base, Y-64 at Mainz. As Operations Officer, I led the planes to what proved to be the closest thing we had seen to a real honest to goodness airfield, not the farmers fields covered with chicken wire for runways. This had been a Jerry base and it was nearly undamaged. While waiting for the rest, I began setting up an operations office in a real hangar. I was sitting at a desk in this office when 'Tex' walked in. He had been hauling equipment from our old base in several runs. "Is the Major here?" he asked.

"No, Tex. He's back at Saizerais."

He looked a little befuddled, then said, "OK" and started to leave. I could tell he was troubled. "Is there anything I can help you with, Tex?"

"Well," he drawled slowly, "Maybe I should tell you before someone else does. I runned over a guy and killed him."

I literally tipped my chair over backward. "For God's sake, Tex! Who? Where?"

He held a hand out reassuringly, "Don't worry. It's just a German."

I got the story on the way to the accident scene. He was wheeling a 2½ ton truck into the gate when a civilian bicyclist pedaled across in front of him. He said he got out and looked and then drove to my office. By the time we reached the gate, the M.P.s had found the victim and the medics had taken the body away. I said Tex did report it to the first officer he found and everyone seemed satisfied. The legend of Tex continued to grow.

What a guy! The following had happened earlier in the war.

All mail from the war zone was subject to censorship. Our own unit officers did all mail from our enlisted while, as officers and gentlemen, we were allowed to sign our own. Even then an occasional letter arrived home with signs of having been checked by someone. Pilots were not excused from this duty. Seldom was there a need to change anything other than cut out the name of a town near our base or some other slip.

One particular evening, a half dozen of us were pouring over a hundred or so outgoing letters. Contents were never discussed, but on this occasion, there was an exception. Somebody stopped the proceedings by saying, "Hey, you guys. You aren't going to believe this!"

What he passed around was an unbelievable communication from Tex to a girl he had met in London. It was crude to the 'nth' degree. But since we had no previous indication that he could write at all, maybe it wasn't all that bad. The censor started to seal the letter when someone suggested a better idea. To save the reputation of America's soldiers in the eyes of this English lass, to put Tex's thoughts into more appropriate language with proper spelling and punctuation.

He had said something like: "It was fun. I want to do it again. Luv, Tex," but the words were misspelled, punctuation missing, as were capital letters. We re-wrote it as:

"My dear Cynthia,

I cannot remember when I have enjoyed an evening more than this past Saturday, spent with you.

If you are free on my next trip to London, I would certainly enjoy seeing you again. Please tell me it would be possible!

Hopefully,
Tex"

Sworn to secrecy, the conspirators sealed that letter and mailed it. Unfortunately we never found out if Tex got another date or not.

We are pressing on deep into the "Third Reich" territory and evidence is everywhere. At our new base we have permanent quarters in a real building, not wooden, not canvas, but one put up by real masons. Gil and I had a room at the end of the hall, a little larger than the others. My bed was in what used to be a walk-in closet, huge and private. Gil's was outside in the main room that also served as our 'living quarters', a couch and a couple of chairs.

The club and dining room was separate in quite a nice building and has served the Luftwaffe in the same capacity.

What made everything really exciting was the liberated D.P. (displaced persons) camp adjoining the airfield. In it were a thousand or so souls – the victims of war. They could not be freed until the slow moving wheels of governments determined who they were and where they would go.

Our ever-ready, finagling Group Executive, Bowers Espy, requisitioned dozens of the younger females to serve in various capacities in the kitchen, in serving capacities and as maids in the officers quarters.

He and his staff gained entry into the compound where they lined up the females and selected the youngest, the healthiest and of course, the most attractive.

Step two was to cleanse them and delouse them. The chosen group was marched to the barracks where they were disrobed, sent to the showers and then to a room where our four flight surgeons sprayed each with DDT or something to make sure they could not contaminate our fighting men. Doc Start told me of the plan and I pleaded – PLEADED with him, "Let me help, Doc?" No soap. I didn't get in. Then the young ladies were assigned to tasks for which they were paid, probably handsomely in their eyes. Gil and I got a tall, willowy blond probably 17 or 18 years old that spoke zero English and seldom said a word in any other language. I think she was Polish, tho. We had a lot of sign language and no sex, but the beds got made and the room as clean as a whistle.

A bunch of the others worked in the Mess Hall and slept in the upper floors of that building, probably our gal did, too. While we never caught our young lady, some did. One pilot bragged at dinner that he had a fine relationship and then to make us jealous, he said, "She has the biggest tits I ever saw. They're beautiful!"

"Oh, yeah, I'll bet!"

"I'll prove it. Give me five hundred francs and I'll leave the shade up a little! We argued a little, then passed the hat until we had raised his fee. "Okay. I'll leave the shade up enough to see. My room is the third down, ground floor, East side. You have to be there at 2000 hours"…and we were!

The young lady was quite attractive. He hugged her for a minute then raised her sweater and she pulled it off. Then she undid the bra and freed two huge boobs. We got our money's worth as he juggled one in each hand for a moment. Then when she started to undo her skirt, he walked over and pulled the blind down. One sorehead rapped loudly on the window. We heard her scream and the lights went out. We ran.

The next day he told us, "You got everything you paid for!" Yeah! War *is* Hell!

Every issue Stars and Stripes carried news of Patton's 3rd Army in its unstoppable rush across Germany. We heard that a huge POW Camp had been overrun and that possibly, a number of our missing pilots were there. Doc Start and I hatched a scheme.

It seems as though the armored division that overran this stalag had simply knocked down the gate with a tank and allowed 10,000 prisoners to pour out – many after years of captivity. The nearest German village bore the brunt of their anger and frustration – not to mention hunger for both food and sex. The village was sacked and nearly every female raped multiple times before Army authorities rounded up as many as could be found and put them back in the camp until proper identification and release could be arranged. The good doctor and I decided to expedite that for our people.

We first typed phony but very official looking orders to allow us in the camp. Then we loaded an ambulance with several blankets, a good supply of available whisky and several snacks, and headed for the camp. Doc drove and I carried the orders that I presented to the sentry as we arrived. The story was that we had been notified of a prisoner in immediate need of treatment. It worked like a charm. The gate opened and we drove in. I was not prepared for what we saw.

The first barracks-type building we entered had only one occupant. Gaunt would not describe him. He looked somewhat like a skeleton with dried skin covering. He sat at a wooden table eating something from a small plate that had been crafted from a tin can. When we entered, he crouched over the plate – guarding it by crooking an arm around it. His eyes appeared as those of a trapped animal. We left after nodding and waving in a try to reassure him we were not after his food.

We probably searched a dozen buildings before we found a pilot from our group, Ken Gorman, of my 355th Squadron. He and a dozen other prisoners had a large piece of cheese and a loaf of black bread and were trying to portion it evenly. He saw and recognized me, and seeing my side arm, knew he was free. While obviously underweight he was not as bad as some we had seen. We put him in the back of the ambulance, covered him with blankets and exited the camp. I had seen enough for some bad memories.

Safely away from there we stopped to uncover and welcome Ken to freedom. I opened the bourbon bottle Doc had thoughtfully provided and a power bar from an escape kit. His joyful attitude made the trip worthwhile. He knew of no other Group members in the camp.

When we reached our base, he was given fresh clothes offered by volunteers – a chance to clean up and a gourmet dinner of steak and all the trimmings. An hour later, he was in the hospital. We had slightly overdone the welcome home and his system was not ready for that.

CHAPTER 38

# WINDING DOWN AND IT ENDS

On April 2nd Deacon Talbot led the group and I went down to see them off and having nothing else to do, Jeeped back to another new 'home'.

Never had we had quarters so good since the day the Althorn Castle docked in Liverpool and put us in the war zone. It was a real cottage with two bedrooms, a living area, a kitchen and even a basement. The latter was so dark and dank that we looked once and let it go at that. We managed to 'liberate' enough furniture to comfortably furnish it so on this Thursday morning, I was able to 'conk out' on a couch. I had dozed for God only knows how long when a knock on the door shook me awake. I muttered a few obscenities regarding people who would interrupt such an important rehabilitation break – then opened the door. Two people having just dismounted their bicycles were before me. The first, a short elderly man dressed in suit, tie and an important looking sash across his frocked coat, stood on the entry step. Behind him, with head bowed, was a quite attractive young woman whose golden tresses made her surely, one of Hitler's pure Aryans.

The man spoke in halting, but understandable English. "Sir, I am the Burgermeister of whatever damn German city we were near. This is Frau Schmidt," (or some other typical German name). I was looking more than listening and in a moment, couldn't remember what he had said. "Her husband was a Luftwaffe pilot who was unfortunately lost. This was their home. She has insufficient food, as do most of us, and she wondered if she could look for the potatoes she had stored beneath the basement stairs."

In our investigation of that dungeon when we moved in, I hadn't noticed potatoes or anything else but if they were there, she was welcome to them. They came in. She would not look directly at me but murmured a "Danke" and went down the steps. I used a flashlight to illuminate the way. What she found was a pile of truly rotten spuds. I wouldn't have eaten one on a bet but she eagerly filled her apron with all she could carry. Watching her struggle up the steps, I truly felt sorry for the enemy for the first time since I got into this affair. I found thought running through my head to tell her to dump that garbage and I would get her some real food. Noticing again her trim figure, I even entertained a mental offer to let her move back in with us – me in particular!

She dumped her loaded apron into her wire basket on her bicycle. Some were so soft they tried to squeeze through the openings in the carrier. She said not one word and still refused to look at me directly. The Burgermeister bowed deeply and thanked me profusely. "'S-alright" I said brilliantly.

They rode off with me watching from the front step still musing the situation. If she were that hungry, would she have accepted an offer to live better? I could surely have used some soft companionship, but wondered. If she loved her husband and one of us had killed him, maybe even me, would I get a kitchen knife in the back instead of a soft love. She and the Mayor left my life and I went back to the couch.

★ ☆ ★ ☆ ★

I completed my second combat tour when I landed from three-hour plus fighter sweep on April 25th. As usual, we had found nothing to shoot at. Now if I don't "screw up" in some other way, I have lived through the war in Europe!

Late in April and early May, our missions did not carry bombs. Many times we dropped leaflets which suggested in German, that the finder surrender. The back of each was in English and to be shown to the first American soldier contacted. It stated the bearer was to be granted safe passage to the nearest POW clearinghouse.

The group flew 20 missions of that sort in the first week of May and lost two planes, one damaged in a ground strafe action but was able to 'belly-in' upon return. The last official loss for the group was Andrew Kevacek of the 356th Squadron on a May 6th mission, but he returned a day later, May 7th.

I flew again on May 8th. A Sergeant from our Squadron was to be married to an English girl and I flew him there in Stars Look Down, the two-seater. We were on the end of the runway at noon but were told to back off for a combat mission of eight P-51's. After their departure, we lifted off and began the three-hour flight it would take to the big city. With all guns, ammunition and armor plate taken out of GQ-Pi, it was easily 50 miles an hour or more, faster than all our others were. I gave Sarge a sightseeing tour. One area in particular was mind boggling. We circled what had been a small German City or village. There were roads leading in from four directions, but what they led to was nothing – zero! There was not even *part* of a building left standing; a great demonstration of the horrors of war!

We landed at the big British base just east of the city. Unbelievably, nobody met us. Where the hell am I supposed to park? We could not find a living soul in view. I taxied around looking, sometimes with tail up to cover more ground. Finally, we gave up looking and I stopped near a cluster of buildings. We entered one, still no one in sight but could hear noise in the distance and followed it. What we found was a king-size party. The war in Europe had ended while we were in the air. We joined the party.

I was enjoying myself, but Sarge was antsy and wanted to get to his fiancée' so I did find one celebrant who promised to see to my aircraft. We found another who delivered us to the nearest transportation downtown. That in itself was an experience. What should have been a thirty-minute trip took over three hours, more time than it had taken to fly from Germany to London. Then to compound Sarge's problems, all offices had closed and he didn't have his marriage license yet. When would they reopen? Nobody knew. I left a very sad soldier and headed for Madam Morton's. I never found out if Sarge got married.

It was dark by the time I reached her flat. The Cities' celebration was still in full swing. The sidewalks were so crowded it was difficult to move. No more black outs. The lights of London were blazing. I found my lady friend smiling, but with tears. They were of happiness for her desire to go home to France that might now be possible. We poured drinks of wine and went to the roof of the building to watch the celebration. What seemed like a hundred searchlights were weaving across the sky – no longer searching for the enemy, but making up for the years of darkness in the City.

The next day I made my way back to the airport where the usual English decorum was still lacking. I was able to fuel and take off for my own base where I guessed another party would be in progress. I was right.

The celebrations were not without cost and some stories were sad. At one field, a group of celebrating pilots piled ten into and on a Jeep to race around the base. One sitting on the hood waving his glass and happily toasting the world until the drunken driver ran into a wall and neatly amputated both of his legs below the knee. Live through the war and go home a double amputee!

At a B-17 base someone decided to climb into the top turret and add to the festivities by arching fifty-caliber tracers into the sky. The clatter of gunfire led others to investigate and decided that it looked like fun and join in. The tale we heard was that with numerous guns blazing, someone lowered their trajectory and eventually, some were firing at each other. I don't know of casualties, but several B-17's were shot up before the commander put a stop to it. SHAEF eventually sent orders to all bases with dire threats to any that persisted in this type of celebration.

April 1945 LOSSES:

| | |
|---|---|
| Earl H. Marshall | KIA |
| Charles W. Moore | MIA |
| Lloyd E. Bates | RMC |
| William F. Harker | MIA |
| George W. Hawkins, Jr. | POW |
| Mortimer A. Reed | POW |
| Robert J. Black | MIA |
| Francis J. O'Connell | MIA |
| Harry D. Brown | POW |
| Rene J. Ramos | MIA |
| Edward H. Rushmore | MIA |
| Joseph R. Holcomb | MIA |

354th AIR CLAIMS THROUGH APRIL    GROUND CLAIMS
    943 destroyed    254/7/161
    53 probably destroyed
    426 damaged

May 1945 LOSS:
 Lt. Kevacek                                    MIA

354th AIR CLAIMS THROUGH MAY, 1945   GROUND CLAIMS
  949 destroyed                        255/7/161
  53 probably destroyed
  428 damaged

FOOTNOTE: The Victory Credits Board reviewed each claim using gun camera film and witness testimony. Final awards were less than claims. Final official confirmed victories for the top three scoring groups in the ETO were:

FINAL OFFICIAL CONFIRMED:
  354th F.G.                 701 Air / 255 Ground
  56th F.G.                  677 Air / 328½ Ground
  4th F.G.                   539 Air / 463 Ground

CHAPTER 39

# TRIP HOME AFTER V-E DAY 1945

VERY SHORTLY AFTER THE cessation of hostilities, I got a chance to go home. It was accompanied by an offer that gave momentary pause to my decision to leave. If I would stay with the group in their Occupation Forces Duty, I would finally get my field grade promotion, something I felt I deserved much earlier. It took me almost a minute to say no. My marriage was thirty-five months old. I had spent all of fourteen of those months with Gwen. I wanted more!

Today's forces would not believe the casual arrangements to get us home. I had orders home. They generally said find your own way. There were only a few hours to pack and leave. The packing fit into a B-4 and two barracks bags. Then I discovered that I was responsible for their transport just as we had been on our first trip over. I put the essentials in the B-4 and left the rest. That was a mistake, maybe. Because of my poker winnings and lack of anything to really spend money on, I had accumulated many things, like shoes. If a pair of brown oxfords got dirty, I bought new ones. I left fifteen pair of practically new 8½ D's. After we reached Paris, I met another returnee who told me worn out shoes were selling for $100 a pair, those with no holes in the soles for twice that. I calculated that I left roughly the equivalent of five or six months pay in one of those bags!

LeBourget in Paris was a mad house. Transports for England and a ship home were coming and going every few minutes. Standard procedure was to talk one of the pilots into taking you. I found a nice C-47 driver who was willing, but already had a maximum load. No problem. Several of us were told to get out to the end of the runway and we'd find the door open and help boarding. That's what we did. Throw your bag into the bird, then helping hands reached out to lift you in. Others must have heard our plans, because at least a dozen more illegals boarded, some on the run before take-off. I couldn't believe the overload once I was on. Without the strong urge to get home, I would have jumped back off. Instead, I prayed until I felt that beautiful old 'gooney bird' break free of the ground and start to climb. My seat was the top of my bag. What seat belt? I was on my way!

We landed in London and immediately set out hitchhiking for Liverpool where we were to catch a boat home. No chance to see Mme. Morton.

In Liverpool – the usual… "Can't tell you how long it will be". It finally happened. Getting on the ship was different this time. Finally, after most of two years in combat, I was going home. Germany was done and while the Pacific war was still going, it's half a world away. Who cares! I'm headed home and the prettiest girl in the world is at the end of this trip for me.

Even the ship was different than my three previous crossings. It was smaller, newer and American…one of the many Kaiser had been turning out. We would have no escorting destroyers and no periodic interruptions when five-inch cannons were fired for practice. Hopefully, all the U-boats patrolling the Atlantic had been notified that hostilities were over. Dear God, I hope so! Wouldn't it be something to run into a die-hard Nazi bent on a private war? That thought lasted no more than a fleeting moment.

There was a bad part to this ship but it could be tolerated. There were thousands of Americans waiting to go home. We found that out in the days we waited in the debarkation base waiting for a ride. Ergo, the ship was overloaded, not with shifts for the bunks as on trip one, but crowded enough that officers were bunked in a hold. Luck of the draw. The one I drew was probably the worst of all. We were in the farthest hold forward and the lowest. The only thing below us was a trap door to the paint locker, something we were to rue later on the ride home. Also, in the absolute bow of the ship, there was only room for one row of bunks. All rows were six beds high. I liked the relative privacy of that forward row so I staked out the bottom bunk. Again, I found out a few days later, not the wisest choice.

Now, there were some good parts as well. Our first meal aboard was dinner and to me, it was a genuine signal that the war in Europe was truly over. Officers were given a private dining room, small but adequate when scheduled for three sittings. I had the first one. We found a table, a round one with linen cloth and silver. There was a menu and I gave out an ungentlemanly whoop when I read it. Main course – bacon wrapped filet mignon! The next whoop came when the server asked what I would like to drink. "Whadayagot?" He listed various choices, one of which was milk. "Powdered?" I asked. "No, fresh." I hadn't had a fresh glass of milk for ten months. I was in heaven. "Are eggs for breakfast real, too?" "Yes sir."

I could care less what sleeping quarters were like from that moment on. Not all meals were as good as that first one, but they were good and they were American.

I searched for a poker game that first night, but didn't find a good one and my heart wouldn't have been in it anyway. I had a pocketful of money and my Lloyds of London bank account still had a few thousand or so left in it. I was too excited about thoughts of Gwendolyn to concentrate on gambling. As Talbot, Fisk and Depner and I had done on the first ride home, we played bridge night and day. The only space in our "officers hold" was directly below the fire escape-type of stairs that the Navy people insisted was a "ladder". We had enough players that we took turns, losers out and next team in. The game went most of sixteen hours a day and my partner Capt. Radar Jolme, and I got our share of wins. Maybe one too many, as things turned out. About the fourth day out, we were playing when a sailor hurried down the ladder, unlocked the door to the paint locker and lifted out a five-gallon bucket of 'battleship gray' paint. I am sure of the color because a few steps up on his hurried return, the handle came off, or he just plain dropped it. The lid came off and the whole damn bucket of sticky, icky gray paint cascaded through the slots and ruined a good blanket, four players uniforms, not to mention hair, faces and hands and the only deck of cards we had in the entire bay.

"Sorry" said the sailor, carefully stepping over a little paint remaining on the ladder, going back for another bucket. The game had ended for the rest of the trip but who really needed it when heading home. I had enough uniforms to throw that one away. It took me days to get it out of my hair and some off my hands. Fortunately I had had my head down in concentration so little soiled my face.

Next, I found out a little bit about Atlantic storms, from probably the worst place on board to experience one. On day four, we ran into a 'dilly'. The bow of the ship, where I bunked, rose to about a forty-five degree angle as we hit a gigantic swell. Then as we passed over that, it would head 45 degrees down the other side. My guess was at least two-thirds of my mates got sick and that didn't help any. I didn't, but it was touch and go for awhile. For awhile, I found if I lay on that narrow bunk facing forward and holding onto both sides, I could ride out the shudders as the bow ploughed down into the sea. I visualized a giant teeter-totter, but had to keep my eyes open. In an hour, the seas calmed. Again, those of us who hadn't been seasick went back to sleep. I talked myself to sleep. "Yep, I made the right decision when I chose the Army Air Corps over Navy."

In between the three meals a day of good American food and the bridge games until the paint ended that bit of recreation, I found a library. I like to read and other than the porno-type book I read on the first voyage over, I hadn't read anything, but Ops orders and Stars and Strips in two years. I spent an hour or so each day in that quiet solitude, catching up.

On one such day, I became aware of the sound of hilarious giggling nearby. Initially, I tried to ignore it, but the sounds persisted and I had to investigate. Across the hallway was a small bay with a barred door. There were a dozen men in bunk tiers, obviously prisoners. The sounds that caused me to investigate came from two men, lying in the same bunk and tickling each other. I was shocked. In my innocence, I could not believe or understand what I saw. I collared an MP passing and asked him. "They're fags going home on Section Eights." Man, there is a lot I don't know about life and people.

Some guys spent the sunny days, when we had them, sunning on the top deck. Coming home as heroes would be great, but having a good tan would make it better, I guess. Since I burn and never tan, I didn't try it. I wanted to impress only one girl anyway. One of the guys should have done the same. He fell asleep and lay for hours in the sun and it earned him a severe burn and most of the ride home in sick bay!

A lot of things make your heart pound in combat interactions, but nothing had affected me like the thought of being with my wife again.

We married on Flight School Graduation Day. She was 18 years old and beautiful. We celebrated our first anniversary on September 6, 1943 and three weeks later; I bid goodbye as we headed east on our way to the war. I finished my first 200 combat hours and started home in July 1944. I made the boat and train trip home in time to celebrate our second anniversary. My thirty-day leave allowed me to re-acquaint myself with one I considered the most beautiful girl in the world.

Then a week later, orders send me back to my unit in Europe for another combat tour. When the ETO war ended, I eventually had orders home again, – by slow ship and slow train. My orders were to Ft. Lewis, Washington and the train would go through Spokane. I called her every time that Trans-continental train stopped. We made arrangements for her to board though no berths were available! For six days across the USA my heart rate increased – hourly. I had visions of her constantly.

In the evening of that sixth day, we pulled into the same station I left family in 1943. Gwen boarded. I had married this beautiful girl in 1942. In 1945 she had matured into a woman – a gorgeous lady. My heart was pounding!

We sat in a crowded coach car the entire night. I can't remember a word of what was said. Maybe I just looked. When we arrived in Tacoma the next morning, 2½-ton trucks greeted the military personnel, for transfer to Ft. Lewis. Gwen headed downtown to a hotel we pre-arranged.

They crowded over a dozen officers in the back of a truck. As ranking officer, I claimed the seat closest to the tailgate. An hour later, we finally reached our destination base and were greeted by a corporal with a clipboard. I had one foot out of the truck when he stopped me.

"You gentlemen all have enough points for discharge and I need to know if you want to stay in or get out." I was stunned!

Since Pearl Harbor four years earlier, I had not dreamed of being a civilian again. The war in the Pacific still raged and I expected to be sent there.

"I will call my wife and let you know," I said. "No, Sir! I have to know before you get out of the truck!" he replied.

I turned to my new boat and train friend, Capt. Radar Jolme and said, "If this is what the peacetime Air Corps is like, I'm out of here!"

Then to the Corporal, "Gross, Clayton K. 0-663512; I'm out of here." And I jumped to the ground.

My first stop was a pay telephone and a call to Gwen. "Guess who this is?"

"Why are you being silly?" she replied.

"No. It's not Captain Gross. It's MISTER Gross. I'm home for good, Honey!"

Silence.....

We celebrated civilian status and discussed our future that night in the hotel. The next day we took a train home to Spokane.

None of my civvies fit after four years of hanging in the closet. I bought two new suits and a bunch of accessories. I transferred my Lloyds of London bank account to one in Spokane. I placed an ad in the classified section of the Spokesman Review, "Returning veteran with $10,000 savings looking for opportunities." I got lots of answers – most seemed interested in my money.

A bedroom in my folks' home, across the hall from theirs, did not seem adequate. Most days we shopped for our own and found one a few blocks away.

Les Kauffman of Kauffman Buick was a family friend and arranged for me to buy one of the first available new ones, a 1946 Buick Special.

I bought a beer tavern and got the vacant state license to promote Professional Boxing.

I was still on terminal leave from the Air Corps when we

dropped the atom bomb on Hiroshima. Nagasaki followed and then the Japanese surrendered. The world was at peace! That day I put my uniform back on resplendent with wings and medals and we went downtown to join the celebration. That night I took it off and assumed it was for the last time…However, a few weeks later I got a call from the Washington National Guard. The 116th Fighter Squadron had newly-assigned P-51 Mustangs and would I be interested? I was!

My dear brother Orien was out of his wartime assignment in the ATC and like all pilots with wings, he wanted to be a fighter pilot. He joined as well. After he checked out in a Mustang we had a few dogfights and he did well for a high time pilot who hadn't used rudders and a stick together. I was afraid, however, that I would kill him. The mental picture of the B-17 veteran, who talked his way into fighters and died pulling his wings off in training, came vividly to mind. Orien and I flew some "no decisions".

A year later Gwen and I sold the tavern and headed for Southern California to find our fortune. I resigned my National Guard Commission. Though I tried desperately to reactivate it in 1950 for the Korean War, no success. I never donned a uniform again. But, in my heart, I remain a 'fighter pilot' forever…..

**End of Story!**

# POSTSCRIPT

MY FIRST VISIT WITH the Gemeinschaft der Jagdflieger as President of the American Fighter Aces had given me so much excitement that I have returned five more times over the years – several times leading a contingent of American Aces. On one of those forays, I was introduced to the ME-262 pilot I had shot down on April 14th.

Originally an American historian had identified my victim as Hauptman Eric Steinberg who unfortunately was killed that day. I was sad to hear that news because the pilot had bailed out and could have survived the war that ended a month later.

Kurt Lobgesong was actually the pilot and had been wounded in my attack, but was able to eject and survive. He was taken to a field hospital which in his words "had so many wounded by the Americans in the West and Russians in the East that no one had time to examine and treat his wound" (in his left side). After waiting for some time, he put a towel over his wound and hitchhiked back to his base where he 'borrowed' a light observation plane and hedgehopped to

Czechoslovakia where he found treatment. Unfortunately, the Russians soon established the "IRON CURTAIN" and trapped him in that country. He returned to his schooling and eventually taught Math in high school and married there.

When America's policies under Reagan brought down the wall, he was able once more to attend meetings with his fighter pilot friends from WWII. Someone gave him a stack of back issues of the "Jagerblatt", the journal of their Association. In one of those he read of my search for the pilot of my jet victory which ended when I found Hauptman Steinberg had died. He corrected that information. And so it was we were able to meet and discuss the battle in 1995.

Both Kurt and his smiling 'Frau' thanked me because, again in his words,… "because of my wounds, I did not fly anymore in the war. You saved my life!"

I couldn't do anything but smile. I wanted to say, "Anytime, Buddy, anytime!"

# EPILOGUE

**W**ERE YOU GUYS SCARED doing your fighter thing? I've heard that question more than once. I've heard and read of other combat pilots' who reported that they were indeed scared. A popular fighter video on public television a few years ago quoted the author, "We were all scared – all the time. Sometimes I returned from a mission so drained that I had to be lifted from the cockpit."

Except for a 30-day leave and another thirty plus for travel time between my two combat tours, I flew combat from the end of 1943 until the war in Europe ended on May 8, 1945 in 105 combat missions. I've examined my conscience many times since. Was I scared? I seldom felt it. I didn't see it evidenced with our other guys, either.

In my first few missions, I admit to a high degree of excitement, nearly wetting my pants on the first one. Still, I think it was only the venture into the unknown MAGNIFIED by the terrible weather.

On one of my first few forays into enemy territory, I detected an inconsistency in the performance of my Merlin engine. I aborted. After returning to the base, I questioned myself about the reality of my diagnosis. Did I imagine rough engines or are they actually less than what I might need to get me there and back? I sat in the cockpit on the ground and ran it up several times trying to convince myself it was not right. Inconclusive! Still, I was not frightened to climb in and try again on the next mission.

I have closed my eyes and relived many times the Lufbery Circle experience with the very good ME-109 pilot. I can see, quite vividly, that 20-mm canon spitting at me until he must have run out of ammunition. I knew how close those shells had to be coming at me! But I lived to get home and I jumped out of the cockpit to find out where the hell my wingman had gone.

How many times did Smitty and I find battle damage from enemy fire; some that made me exclaim, "Holy Simoly. That was close."

On my near downing by friendly fire one fifty-caliber shell came within a millimeter of penetrating the armor plate behind my head. After limping home with severe damage, my mindset was anger, not fright. I *bounced* out of the wounded bird and into a new P-51 to fly to challenge the pilot whose error might easily have killed me.

Maybe some of my squadron pilots were scared, but I didn't see it. As Squadron Operations Officer, I wrote mission schedules. More often than not, I had a dozen pilots hanging over my shoulder when I wrote in the last few names for the next mission, and those not listed, complained loudly that they deserved one of the remaining slots.

I know part of that was the confidence that permeated our fighter group – borne out of our early successes and handed down to every replacement pilot so the level never decreased. We were the best fighter group of the war measured by enemy aircraft destroyed in aerial combat. Still, we could not help but notice our losses. We left the USA with 80 plus pilots and we lost 187 killed or captured. Did the rest of us want out? Au contraire…

I was desperately in love with my beautiful Gwendolyn and ecstatic about my 30-day leave from the war zone to experience my love. Still, I was piqued to have missed the 'good hunting' I missed during my leave!

I left the service in 1945 and re-signed my reserve commission to fly P-51's with the Washington National Guard. Then, I had to resign that commission a year later when I moved south to Los Angeles.

In 1950, the Korean War erupted and I logged a few thousand miles driving around California searching for a fighter unit that could or would use a successful re-treaded ACE. It never worked, but in retrospect, I feel I was right. Aerial combat did not scare me. It excited me!

# GLOSSARY

| | |
|---|---|
| AA | Anti-aircraft |
| AC | Air Corps or Aviation Cadet |
| ATC | Air Transport Command |
| BOQ | Bachelor Officer Quarters |
| C.O. | Commanding Officer |
| CPT | Civilian Pilot Training |
| E.A. | Enemy Aircraft |
| EM | Enlisted Men/Man |
| ETO | European Theater of Operations |
| FFI | Free French (Resistance against Germany) |
| GI's | Government Issue or Enlisted men |
| IO | Information Officer |
| KIA | Killed in Action |
| KIFA | Killed in Flying Accident |
| KP | Kitchen Police/Patrol |
| LST's | Landing Ship Troops |
| MAG | Magneto |
| MIA | Missing in Action |
| MP's | Military Police |
| MPH | Miles Per Hour |
| MAE WESTS | Individual Floating Vests |

| | |
|---|---|
| NON-COMS | Non-commissioned |
| 'O' CLUB | Officers Club |
| OP'S | Operations Office |
| PAAB | Portland Army Air Base |
| PFC | Private First Class |
| POW | Prisoner of War |
| PR | Public Relations |
| PX | Post Exchange |
| RAF | Royal Air Force |
| RECCE | Reconnaissance |
| RECON | Reconnaissance |
| RHIP | Rank Has Its Privileges |
| R.T. | Radio Transmitter |
| RTU | Replacement Training Unit |
| RON | Remain Over Night |
| SHAEF | Supreme Headquarters Allied Expeditionary Force |
| TO | Take Off |
| UK | United Kingdom |
| USAAF | U. S. Army Air Force |
| WAAF | Women's Auxiliary Air Force |

# INDEX

## A
Allen, Gus W. 152, 256-259, *photo*

## B
Beerbower, Don M. *photo*
Bickell, George R. 58, 62-64, 68-70, 85-87, 90. 113, 175. 177, 178, 187, 209, 214, 235, 248, 249, 251, 253, 254, 257, 279, *photos (2)*
Blakeslee. Col. Don, 4th F.G.110, 139
Bonotto, Caryl P. 161-163
Bradley, Jack 1, 106, 140, 141, 161, 194, 195, 213, 239, *photo*
Bradley, Gen. Omar 192
Brooks, Gen. John D. 19, 20-21, 31-32, 42
Brown, Arthur F. 190, 222
Brueland, Lowell K. 68-70., 97. 105, 127. 128. 145, 146, 150, 147. 164, 191, 244, 279, *photos (2)*
Buer. Glendon J. 137, 138. 187
Burris, Major I. *photo*

## C
Cahill, William M. 81, 222
Cloke, Marshall 266-268
Cocker, Lynn W. 157, *photos (3)*

## D
Dalglish, James B. 113, 131, 132, 137, 157
Davis, Wm. 'Bill' 157, 271, 272, *photo*
Dernpsey, Don (Sgt. Pilot) 129
Depner, Earl G. 194 195 218 295
Dickson, Dorothy 117, 118
Dietrick, Virgil 97
Disiere, Alfred Joseph, Jr. 181, 182

## E
Eagleston, Glenn T. 1, 139, 194, 195, 247, *photo*
Edward, James *photo*
Elste, Sgt. 263
Emerson. Warren Red' 94, 9S. 97, 105, 127, 128, 157, 164, *photo*
Emmer, Wallace N. *photo*
Espy, Bowers W.176, 237, 252, 282

## F

Fisk, Harry E. 194, 195, 222, 223, 295

## G

Gabreski, Col. Gabby, 56th F.G. 1, 149, 151-153
Goodnight, Robert *photo*
Gorman, Kenneth 285
Gross. Orien Wilford 2. 198
Gross, Orien Wilford, Jr. 7, 18-20, 299, *photos (2)*
Gumm, Charles F. 113, 130
Gunter, Edwin D. 33, 38, *photo*

## H

Hale, Gean B. 33, 38, 45, *photo*
Hall, Norman E. 'Stud' 113
Hamilton, John J. 33, 38, 46, *photo*
Hargis, Wm. G. 265
Harris, Billie D. 'Bucky' 129, 173-175, 213, 247, *photo*
Hasbrouck, Ralph C. 168 169
Hawley, Charles W. 148, 173, *photo*
Hoehn, Geo. J. 'Jr.' 184, *photo*
Howard, James H. (MOH) 135, 139, 246, 247
Howell, Wentworth 'Curley' 248
Hunt, Edward E. *photo*

## J

Johnson, Al 86 - 89, *photo*
Jolme, Radar 295, 298

## K

Kallas, Paul 148
Kenyon, James R 'Dick' 129, *photo*
Kestler, Leland P. 253
Kevacek. Andrew 288

Kinmon, Geo. N. Jr. 224, 263, 264, 275
Kirts, Ben 273
Kline, Russell 275
Knier, Earl *photo*
Konopka, John 136

## L

Lamb, Geo. Max 240, 241
Lanowski, Vitold, Polish Pilot 152, *photo*
Lasko, Charles W. 'Cuz' 118, 182, *photo*
Lobgeson, Kurt xiv. 300, 301, *photo*
Long, Maurice G. 'Maury' 214, 215

## M

Martin, John J. Jr. 22, 29, 32
Martin, Col. Kenneth R. 81, 82, 106, 111, 137-139
McDonald, Norm 137, 139
McLeod, F. Duncan 210, 211
Mellor, Art 184, 185
Meyler, Walt 217

## N

Nacy, William P. 'Pete' 65, 78

## O

O'Connor, Frank Q. *photo*
Orndorff, Uncle Clarence 63

## P

Patton, Gen. George S. Jr. 216, 237, 263, 270, 284
Peters. Bruno 103
Pittard, Robert, Jr. 48, 49
Plath, Bruce, Engineer Officer 156

## Q
Quesada, M/Gen. Elwood 'Pete' 105, 113, 261

## R
Radojits, Tony T. 82, 86, 88, 131, 132 137, *photo*

Rhing, Vern 82, 86, 88, *photo*

Richards, Danny 147, 148, 164, 165

Ryan, Edward R 82, 158, *photo*

## S
Seaman, Owen 115

Shirley, Thomas DDS 216, 219, 220

Simmons, William J. 147

Slaven, M. J. 242

Smith, C. E. 'Smitty' 59, 112, 121, 138, 144, 145, 155, 156, 199, 213, 216, 303, *photos (2)*

Start, .Dr. Gwyn H. 75, 111, 198, 216, 218, 220, 283, 284

Stephens, Bob 106, 129, 144, 151, 157, 161, *photo*

## T
Talbot, Gilbert F. 126, 129, 185, 194-196, 199, 201-203, 207-210, 213, 216, 219-220, 237, 253, 267-268, 282, 286, 295, *photo*

Teschner, Charles G. 145

'Tex' 247, 248, 280-283, *photo*

Turk, Jack B. 131, 137

Turner, Richard E. *photos (2)*

## W
Weissinger, Bob 60

White, Horace Bedford 128

Widdoes, Eugene W. 263

Wulff, Earl 62, 63, *photo*